Lecture Notes in Information Systems and Organisation

Volume 14

More information about this series at http://www.springer.com/series/11237

Daniela Mancini · Renata Paola Dameri
Elisa Bonollo
Editors

Strengthening Information and Control Systems

The Synergy Between Information Technology and Accounting Models

 Springer

Editors
Daniela Mancini
University of Naples "Parthenope"
Naples
Italy

Elisa Bonollo
University of Genoa
Genoa
Italy

Renata Paola Dameri
University of Genoa
Genoa
Italy

ISSN 2195-4968   ISSN 2195-4976   (electronic)
Lecture Notes in Information Systems and Organisation
ISBN 978-3-319-26486-8   ISBN 978-3-319-26488-2   (eBook)
DOI 10.1007/978-3-319-26488-2

Library of Congress Control Number: 2015955375

Springer Cham Heidelberg New York Dordrecht London

Printed on acid-free paper

Springer International Publishing AG Switzerland is part of Springer Science+Business Media (www.springer.com)

Contents

Looking for Synergies Between Accounting and Information Technologies

D. Mancini, R.P. Dameri and E. Bonollo

Abstract The research works published in this book are a selection of the papers submitted at the XI Annual Conference of the Italian Chapter of Association for Information Systems (ItAIS 2014), which was held in Genoa in November, untitled "Digital Innovation and Inclusive Knowledge in Times of Change". The volume contains 17 research works that were accepted at the conference after a double-blind review, and were mainly presented at the Accounting Information Systems track.

Keywords Accounting information systems · Strategic management · Management control systems · Digital innovation · Synergies

1 Introduction

The research works published in this book are a selection of the papers submitted at the XI Annual Conference of the Italian Chapter of Association for Information Systems (ItAIS 2014), which was held in Genoa in November, untitled "Digital Innovation and Inclusive Knowledge in Times of Change". The volume contains 17 research works that were accepted at the conference after a double-blind review, and were mainly presented at the Accounting Information Systems track.

The aim of the book is to introduce the current debate in Italian research community of information systems on the relationship between accounting information systems and digital and technological supports. Contributions come from academicians, young researchers, PhD students, experts and practitioners specialized in the field of financial

D. Mancini
Parthenope University, Naples, Italy
e-mail: mancini@uniparthenope.it

R.P. Dameri · E. Bonollo (✉)
University of Genoa, Genoa, Italy
e-mail: bonollo@economia.unige.it

R.P. Dameri
e-mail: dameri@economia.unige.it

© Springer International Publishing Switzerland 2016   1
D. Mancini et al. (eds.), *Strengthening Information and Control Systems*,
Lecture Notes in Information Systems and Organisation 14,
DOI 10.1007/978-3-319-26488-2_1

accounting, management accounting, internal control systems, organization, strategy and management, interested to discover the helpful use of Information and Communication Technology (ICT) in managing accounting information required to support decision and control processes.

Usually accounting information systems research investigates the link between financial/management accounting and information technology, in order to highlight the implications of technology on administrative/accounting processes, accounting models, accounting knowledge, accounting skills, performance measures, and so on [1–3]. Previous research demonstrates that information technology has various implications on accounting, in particular it is a useful tool for managing accounting processes, automating some control mechanisms, and producing accounting and performance information for control aims in a more efficient way. Information technology is also a mean useful to elaborate more effective information, in order to improve decision making processes and to enhance companies' ability to compete [4].

Scholars and practitioners highlight that information technology can be useful applied to decision-making processes. In particular, the more a process is standardized, is characterized by a clear definition of data and information required and is based on a well-known decision model [5], the more that process can be automated and information technology can be an efficient and effective support. Afterwards research works stressed the importance of integration between data, IT, information processes in order to grasp the advantages coming from the extensive use of technologies [6]. Scholars underline the role of information technology to help integration between several components of information systems (data, information, human contributions, procedures), to improve integration of information flows between each organizational level inside companies, and to support integration of information sharing inside and outside companies [7, 8].

During the latest years, ICT provided new opportunities for companies through Internet, digital technologies, the convergence between several media tools (audio, video, and so on), the development of some social utilities, such as wiki, chat, forum, instant messages, tweets, and social networks. These innovations required additional research efforts, also in the field of financial, management and strategic accounting, because companies need to discover if, how and where these new technologies can be applied. Additional investigations are required to understand how companies can employ integration and convergence between several ICT tools in order to enhance their ability of managing information, of taking better decisions, of improving organizational control and coordination, of being proactive and value adding.

The leitmotif of this book is that these innovations require the shift of the focus from integration to synergy between accounting and ICT. Companies, and their managers, need to understand these new technologies and create an environment, in which ICT cooperate with the other components of accounting information system, in order to strength companies' ability to guide activities towards objectives. Each contribution, included in this book, proposes different ways in which companies can create and exploit synergies between information technology and accounting information systems (processes, models, knowledge and skills) in order to enhance the ability to manage information and to improve the capacity of controlling and guiding activities towards objectives.

The book is ideally articulated in three parts. The first deals with the search of synergies at the strategic level, the second considers the management control level while the third regards the operational and transactional level.

2 Using AIS for Supporting Strategic Management

ICT is more and more pervasive in organizations, firms, accounting systems. During the latest years, especially ERP systems have been increasing their role not only in supporting accounting processes, but also in driving a deep reorganization mainly interesting large corporations [9]. For a decade and more, ERP has been a key instrument to improve efficiency, effectiveness and appropriateness of operations and business activities; and for implementing a process-oriented business model adopted in large companies all over the world [10, 11]. This trend is characterized by a strong accent on standardization: standard processes, standard data, standard business models and value chains; discretion reduction, and finally rigidity; and the pivotal role of few vendors, global leaders imposing their own enterprise systems [12].

At present, this trend is quite exhausted, even if continuous improvements are applied to gain ever better returns from ERP implementation. But a new trend has been starting, suggesting information systems focused on complexity, aiming not at reducing it through standard answers, but at facing it thanks to flexible, tailored ICT applications used to process big data and unstructured information in an innovative way. These systems are conceived to support strategic management, instead of operational processes [13, 14].

This topic is not new: Nobel Prize Herbert Simon in Sixties theoretically defined a framework of using ICT in management [15–17]. He described three types of problems: structured problems, that can be automated and solved thanks to the direct action of ICT, able to replace the human being; and semi-structured and unstructured problems, where computers, unable to replace the man, deliver to the manager processed data to create knowledge and support the best decision making for the company.

From the Simon's theory, several streams of research have been developed in the following years; two of them are especially relevant for our work: human-machine interaction and decision support systems [5].

At that time, it was not possible to concretely implement the Simon's vision about the role of computers in strategic management, owing to the limits of the available technology. Nowadays innovation in ICT permits to apply smart technologies also to unstructured problems, facing complex decisions and processing sometimes scarce, some others redundant, information.

This field is known as Business Intelligence (BI), that is, the application of smart and sophisticated instruments to drive strategic decisions in complex environments

[18–20]. BI offers a very rich portfolio of applications and solutions, linking several heterogeneous managerial aspects in an ever new way:

1. "Multi" data: multimedia, multidimensional, deriving from multiple sources;
2. High computing capacity, able to process big data in few seconds;
3. Managers aware about the potential role of ICT in supporting their firm management.

All these aspects are supported by smart devices wired 24/7, easy to use and strongly integrated in daily working and personal life. Technology is more and more enabling all the tasks and operations in firms, but it requires well-conceived managerial and accounting models to profitably use this technology. The result is just the opposite respect to the ERP era: no more standardization, but flexibility and agility. Solutions should be designed not in a rigid way, but able to be easily adapted to different situations, to support firm-specific strategies and face fast and changing markets and competitive arenas.

This panorama emerges also from a subset of papers submitted to ItAIS 2014, Accounting Information Systems track. The use of ICT to support strategic management is considered not only pivotal to better exploit the synergies between business and technology, but also a crucial aspect to empower global companies to face an increasing complexity. The topic regards large corporations, but also SMEs, independently from the industrial sector or the country in which they work. Also the public sector is involved, looking at new models to support strategic decisions for better using scarce resources to create public value.

At a first glance, this subset of five papers look very heterogeneous; it regards both large companies and SMEs; industrial, banking, or services sectors; companies in Italy, but also in USA, or in Portugal, Hungary and Slovakia; and also universities or academic spin-offs. On the contrary, a fil rouge links all the papers, that is, the research of innovative way for using ICT not to simply automate, but to create knowledge and managerial competences thanks to a rich management-technology interaction.

Inghirami and Scribani put the basis for understanding what Strategic Management Accounting (SMA) is. Their paper defines the boundaries of this topic, but clarifies that a shared definition doesn't exist, especially because the content of SMA varies and evolves along with the evolution of accounting and managerial conceptual models. For this reason, SMA is more interesting and promising respect to financial accounting, a standard model not evolving nor flexible respect to the different needs and expectations of firms in different strategic positioning. The empirical investigation of the Nespoli case highlights the role of SMA in supporting a global group with a differentiated multinational ensemble of entities.

Aureli, Ciambotti, Joczik, and Sasvari face two basic concepts. The first regards the correlation between the use of ICT and the value creation: from Solow to Carr, this correlation has been considered difficult or sometimes impossible to demonstrate, because "IT doesn't matter". On the contrary, the authors investigate on this relationship and especially on how the use of information systems could support the business success. The latter concept regards the role of ICT in SMEs and the maturity level of adopting business information systems in different European countries; a survey useful also at macro-economic level, to support public policies for ICT implementation in SMEs.

Also Caserio, Panaro, and Trucco have an international field of research; in this case, US companies are examined, about the content of their MD&A depending on financial and economic conditions companies are experiencing. In this case, two advanced IT techniques—data mining and content analysis—are applied to financial disclosure and especially Management Discussion & Analysis to investigate about the quality and fidelity of MD&A and the reliability of MD&A content to forecast future performance of a firm. Language processing and sentiment analysis support these surveys applied to a large set of US companies.

Bruno, Iacoviello, and Lazzini focus their research on banking sector and especially on a case study regarding an Italian bank. IT has ever been a critical component of the credit intermediation business, and recent innovations improved the role of information systems in supporting Risk management: a crucial activity for creating value in the banking sector. This work outlines a very important topic regarding all the strategic management accounting and use of IT: the quality of data. Quality of data and information delivered and processed are a major determinant of the outcome; but it should be considered together with other determinants such as managers education and culture, functional relationships, and appropriate technology resources.

Bassano, D'Aniello, Gaeta, Perano, and D'Eredità consider the public sector and a very particular niche: academic spin-offs. Academic spin-offs are an instrument to transfer academic research output to the market, through the settlement of a newco aiming at embedding innovative technologies deriving from the research activity into products and services offered to the market. As academic spin-offs are based on knowledge, to evaluate the intellectual capital of these companies is fundamental to assess their probability of success. The authors suggest to use a DSS based on fuzzy logic to evaluate the demographic factor in the spin-off founding team, assessing their human capital in order to estimate their capacity of value creation.

Finally, it emerges that all the papers are focused on innovative instruments using ICT and applied to innovative management models. Information systems are no more confined in traditional accounting, such as financial accounting or managerial accounting, but are extended to larger fields for exploring companies and public bodies. Different types of data and knowledge are processed: not only traditional, quantitative data, but qualitative information (demographic data for academic researchers founding a spin-off) or natural data language (as in examining MD&A in US companies). This subset of five papers is therefore an example of how the Accounting Information Systems field of research is changing, linking both managerial evolution and technology innovation.

3 Management Control and Information Technologies: Synergies from Digital Innovations

Management control system is composed by several interrelated mechanisms designed to guide, efficiently and effectively, company's actions towards its goals [21]. According to literature, from a narrow view of this system focused on financial and short term control [22], we pass to a larger view that includes also [23–28]:

- Performance measures based on quantitative and not only financial numbers;
- Long term control based on control models which connect performance measurement to strategic vision;
- Organizational control focused on the power of values, shared principles and myths to guide employees' behaviors;
- Relational control focused on efficiency and effectiveness of intra organizational processes;
- Risk dimension which help to calibrate the level of control to the organization's ability to reach goals.

The development and the sophistication of management control system require an integrated vision of its design and implementation. Nowadays it is more and more difficult to talk about management control system apart from its information system and from the IT tools used to collect and elaborate information. They are different faces of the same wide and coordinated system. The relationship between management control and ICT is very crucial. During the latest decades, some technologies help companies to manage timelier and more accurate information in order to support managers' decision-making. Integrated transaction systems, business intelligence systems, for example, in some cases have represented a great opportunity to improve management control mechanisms and to generate a more effective guide of companies' activities. Today the challenge is how companies can use digital innovation and social technologies to improve their ability to control activities and get better performances. It is not a problem of having better and cheaper information, in term of accuracy, timeliness, cost saving of information process. The question is how companies can add value to new types of data and information (i.e. web metrics, log data) which could have managerial implication and how they can be used and mixed with traditional measures, in order to strengthen companies' ability to guide their business toward objectives.

The papers, included in the second part of the book, highlight how companies can create synergies between new technologies and management control mechanisms. Synergies can come out from different circumstances. New technologies enable companies in easily and conveniently elaborating a huge amount of data and information or in collecting and elaborating several types of row data coming from the measurement of digital or web processes. Consequently, companies have to understand which kind of measures they can add to the traditional ones in order to design a more effective management control structure. Moreover, new technologies

enable companies in easily and economically applying several analytics methodologies, as content analysis and statistical models. New technologies also help
companies in exchanging information with their partners in order to improve the
ability to coordinate and control joint activities.

The second part of the book contains original research works that try to detect
different ways to find and create synergies between accounting information systems
for management control and digital and social technologies.

The paper Castellano and Del Gobbo presents a comparison between the traditional measures to evaluate the efficacy of an advertising campaign based on TV
commercials, and new measures based on web metrics. The paper suggests the
importance to search a synergy between different kind of metrics, traditional and
web metrics, in order to reach a more sophisticated interpretation of the performance of an advertising campaign able to encourage a better alignment between
performance measurement and strategy. This synergy is also important because it
can help to overcome problems of accuracy and availability of data, to obtain
"interesting insights about the reactions of the customers" using quantitative and
qualitative measures.

The paper Varriale and Di Vaio concern the design of performance measurement
indicators to assess e-mentoring programs. The paper give theoretical indications on
the use of ICT for managing on line mentoring program able to overcome "geographic, space and time limitations". The authors highlight the arising issue of
designing a system of key performance indicators able to monitor the efficiency and
the effectiveness of the e-mentoring program and to compare it with traditional
mentoring activities. In this case, digital technologies require the development of
new performance measures able to capture the success of e-mentoring programs and
capable of helping companies to plan and manage synergies with the traditional
programs.

The paper Pozzoli and Gesuele presents a content analysis applied to integrated
reports of Italian public utilities, in order to highlight the state of the art of the
quality of this mean of communication. The work give evidence to two aspects. The
first concerned the emerging interest for integrated reporting as a new form of
"external communication, which incorporates and combines financial and
non-financial material information [...]". Additional research is request to understand how IT tools are able to satisfying data collection and to managing the
information and data flow for integrated reporting. The second important aspect is
the use of the content analysis as a tool for managers able to provide new and
different information for a better design of the integrated reporting. Also in this case
IT is a critical element, able to easily perform the context analysis and compare the
integrated reporting of several companies.

The paper Spano and Bellò concerns the implementation of a business intelligence module in the Sardinia Region in order to highlight factors capable of
exploiting the potentialities of this module in supporting decision-making processes. The case study reveals that important advantages derive from the implementation of the business intelligence module, especially in term of transparency of
information flow for decision makers, in term of homogeneity of reports and

dashboards and in term of timely and easy-to-use information. However, the tool is underuse and the synergy between ICT and management control is underdeveloped because of the negligence in the design phase regarding IT infrastructure, data collection, and training initiatives and communication.

The paper of Di Vaio and Varriale analyses how new technologies can help Port Authorities to exchange information with the other economic operators of the seaport relationship systems, in particular water concessionaries. A multiple case analysis help to understand which technologies are used and how they support Port Authorities to perform their planning, coordination and control tasks on port operations and services, managed by private companies in outsourcing. The study reveals that email remain the first tool employed for information exchange. Despite information technology could be a networking and communication tool, two factors mediate the use of a more sophisticated instrument (for example a digital platform): the participation of Port Authority in the ownership structure of the water concessionaire and the nature of mono or multi-utilities of the concessionaire.

4   IT and Accounting Information System: Synergies and Determinants at Operational Level

Increasing challenges in the current competitive environment lead organizations to constantly face changing conditions. Adaptations, reactions and pro-actions could be supported by decision-making processes capable of being fast and reliable even at operational level.

In this regard, the integration between IT and accounting information system affects the quantity and quality of the available information to support the decision-making processes. Indeed the level of this integration impacts on the collection, classification, processing, communication of data and on the type and reliability of the information used to support operations management [29, 30].

The synergies between IT and accounting information system do not necessarily follow the introduction of IT applications in the accounting information system, but are the result of a progressive accumulation and stratification of experiences, procedures, know-how and mistakes [31–34]. This means that these synergies are not automatic and static, but change in space and time, according to the environment in which organizations are operating [35, 36], and are based on the evolution of the accounting information system or of the IT or of both of them in a two-way relationship. In detail as well known, at operational level, IT applications allow organizations to increase the accuracy and speed of transaction processing, by conducting business operations electronically and so leading to a higher operational efficiency. Furthermore they enable organizations to prepare budget, financial statement and reporting documents in electronic format, with cost savings and reduction of human errors. On the other hand, however, changes in accounting information system, due to legislative or autonomous initiatives, encourage improvements or severe modifications in IT applications.

Synergies between these two elements, even if at operational level, do not just impact on technical aspects, but potentially reveal their effects on the overall management, also and above all on the accountability processes and organization.

Nevertheless there is often a gap between the theory and the actual situation of organizations, especially with reference to unlisted companies and public organizations. In fact, on one hand, scholars have highlighted for a long time IT positive impacts on accounting information system and on other various aspects such as productivity and organizational performance [37–39]. On the other hand, even though organizations have often aligned IT applications with their business operations (thanks to the constant reduction in technology costs), they generally have not exploited the synergies between IT and accounting information system for the benefits of a better accountability process or a harmonious organizational development [40].

The papers included in the third part of the volume are focused on the aforementioned issues.

The first two papers provide an empirical research and a theoretical analysis concerning IT impacts on accounting information systems and, more in general, on business operations.

The paper of Avallone, Ramassa and Roncagliolo focuses on the XBRL technology that could improve the accounting information system, with particular reference to financial reporting process, cost accounting and performance measurement. Nevertheless the authors show that preparers and professionals supporting unlisted companies seem to limit their efforts to mandatory rules to transmit financial statements without exploiting the XBRL potential. The only current benefits of XBRL seem to be for external users of financial information (e.g. financial analysts).

All this highlights that the actual use of IT integrated with accounting information system is above all a cultural problem requiring specific training/promotion initiatives for potential users.

The paper of Aloini, Dulmin, Mininno and Spagnesi investigates whether the development of IT thanks to web based technology can have managerial implications. In detail, the study reviews the current state of academic research about the integration of ERP software and social collaboration tools (e.g. social networks, wikis, mashups and tags). Results highlight potential impacts on the organization, internal and external information flow, management practices, systems of incentives and rewards, decision-making process and intellectual capital sharing.

Changes in the synergies between IT and information system at operational level do not just consist, as already said, in new IT that can potentially change the accounting information system and, more generally, the business operations. They can also derive from the evolution of the accounting information system to be supported by new IT applications. In this case the available IT is at the same time a restriction for the development of the accounting information system and a mean to enhance its information potential.

In other words, the role of IT is not neutral, perfectly adaptable to the peculiarities of the organization. IT applications have restrictions that can affect accounting procedures or even imply a total reorganization [41].

This is the case of the transition from the traditional public accounting system to the accrual accounting in the Italian public universities dealt with by the papers of Giovanelli, Rotondo and Caffù and of Bonollo, Lazzini and Zuccardi Merli.

Specifically Giovanelli, Rotondo and Caffù present the experimentation of Cineca's U-GOV, the IT system chosen to support the accounting change in the University of Sassari. The system is based on the integration and sharing of information between accounting, planning and control system, both before and at the end of the accounting period. The experimentation showed the complexity of an accounting change process dealing with not only technical, but also cultural (e.g. the well known "resistance to change") and organizational aspects.

More in detail Bonollo, Lazzini and Zuccardi Merli investigate the support of Cineca's U-GOV application platform for the management of research projects. The study focuses on the case of University of Genoa and highlights how this University had to reconfigure all the accounting procedures and rethink responsibilities and organizational tasks between peripheral structures (e.g. departments, research centers, libraries, etc.) and central administration, orienting its IT applications to an integrated management of research projects.

Finally we should point out that synergies between IT and accounting information system affect multiple aspects other than technical and, in turn, they are affected by numerous determinants (other than technical).

The last three papers of the third part of the volume focus on determinants of new IT in order to give suggestions to managers, practitioners, regulators, etc.

Corsi and Trucco highlight that skills, job tenure, level of education and main activities of the Chief Information Officers impact on the ERP implementation and management in the Italian context and contribute to improve firm's performance (in terms of reliability and timeliness of data and improvement of quality of the internal control system).

Mazza, Azzali and Brooks investigate the determinants of IT controls (ITC) quality. The authors identify four classes of independent variables: ITC staff, complexity, internal control resources, corporate governance. Results show that industry, internationalization and diversification, outsourcing strategy, market capitalization, firm age and corporate governance play a relevant role in determining the efficiency and efficacy of ITC.

Gesuele investigates the determinants of web based technology in Spanish local governments. Specifically the author identifies as e-disclosure key drivers the size, internet visibility, media interest, citizens wealth and leverage. These factors are able to influence the transparency via web of the Spanish public organizations analyzed.

References

1. Marchi, L.: I sistemi informativi aziendali. Giuffrè, Milano (1993)
2. Poston, R.S., Grabski, S.V.: Accounting information systems research: is it another QWERTY? Int. J. Account. Inf. Syst. **1**, 9–53 (2000)
3. Ferguson, C., Seow, P.-S.: Accounting information systems research over the past decade: past and future trends. Account. Financ. **51**, 235–251 (2011)
4. Porter, M.E., Millar, V.E.: How information gives you competitive advantage. Harvard Bus. Rev. **4**(63), 149–160 (1985)
5. Gorry, G.A., Morton, M.S.S.: A Framework for Management Information Systems, vol. 13. Massachusetts Institute of Technology, Cambridge (1971)
6. Rom, A., Rodhe, C.: Management accounting and integrated information systems: a literature review. Int. J. Account. Inf. Syst. **8**, 40–68 (2007)
7. Nicolaou, A.I.: A contingency model of perceived effectiveness in accounting information systems: organizational coordination and control effects. Int. J. Account. Inf. Syst. **1**, 91–105 (2000)
8. Mancini, D.: Il sistema informativo e di controllo relazionale per il governo della rete di relazioni collaborative d'azienda. Giuffrè, Milano (2010)
9. Kanellou, A., Spathis, C.: Accounting benefits and satisfaction in an ERP environment. Int. J. Account. Inf. Syst. **14**, 209–234 (2013)
10. Madapusi, A., D'Souza, D.: The influence of ERP system implementation on the operational performance of an organization. Int. J. Inf. Manage. **32**, 24–34 (2012)
11. Soh, C., Kien, S.S., Tay-Yap, J.: Enterprise resource planning: cultural fits and misfits: is ERP a universal solution? Commun. ACM **43**, 47–51 (2000)
12. Davenport, T.H., Harris, J.G., Cantrell, S.: Enterprise systems and ongoing process change. Bus. Process Manag. J. **10**, 16–26 (2004)
13. Barbucha, D., Nguyen, N.T., Batubara, J.: New Trends in Intelligent Information and Database Systems (vol. 598). Springer, Berlin (2015)
14. Mancini, D., Vaassen, E.H., Dameri, R.P.: Accounting Information Systems for Decision Making. Springer, Berlin (2015)
15. Simon, H.A.: A behavioral model of rational choice. Q. J. Econ. **69**, 99–118 (1955)
16. Simon, H.A.: The new science of management decision. The Ford distinguished lectures, vol. 3. Harper & Brothers New York, NY (1960)
17. Simon, H.A.: Administrative behavior (vol. 4). Free Press, New York (1965)
18. Luhn, H.P.: A business intelligence system. IBM J. Res. Dev. **2**, 314–319 (1958)
19. Watson, H.J., Wixom, B.H.: The current state of business intelligence. Computer **40**, 96–99 (2007)
20. Chen, H., Chiang, R.H., Storey, V.C.: Business intelligence and analytics: from big data to big impact. MIS Q. **36**, 1165–1188 (2012)
21. Malmi, T., Brown, D.A.: Management control systems ad a package—opportunities challenges and research directions. Manag. Account. Res. **19**, 287–300 (2008)
22. Johnson, H.T, Kaplan, R.S.: Relevance lost: the rise and the fall of management accounting. Harvard Business Press, Cambridge (1991)
23. Kaplan, R.S., Norton, D.P.: The Balanced Scorecard: Measures that Drive Performance, pp 71–79. Harvard Business Review (January–February) (1992)
24. Mancini, D.: L'azienda nella «Rete di imprese». La prospettiva del controllo relazionale, Giuffrè, Milano (1999)
25. D'Onza, G.: Il sistema di controllo interno nella prospettiva di risk management. Giuffrè, Milano (2008)
26. Corsi, K.: Il controllo organizzativo. Una prospettiva transazionale, Giuffrè Milano (2003)
27. Lamboglia, R.: La componente immateriale e organizzativa del sistema di controllo aziendale. Giuffrè, Milano (2012)
28. Ouchi, W.G.: Markets, bureaucracies, and clans. Adm. Sci. Q. **25**, 129–141 (1980)

29. Marchi, L.: I sistemi informativi aziendali. Giuffrè, Milano (2003)
30. Mancini, D.: Modelli e strumenti per l'acquisizione dei dati contabili. In: Marchi, L., Mancini, D. (eds.) Gestione informatica dei dati aziendali. Franco Angeli, Milano (1999)
31. Hopwood, A.G.: Accounting and organisation change. Account. Auditing Account. J. **3**, 7–17 (1990)
32. Steccolini, I.: Accountability e sistemi informativi negli enti locali. Giappichelli, Torino (2004)
33. Hopwood, A.G.: The archaeology of accounting systems. Acc. Organ. Soc. **12**, 201–234 (1987)
34. Hopwood, A.G.: Accounting and the domain of the public-some observations on current developments. In: Guthrie, J., Parker, L., Shand, D. (eds.) The public sector- Contemporary readings in accounting and auditing. Harcourt Brace Jovanovich, Marrickville (1990)
35. Wickramasinghe, D., Alawattage, C.: Management accounting change. Approaches and perspectives. Routledge, London (2007)
36. Venkatraman, N.: IT-enabled business transformation: from automatism to business scope redefinition. Sloan Manag. Rev. **35**, 73–87 (1994)
37. Pan, G., Pan, S.L., Lim, C.Y.: Examining how firms leverage IT to achieve firm productivity: RBV and dynamic capabilities perspectives. Inf. Manag. **52**, 401–412 (2015)
38. Melville, N., Kraemer, K., Gurbaxani, V.: Review: information technology and organizational performance: an integrative model of IT. MIS Q. Manag. Inf. Syst. **28**, 283–322 (2004)
39. Stiroh, K.: Information technology and the US productivity revival: what do the industry data say? Am. Econ. Rev. **92**, 1559–1576 (2002)
40. Chen, Y.C., Wu, J.H.: IT management capability and its impact on the performance of a CIO. Inf. Manag. **48**, 145–156 (2011)
41. Mancini, D., Vaassen, E.H.J., Dameri, P.R.: Trends in accounting information systems. In: Mancini, D., Vaassen, E.H.J., Dameri, P.R. (eds.) Accounting information system for decision making. Springer, London (2013)

Towards Strategic Management Accounting: The Nespoli Group Case

Iacopo Ennio Inghirami and Giuseppe Scribani

Abstract The process to implement a Strategic Management Accounting (SMA) system is quite long and complex. SMA is not a separate item: it should be linked and closely integrated with the rest of the Accounting Information System (AIS). Firstly, the core of the AIS, the ERP system, should work properly, acting as the main source for the SMA system. Secondly, it is necessary a great empowerment of the management, which is supposed to operate directly the SMA system. The first part of the paper describes the SMA theoretical framework, discussing the more recent theories. The second part describes a medium-size company and its experiences in implementing a SMA system. In particular, we will describe the Nespoli Group, which comprehends 45 medium-size firms localized all-over Europe and the issues linked to the management of such a differentiated multinational ensemble of entities. The third part highlights the specific characteristics of the Nespoli Group SMA system. Several final considerations conclude the paper.

Keywords Accounting information systems · Strategic management accounting · Business intelligence · ERP systems

1 Introduction

Most textbooks of Management Accounting define the discipline in terms of its decision-making role. It is generally stated that since managerial functions involve using information for better planning and control, Management Accounting principles are very important for effective and successful management at all levels. In this paper, we will review the role of Strategic Management Accounting (SMA) that claims to be the future of Management Accounting discipline.

I.E. Inghirami (✉)
University of Milano-Bicocca, Milan, Italy
e-mail: iacopo.inghirami@unimib.it

G. Scribani
Gruppo Nespoli, Como, Italy

© Springer International Publishing Switzerland 2016
D. Mancini et al. (eds.), *Strengthening Information and Control Systems*,
Lecture Notes in Information Systems and Organisation 14,
DOI 10.1007/978-3-319-26488-2_2

The purpose of the paper is to analyse the definition and the use of the SMA in a medium sized company: the Nespoli Group Spa. The Nespoli Group is a world-wide family-owned Italian company, mainly operating in the "Tools for painting" market.

The Nespoli Group's established position on domestic and international markets increases the interest on the analysis of the company's performance measurement models. Some research questions emerge from this analysis:

1. What are the peculiar characteristics of the SMA model in Nespoli Group?
2. What is the role of SMA in the implementation of the Nespoli Group's strategy and what is the contribution to the achievement of leadership position?
3. What are the techniques that make up the SMA system of the Nespoli Group?

2 Mutual Relations Between Accounting Information Systems and Strategic Management Accounting

2.1 Accounting Information Systems and Strategic Management Accounting: Some Definitions

The definition of Accounting Information System (AIS) depends on the definition of Accounting itself. It is possible to distinguish between two kinds of accounting: Financial Accounting and Management Accounting. Financial Accounting is defined as:

> The art of recording, classifying, and summarizing in a significant manner and in terms of money, transactions and events which are, in part at least, of financial character, and interpreting the results thereof [1],

Likewise, Management Accounting is defined as:

> The process of identification, measurement, accumulation, analysis, preparation, interpretation and communication of information used by management to plan, evaluate and control within an entity and to assure appropriate use of and accountability for its resources. Management accounting also comprises the preparation of financial reports for non-management groups such as shareholders, creditors, regulatory agencies and tax authorities [2].

The aim of Financial Accounting (FA) is to gather and summarize financial data to prepare financial reports, such as a balance sheet and income statement, for the organization's management, investors, lenders, suppliers, tax authorities, and other stakeholders. FA main recipients are external users, and financial reports must follow precise layouts and rules. In fact, FA must accomplish national and international principles, such as the Generally Accepted Accounting Principles (GAAP) or their equivalent in each different country. The focus of FA is to exhaustively represent all the events that occurred by means of reports produced every month, quarter and year.

The theories and the reference models adopted by FA have been defined from a long time and will not to change in the future. Hence, FA systems are stable and do not evolve, particularly when comparing this field with other management topics. Once the organization has introduced and implemented a system, FA can run for several years with very little or no changes at all, unless there is a change in external requirements such as new rules, principles or laws.

While FA is oriented towards the request of external users, Management Accounting (MA) focuses on the needs of managers. In literature, it is possible to find several conceptual models that may be useful in providing information to managers. These well-known and well-defined models are designed for planning activities and, after the execution of the activities themselves, to control the obtained results and to report discrepancies, if any. Garrison et al. present this non-exhaustive list of reference models [3]:

- Cost classification;
- Job-order costing;
- Process Costing;
- Cost behaviour;
- Cost-Volume-Profit relationship;
- Variable costing;
- Activity-based costing;
- Profit Planning (Budgeting);
- Capital Budgeting;
- Advanced reporting.

In the mid-80s major complaints versus MA emerged in the literature [4]. In fact, although MA is considered essential for informed management activity, MA itself seems to have some flaws, particularly arising from its roots in Cost Accounting, as it is possible to observe in the above reported list. As a matter fact, traditional MA approach considers cost classification and analysis, Cost-Volume-Profit models, Profit Planning (Budgeting), Capital Budgeting and advanced reporting.

Researchers [5, 6] argued that: (1) MA had not evolved over the past decades; (2) MA is too focused on costs; and (3) MA is not very useful for managers, because it is not focused on strategy and on market opportunities. Manager risks to undertake incorrect decisions based on inadequate and obsolete management accounting data. The lack of attention to clients, competition and performance, together with a poor or even non-existing strategic approach could lead to inca- pacity to cope with the new highly competitive environment [7].

Strategic Management Accounting (SMA hereafter) is a promising and well-acquainted evolution of Management Accounting [8]. SMA tries to address all the above-mentioned criticisms levelled against Management Accounting. SMA was initially proposed by Simmonds at the beginning of the '80s [9] and it was not taken seriously until the late '80s. Simmonds argues that SMA greatly differs from MA because of its focus on the comparison of the business with its competitors. Langfield-Smith affirms that there is no agreed definition of SMA in literature [7].

Table 1 Traditional management accounting versus strategic management accounting

	Traditional MA	Strategic MA
1	Historical	Prospective
2	Single entity	Relative
3	Introspective	Out-ward looking
4	Manufacturing focus	Competitive focus
5	Existing activities	Possibilities
6	Reactive	Proactive
7	Programmed	Un-programmed
8	Data oriented	Information oriented
9	Based on existing systems	Unconstrained by existing systems
10	Built on conventions	Ignores conventions

However, Wilson declares that that MA differs from SMA in several aspects (see Table 1) [10].

An interesting definition of SMA has been proposed by Bromwich [11], who argues that SMA is:

> The provision and analysis of financial information on the firm's product markets and competitors' costs and cost structures and the monitoring of the enterprise's strategies and those of its competitors in these markets over a number of periods.

Ma and Tayles argue that SMA finally bridged the gap that existed between MA and strategic management [12]. SMA moved MA from monetary issues to a more multi-dimensional approach. It is not simply a new orientation, which is aimed towards strategy, it is a radically different way of re-thinking MA around strategic concepts [8]. In fact, according to Lord [13], the functions commonly associated with SMA are:

1. To collect information related to competitors.
2. To use accounting for strategic decisions.
3. To cut costs on the basis of strategic decisions.
4. And, to gain competitive advantage through it.

2.2 Strategic Management Accounting: An Empirical Perspective

A straightforward characteristic of the SMA literature is the paucity of empirical research [14]. Actually, most of the literatures regarding SMA were at conceptual level and with a prominent academic emphasis. The main concern is that SMA adoption cannot be measured directly: it is in fact necessary to investigate the adoption of those techniques that can be reconnected to the SMA concept. This is an alternative way to define SMA. While researching the link between SMA and strategy, Cinquini and Tenucci [15], proposed to define the ensemble of techniques that companies really implement instead of trying to measure the implementation of

SMA itself. Cinquini and Tenucci measured the adoption of one or more of the following techniques:

(1) Activity Based Costing/Management (ABC/M); (2) Attribute Costing; (3) Benchmarking; (4) Competitive Position Monitoring; (5) Competitor Cost Assessment; (6) Competitor Performance Appraisal on public financial statements; (7) Customer Accounting; (8) Integrated Performance Management Systems; (9) Life Cycle Costing; (10) Quality Costing; (11) Strategic Costing; (12) Strategic Pricing; (13) Target Costing; (14) Value Chain Costing.

Actually, organizations hardly understand the meaning of SMA concept, hence it is easier to ask them if they currently implement some of the above-mentioned techniques and then evaluate if they are de facto applying a SMA approach. Several researchers followed this course: Guilding et al. [16] created a report based on the survey of twelve SMA practices in different countries and concluded that the extent of diffusion was not uniform in New Zealand, UK and USA. Fowzia [14] measured the implementation of fourteen SMA techniques and in this way measured business strategy and strategic effectiveness of manufacturing organizations in Bangladesh.

3 Methodology

The methodology used is the Case Study research approach, following the methods recommended in the literature. The decision to analyse a single case study [17] may be useful for giving a detailed outline of the grounds and distinctive features of the development and subsequent implementation of the internal reporting model represented by the SMA.

The case study approach [18] is interesting since it may offer the option of constructing theories and generalizations based on the study of a single operational case [19–21]. In the case examined, the benefits of such an approach can be seen in the ability to illustrate the factors that drove the company to adopt the SMA and the consequences within the planning and control function.

In fact, there is no literature regarding SMA implementation difficulties and costs. For this reason, we were searching for an empirical case to deeply investigate the implementation of a SMA system. The selected company was interested in developing a SMA system; hence, we followed systematically the implementation of the new system.

The research carried out features aspects of a qualitative and quantitative nature: the data examined are based on interviews, the company's economic and financial documentation made available to the public on the company's website and on internal reporting documents. The period analysed concerns the period from 2011 to 2014. The interviews were conducted with the Head Quarter CFO and those responsible for management control: the questions were designed to explain the various stages of the SMA's implementation to illustrate the progress achieved and the benefits in terms of company results achieved.

The interview as opposed to the questionnaire approach offers greater flexibility even if the results were characterized by a certain degree of subjectivity due to the difficulties of interpreting the answers. However, this was useful for understanding the competitive context in which the company operates and the particular features of the sector to which it belongs.

The contribution of the paper to the literature is motivated by the lack of surveys about the SMA implementation. The major limitation of this research is that results are related to the analysis of a single case study. This study cannot lead to general conclusions and it will be necessary to conduct a comparative study between the observed company and other companies. Thus, this study represents a starting point for further research in the application of SMA concepts.

4 Strategic Management Accounting in Action: The Nespoli Group Case

4.1 Presentation of the Nespoli Group

The Nespoli Group was founded in North Italy right after the Second World War. At the end of the 40s, Oreste and Bruno Nespoli started what was called "Pennellificio Nespoli" (the Nespoli Brush factory). Initially the company was made of a few artisans working with clear and simple rules: serious work and customer satisfaction.

The company grew steadily and at the end of the 70s, it passed from being a small business to becoming an industrial sized complex. At the end of the 90s Nespoli Group started a series of acquisitions in the paint tools sector throughout Europe (see Table 2).

The first strategic acquisitions have been made in Spain, France and Germany. Together with the acquisition of Franpin Group, it acquired ZFI (Zhongshan Franpin Industries) its China based factory. Later on, Nespoli Group decided to diversify its offer and made further acquisitions in the sector of Aerosol Paint Spray with the acquisition of Italideal and CIA in Torino (Italy).

In addition, Metal Tools become part of Nespoli Group business with the acquisition of Milbox in France in 2006 and of Techno in Germany in 2008. Nespoli Group entered in the business of Wood and Leather Treatment through the acquisition of Gubra and Grand Chic (Italy). In 2010, it was created another business unit for Cleaning Tools, driven by the acquisition in Italy of the well-known PIPPO and Eurostile brands. Today the Nespoli Group, led by Luigi and Alessandro Nespoli is the first European group in the market segment of "Tools for painting", in terms of sales figures, production volumes and market size. Entering in UK, Poland, China, Russia and Turkey markets the Group had a turnover approaching 350 million Euro with over 2000 employees. The Nespoli

Table 2 Nespoly group acquisition history

Year	Country	Company
1996	SPAIN	Rulo Pluma s.a.
1999	FRANCE	Roulor s.a., Monitor s.a., Le Herisson s.a.
2001	GERMANY	Schabert Gmbh
2004	FRANCE	Franpin Group
2005	GERMANY	Friess Gmbh
2006	FRANCE	Milbox s.a.
2008	FRANCE	Mancret
	ITALY	Gubra s.r.l.
	GERMANY	Techno
	ITALY	Gaia s.r.l.
	ITALY	Italideal—Cia s.r.l.
2009	ITALY	Grand Chic s.rl.
2010	SPAIN	Castor
	ITALY	Pippo Brand
	ITALY	Eurostile
2011	GERMANY	Noelle Group

Group owns several renowned brands such as Nespoli, Roulor, Franpin, Rulo Pluma, Friess, Techno, Pippo and Coronet, and it manufactures tools for several "private labels".

4.2 The Nespoli Group's Control Model

The Nespoli Group has to manage a complex and articulated reality composed by an ensemble of mixed entities. Top managers have to clearly define not only the overall goal of the Group, but they also have to define the common rules that will to be utilized to manage all the figures. It is necessary to predispose two main sets of information, one related to the Statutory Vision of the Group, and the other presenting the Managerial Vision of the Group itself.

The Statutory Vision of the financial figures has to deal with the local accounting principles of each company. We may talk about a "Local GAAP" approach: each company produces financial accounting data following its national rules. In order to achieve Consolidated Financial Statements for the Nespoli Group, it is necessary to "homogenize" the data coming from each company.

The Managerial Vision of the figures is implemented by means of two sets of documents: (1) Management Reporting, based on business-specific control model; (2) Management Consolidation—Directional Reporting, which contains the Group consolidation figures (Group indicators and Business indicators).

The Control Model reporting is articulated according to two main levels: the Legal Entity level and the Group level.

- Legal Entity Level

  - **Top Management Reporting:** concise presentation of economic, patrimonial and financial situation of the Legal Entity; it is possible to have separate reports for Business Unit and Areas of Activity; quantitative and qualitative indicators are utilized.
  - **Operational Reporting:** it is used by operational managers and complete the information provided by Top Management Reporting; additional quantitative and qualitative indicators are utilized.

- Group Level

  - **Top Management Reporting:** concise presentation of economic, patrimonial and financial situation of the Group, divided by Business Unit and Areas of Activity; presentation of intra-group activities; quantitative and qualitative indicators show a complete description of Group's dynamics.

The specific characteristics of each business require diverse Control Models, distinguishing between the peculiar activities of each area results and the activities common to the entire Group. In particular, Group financial and fiscal planning activities are considered common to the entire Group itself. Conversely, business' specific and support activities will be referred to the autonomous administration of each Legal Entity.

4.3   The Implementation of Nespoli Group's SMA System: Architectural and Theoretical Aspects

In recent years, Nespoli Group started a relevant project with the aim to provide Top management and Business analysts with reporting information and key indicators that are common across the entire group and that could be analysed in a consistent way with various level of details.

Dr. Bosisio, the Nespoli Group Chief Information Manager (CIO), declared that DataManager is the powerful and flexible tool utilized for getting deeper into business information, empowering business analysts with OLAP technology. As we said earlier, SMA should be fed by various sources of data; however, the principal source remains a sound and well-running ERP system. Here a problem arises, because the various companies that compose the Nespoli Group are actually running diverse ERP systems, such as Legacy Systems (IBM AS400), SAP, Oracle, MS Dynamic. Therefore: (1) In the long term, the Group has to choose a single ERP system and all the companies have to gradually switch to it; (2) In the short term, it is necessary to create a system that can receive data from several sources, clean it and consolidate it.

4.3.1 The Common Nespoli Group's ERP

Dr. Bosisio stated that several considerations forced Top Management to adopt a unique ERP system throughout the Group: (1) To unify processes and data of all the Legal Entities; (2) The obsolescence of Hardware and Connectivity; (3) Increasing number of malfunctions and difficulties in finding spare parts; (4) Non updateable Software; (5) Decreasing performance; (6) Decreasing security.

During 2012, the Group has started a major project for an ERP common to all the companies of the Group itself. A "steering committee" expressly created for this task: (1) has defined the specific characteristics that the new software should possess; (2) has performed a software selection; (3) has chosen the Hardware architecture and the related organisational aspects.

The Steering Committee has stated that all the companies of the Nespoli Group have to move towards the implementation of Microsoft's Dynamics NAV ERP system in external Data-Centres. This system will unify the bookkeeping and the fiscal accounting of each Legal Entity composing the Group. Moreover, the Steering Committee decided to perform a "pilot" implementation in Noelle Group, Nespoli Deutschland and Coronet Germany, treating them as "Model Company", and considering from the beginning the needs of all the Group's companies. The project started in September 2012 for Noelle Group, in January 2014 for Nespoli Deutschland and in June 2014 for Coronet Germany.

4.3.2 The Nespoli Group's SMA

Waiting to have a unique ERP system in all the Group's companies that will ease the data gathering phase, it was necessary to predispose a sound SMA system to support Top Management's activities. For this purpose, it has been developed a proprietary system called DataManager. This system gathers fiscal and managerial data from every company's transactional system. DataManager extracts final data by means of appropriate interfaces from those transactional systems. Utilising listed processes and documented rules, it consolidates the gathered data and it arranges data sets that can be analysed from final users. This final data allows managers to prepare budgets and forecasts regarding Sales, Purchases, Stock and Manufacturing.

The outcome of the Nespoli Group's SMA system consists in several managerial reports regarding Cost classification, Job-Order Costing, Process Costing, Activity-based costing, Profit Planning and Budgeting and Advanced Reporting. In particular, managers can access SMA via an Excel interface and analyse information. However, it is possible to modify reports, and dynamically choose Legal Entities, time periods, etc. freely picking the desired dimensions of analysis.

A non-exhaustive list comprehends:

- Business Unit Analysis;
- Market Channel Analysis;
- Customer Chain Analysis;
- Trend Analysis;
- Stock Analysis—Expiring/obsolete product, Consumption spread, ABC Analysis, Stock Health Evaluation.

4.4 The Implementation of Nespoli Group's SMA System: The Service Level Agreement and the SharePoint Pilot Projects

In the last ten years, the Nespoli Group is grown exponentially through acquisitions in Italy and abroad. In a first step, the model of development has been to acquire new companies, leaving the dedicated local management of the acquired companies. The dual advantage was to maintain business continuity and to have a simplification of the chain of command; the disadvantage was the maintenance of an identity of the acquired companies that was not merged into the "Nespoli vision", as stated by Dr. Ripamonti (Group Planning and Control).

In recent years, the size and complexity of the Group have become such as to require a change in the Group's vision; hence, it was created a Head Quarter structure with the goal of:

- Steer the group as a single entity;
- Act as a chain of transmission between strategies identified by the Ownership and Group companies;
- Develop the Business Unit that represent the main product lines (Paint tools, Metal Tools, ...) by focusing on the needs of customers;

The Group's strategy continues to be a growth strategy, walking in two directions:

(a) MARKETS: strength in markets already served and further geographic expansion into new high-growth markets such as Turkey, Russia and China;
(b) BUSINESS: Diversification in products for household cleaning, spray paints, in specific products for the construction industry (Metal tools), in products dedicated to the care of the wood and leather.

Dr Scribani, the Nespoli Group Chief Value Officer (CVO), explained the growth path for products: firstly, these are complementary products; secondly, they are often purchased from the same "Buyer"; and thirdly, they fall into the Nespoli Group "Mission".

Similarly, the growth path in the new markets is aimed: (1) to exploit the competitive advantages already acquired in the markets currently occupied. It is possible to adopt a "Copy and Paste" strategy; (2) to exploit the high rates of growth in emerging countries; and (3) to follow Nespoli Group main customers in their international expansion.

In order to develop this vision, the Group has started to implement IT tools that allow setting up basic information on the subject of strategic planning and control. Furthermore, the Group has chosen to implement a "Pilot project" to test the real potential of the system itself. This project is based on two separate project: the first is a system capable to evaluate the "Service Level Agreement"; the second is a system that eases the collaboration between managers, the "SharePoint Board".

4.4.1 The Service Level Agreement System

One of the fundamental reasons why the Nespoli Group is a European leader is the attention to the quality and level of service to its customers. In the field of Large Retail Groups, customers require that the rates of delivery on time of ordered products is greater than percentages of 95 %. Delays and bad deliveries create revenue loss to the customer that rebates substantial penalties to its suppliers.

The daily collection of information for each order, for each shipment, for each customer indicating the level of service and the causes that have led to any stock-outs (delays by suppliers or production), allow a better control of the Supply Chain. This information allows also presenting to their actual and prospect the reasons why the Nespoli Group should be considered a partner and not just a supplier.

Service Level Agreement (SLA) key measures are integrated into a Supply Chain Scorecard that is consistently measured across the organization allowing benchmarking inside the Group. The main KPI analysed in SLA report are:

- Forecast accuracy
- Stock levels
- Internal/External supplier delivery performance
- Transport provider measurements
- Warehouse Operation measurements
- Order Fill rate
- Product Availability or Stockout rate
- Days Sales Outstanding
- Customer delivery transport measurements
- Customer Order Outstanding analysis

4.4.2 The SharePoint Board System

The SPB is a collection of interrelated tools that allow an integrated and systemic tool aimed at collaboration. It comprehends:

- Extented Enterprise Resources Planning (EERP) systems, implemented using Microsoft Dynamics NAV;
- CPM Corporate Performance Management (DataManager);
- Collaboration and publishing system (Microsoft SharePoint);
- Customer Relashionship Management (Microsoft Dynamics CRM)
- Other office management tools.

The Group must be governed as a single entity by creating synergies and effi-ciencies. The Nespoli Group has full coverage with companies throughout Europe and in many countries around the world. The language used in the group are many —Italian, English, German, French, Spanish, Portuguese, Turkish, Czech, Polish, Portuguese, Chinese—and it was a priority to create a point of convergence, a virtual marketplace in which everyone could easily access to get to know and to work together.

SharePoint Board is this place in which the Group publishes:

1. Relevant information at Group level (official communications, calendar reporting and budget);
2. The rules and the procedures of the Group, as they are formalized (Head Quarter organization and corporate governance of companies, procedures for transfer pricing, purchasing, year-end bonuses, items returned, item charge allocation, forecast sales, and so on).

This board has the benefit of showing the official versions of documents, eliminating hundreds of e-mail, to give unity and consistency for the behaviour to various levels of the company. Obviously, this process of formalization of the rules is a long journey because it implies that the rules are shared, accepted and implemented in the company, and that they are followed and respected.

In addition, Sharepoint board is used to manage group-wide strategic projects: within the three-year plan that is developed and approved at the end of July each year, the Head Quarter identifies 3–4 projects that have strategic value and involve more companies in the group. The projects, once approved by the ownership, become executive projects with a manager who has the task of articulating them, identifying the human resources involved, defining the time and investment required and the benefits. These projects are entered and managed using SharePoint Board. All the activities are traced and documents are stored in the official website, giving transparency to the whole project. Any delay must be justified and activities/resources are reprogrammed accordingly. It is a transparent, clear and organized way to translate the business strategy into action and to follow up the progress of projects constantly monitoring them.

Some strategic projects started and managed in SharePoint Board are:

- Development of the Business Units;
- Development of the ERP system of the Group;
- Stock performance management.

The stated aim of the CVO for the future is to develop a system of scorecards that within SharePoint Board allows to fully managing the Group's activities, linking:

- The strategic vision spelled out in the Three-year Plan;
- The articulation of the strategy (filleting and completing the projects that have been included);
- The segmented information through Business Intelligence System (e.g. margins per customer and analyses for "make or buy" decisions);
- The operational processes with a view to Best Practices such as the technology of item (PDM, Total Quality System, Product industrialization and rationalization of overlapping productions and uncompromising standards of productivity).

5 Evaluation of the Nespoli Group's SMA System and Conclusions

Several considerations can be done about the Nespoli Group's experience. However, it is important to stress that what we described is only the initial part of a long and challenging process. The final goal is to implement a rich set of procedures not only aimed to support the management, but that will also evaluate the Group's performance.

The Nespoli Group is a multinational, multilingual ensemble of companies, formed over a quite long time. The definition of a common SMA is the first effort to implement a common management background. A relevant aspect has been the definition of a common timing for data collection and subsequent elaboration of reports and documents. The SMA system homogenizes the data, the process to create reports and reports themselves. Moreover, the system acts as communication media within the Group, and it replaces all other means of communication.

Even if the SMA system was born according to the needs of the Group's Head Quarter, the implementation of the system in all the companies eased dramatically the management of each company of the Group itself. While preserving the autonomy of each Legal Entity, the adoption of SMA eases the coordination within the Group. The SMA facilitates the vertical integration between Legal Entities' Management and Nespoli Group's Management. In this way, it is ensured an effective coordination, and both Local Entities' and Group's strategies can be reached.

In this respect, the Nespoli Group's experience is highly positive. Against a relevant investment in terms of structures and management empowerment, the Group has acquired an invaluable tool that turned to be irreplaceable to manage each Legal Entity composing the Group and the Group itself.

In conclusion, we can answer the Research Questions that we had placed in the introduction:

RQ1: What are the peculiar characteristics of the SMA model in Nespoli Group?

The Nespoli Group implemented a SMA system aimed to support several issues relevant to the management of their customers and to the management of the Group itself. Actually, a pilot project monitors the Service Level Agreement, but in the future, other performance indicators will be added, thus creating a complete SMA system. Similarly, another pilot project, SharePoint Board, eases the communication within the Group.

RQ2: What is the role of SMA in the implementation of the Nespoli Group's strategy and what is the contribution to the achievement of leadership position?

The SMA system allows constant monitoring of the performance of the Group and the individual Legal Entities, thus assessing the effectiveness of the implemented strategies. In other words, the system helps Top Managers to steer the group as a single entity and, at the same time, it acts as a "chain of transmission" between strategies identified by the Ownership and single Group companies.

RQ3: What are the techniques that make up the SMA system of the Nespoli Group?

Nespoli Group has implemented many of the techniques that we have previously mentioned. The most important aspect, however, is that these analyses are used to measure the success of the strategies adopted in terms of customer satisfaction and product success. Moreover, in addition to the accounting aspects, the implemented SMA system presents significant attention to the organizational aspects.

References

1. Singh Wahla, R.: AICPA Committee on Terminology. Accounting Terminology Bulletin, 1, Review and Résumé (2011)
2. CIMA—The Chartered Institute of Management Accountants.: CIMA Official Terminology. Elsevier Science, Amsterdam (2005)
3. Garrison, R.H, Noreen, E.W., Brewer, P.C.: Managerial Accounting. 13/E, McGraw-Hill, New York (2010)
4. Johnson, H.T., Kaplan, R.S.: Relevance lost: The rise and fall of management accounting. Harvard Business School Press, Boston (1987)
5. Cooper, R.: The changing practice of management accounting. Manag. Account. **74**(3), 26 (1996)
6. Parker, L.D.: Reinventing the management accountant. Transcript of CIMA 2002, Glasgow University. http://www.cimaglobal.com/Documents

7. Langfield-Smith, K.: Strategic management accounting: how far have we come in 25 years? Account. Audit. Account. J. **21**, 204–228 (2008)
8. Shah, H., Malik, A., Malik, S.M.: Strategic management accounting—a messiah for management accounting? Australian J. Bus. Manag. Res. **4**, 01–07 (2011)
9. Simmonds, K.: Strategic management accounting. Manag. Account. **59**, 26–29 (1981)
10. Wilson, R.M.S.: Strategic management accounting. In: Ashton, D., Hopper, T., Scapens, R. (eds.) Issues in Management Accounting, pp. 159–190. Prentice-Hall Europe, London (1995)
11. Bromwich, M.: The case for strategic management accounting: the role of accounting information for strategy in competitive markets. Account. Organ. Soc. **15**, 27–46 (1990)
12. Ma, Y., Tayles, M.: On the emergence of strategic management accounting: an institutional perspective. Account. Bus. Res. **39**, 473–495 (2009)
13. Lord, R.: Strategic management accounting: the emperor's new clothes? Manag. Account. Res. **7**, 347–366 (1996)
14. Fowzia, R.: Strategic management accounting techniques: relationship with business strategy and strategic effectiveness of manufacturing organizations in Bangladesh. World J. Manag. **3**, 54–69 (2011)
15. Cinquini, L., Tenucci, A.: Strategic management accounting and business strategy: a loose coupling? J. Account. Org. Change **6**, 228–259 (2010)
16. Guilding, C., Cravens, K.S., Tayles, M.: An international comparison of strategic management accounting practices. Manag. Account. Res. **11**, 113–135 (2000)
17. Dyer, W., Wilkins, A.: Better stories, not better constructs, to generate better theory. A rejoinder to Eisenhardt. Acad. Manag. Rev. **16**(3), 613–619 (1991)
18. Ryan, B., Scapens, R., Theobald, M.: Research method and methodology in finance and accounting. Thomson, London (2002)
19. Mintzberg, H.: An emerging strategy of direct research. Adm. Sci. Q. **24**(4), 582–589 (1979)
20. Yin, R.J.: The case study crisis: some answers. Adm. Sci. Q. **26**, 58–65 (1981)
21. Eisenhardt, K.M.: Building theories from case study research. Acad. Manag. Rev. **14**(4), 532–550 (1989)

Interpreting the Correlation Between the Capacity of Generating Added Value and the Use of Business Information Systems Through the Example of SMEs

Selena Aureli, Massimo Ciambotti, Attila Jóczik and Peter Sasvari

Abstract This research has two main objectives. It aims to investigate the relation between ICT development and enterprise capacity to generate added value and explore the IT infrastructure of enterprises with reference to Hungary, Slovakia, Italy and Portugal. Data have been obtained from international datasets and an online survey including about 300 enterprises classified into microenterprises, small and medium-sized enterprises, and corporations. With reference to company IT infrastructure, findings indicate that enterprises of the two Southern European countries are more developed in relation to the number of workstations, the use of server-based networks and business information systems regardless of their size. Hungarian and Slovakian businesses hardly seem to use any of these systems. In addition, results suggest that business size does play a role in IT adoption in all examined countries. This implies that policy-makers should pay attention to business size and country-specific conditions as these two factors might affect ICT policy implementation.

Keywords Business information systems · Italy · Hungary · Portugal · Slovakia · Small and medium-sized enterprises

S. Aureli (✉)
University of Bologna, Bologna, Italy
e-mail: selena.aureli@unibo.it

M. Ciambotti
University of Urbino "Carlo Bo", Urbino, Italy
e-mail: massimo.ciambotti@uniurb.it

A. Jóczik · P. Sasvari
University of Miskolc, Miskolc, Hungary
e-mail: attila.joczik@gmail.com

P. Sasvari
e-mail: iitsasi@uni-miskolc.hu

© Springer International Publishing Switzerland 2016
D. Mancini et al. (eds.), *Strengthening Information and Control Systems*,
Lecture Notes in Information Systems and Organisation 14,
DOI 10.1007/978-3-319-26488-2_3

1 Introduction

Businesses have been using electronic devices to facilitate their operation since the emergence of computers which helped organizations to improve their information and communication processes. Similarly to all technical innovations, computers were initially only available to large companies that had enough capital to finance their development. Moreover, they were applied only to perform simple computing tasks in a faster and more efficient way [5]. Today, with the robust development of internal computer networks and the Internet, almost all companies rely on some type of information system and large organizations benefit from different corporate modules merged into a single interface designed to manage all internal and external information flows. The information stored in computers has several fields of application, from the automation of production to e-commerce and computers make possible to give answers to questions that had not even arisen before [5]. That is how a business society has evolved by now in which market share is substantially dependent on the IT support behind business enterprises.

With the increase in telephony, transmission and media broadcasting technologies, IT progressed and it was incorporated into the general concept of Information and Communication Technology (ICT) which is an integral part of every business enterprise's infrastructure of today and contributes to business development. The contribution of ICT can be appreciated at the national level in terms of its positive impact on GDP, usually calculated using added value. Although in the seventies and eighties, ICT did not seem to contribute to GDP growth, recent studies have shown that in the 1990s high GDP growth was mainly caused by the technology improvements and wider use of ICT among businesses [24]. Coherently, it might be assumed that in countries where the ICT development level is higher, the enterprises record higher productivity, organizational transformation, higher capability of manufacturing new, more complex and better quality products, which means higher added value.[1]

Nevertheless, it might be possible that this relationship does not work the same way in all countries. Several factors can affect the efficiency of transformation of ICT investments into macroeconomic outcomes [26, 27]. Among others, institutional differences such as market regulation, the legal and infrastructural environment might hinder enterprises to exploit ICT and translate it into higher value added. In countries such as Hungary, the Czech Republic, Slovakia and so on formal institutions deriving from a socialist planning economy have been remodeled from the 1990s but they may still have an impact on the business environment. Also, the information technology infrastructure of local businesses might be

---

[1]Added value at basic prices can be simply defined as the difference between gross output (at basic prices) and intermediate consumption (at purchaser prices) and can be decomposed into the following components: Compensation of Employees; Gross Operating Surplus; Mixed Income; and Other Taxes on Production less Subsidies on Production. OECD National Accounts of OECD Countries 2009, -Volume I, Main Aggregates, OECD Publishing (2009).

different, especially if we consider that small-sized private enterprises may lack enough financial capital to adopt ICT solutions and only formerly state-owned corporations or foreign multinationals may have the necessary financial resources to access advanced technology [10].

Thus, this paper aims to answer to the following questions: (1) Are countries such as Hungary and Slovakia exploiting and transforming ICT into added value as efficiently as other European countries? (2) Are there any differences in the level of ICT adoption in Hungarian, Slovakian, Italian and Portuguese enterprises? (3) Is business size an explanatory variable of ICT adoption?

Since international statistics do not provide sufficiently detailed comparable data on ICT usage among businesses, an online survey was mailed to more than 300 enterprises in which they were classified into groups of micro-enterprises, small and medium-sized enterprises and corporations. The paper proceeds as follows. After a brief literature review, explanations on how to measure ICT development level and its economic impact are provided. In the methodology section, the authors describe how they tested the relationship between ICT and added value with a special attention to the econometric approach which helps to interpret some of the results. The paper concludes with some indications for further research.

2 Literature Review

The relationship between ICT investments and macroeconomic outcomes such as GDP represents an important stream of research in economic studies [3, 9, 21] which have mainly tested this link on developed countries [15, 24]. On the contrary, researches into the formerly Socialist countries revealed a lower impact on economic growth [12, 18, 25, 27], suggesting that some specific factors might hinder these countries to achieve the same return on information technology investments seen in Western European countries. In addition, there are studies indicating that the impact of ICT investments on these economies is not the same. Some authors [18] ascribe differences between Hungary and Slovakia to the diverse historical background and transition process chosen. National differences in institutional context have also directly influenced the ICT adoption level. According to [16], for example, the role of the state in Hungary (which owned several large corporations accountable for the majority of national expenses on IT) and the national information infrastructure policy have strongly impacted ICT production and use, although some surveys comparing Slovakian and Hungarian enterprises in terms of information systems adoption do not find strong differences [29].

ICT adoption among enterprises represents a more narrower research topic, which has been investigated by several authors, especially in terms of Information Systems/Information Technology usage. IS/IT adoption is now considered a mature field of research [30]. However, research papers on transition economies are rare to find in international journals [31]. Surveys usually devote a great attention to business information systems (according to [31] this is the most studied topic, closely followed by electronic applications) because of their great capability to contribute to productivity increase, time saving, cost-reduction, knowledge improvement and value creation [17]. Business information systems are actually fundamental to access, recover, use or manipulate any type of information that the user needs [6]. These systems utilize computer hardware and software, manual procedures, models for analysis and decision-making, which can provide relevant information to support the operations, management, analysis, and decision-making functions in an organization [11]. Moreover, an increasing number of studies focuses on SMEs which have been traditionally labeled as low ICT adopters. This is also true for the countries considered in this study. Smaller Slovakian enterprises seem to lag behind their larger business counterparts in ICT adoption [19] like the Hungarian ones [28, 29], as well as Italian [2, 8, 22] and Portuguese SMEs [7].

3   Methodology

The present study focuses on two former planning economies, Hungary and Slovakia, which are considered similar on the basis of becoming EU member states with the first wave of accession from Easter Europe in 2004 and it compares them with other two Southern European countries, namely Italy and Portugal, which seem to have a more similar ICT development level in international statistics compared to the highly developed Northern European countries. Below a description is provided on how to measure ICT development level and added value created by enterprises in a country. The chosen indicators are used to verify the supposed relationship between ICT development level and added value, by performing a linear correlation analysis. Then, since ICT indices do not strictly refer to enterprises, nor there are statistical data on enterprises' information systems adoption classified for business size, researchers had to carry out an empirical survey to collect information about the current practices of businesses belonging to different size categories.

3.1   The ICT Development Level at a Country Level

To measure the ICT development level two types of indicators can be used [3]. The first type of indicators show the quantitative aspects of ICT development, while the another group of indicators include more complex measures of development such as skills and usage. The first type of indicators are useful to represent the general development level of a country but they do not quite express the real situation. Its appropriate examples are: the number of ICT devices, the number of ICT employees, the number of ICT enterprises, etc. They are used for characterizing the general ICT standards of a country on average. In contrast, complex or integrated indicators do not only put an emphasis on measuring ICT infrastructure but they also take quality issues into account. ICT Development Index (IDI) is an index published by the United Nations International Telecommunication Union (ITU) based on internationally agreed information and communication technologies indicators. It is used to measure the ICT development levels in 155 countries. The index itself, which can be used as an evaluation tool at global, regional and country levels alike, combines 11 indicators grouped into three sub-indices: ICT access, use and skills. The IDI index indicates that Northern and Western European countries occupy the top positions in the EU. Looking at individual countries, the IDI index indicates that Italy is the most advanced country (16th), followed by Portugal (22nd), Slovakia (23rd) and Hungary (24th). None of the four countries here examined is the best performer of the geographical area they belong to. In fact, the Czech Republic and Poland are the most advanced among the Eastern European countries in the EU, while with reference to Southern European countries, the countries achieving the highest score are Slovenia and Malta.

3.2 The Added Value in the European Union

According to EU national statistics [14], the added value created in the EU is EUR 6441 billion. Nearly half of it produced by Western European countries. Countries of Northern and Southern Europe contribute to the EU's performance with EUR 2927 billion while the lowest performance is observed in the case of Eastern European countries by EUR 404 billion. Considering business size categories, we notice that the added value of micro-enterprises and SMEs in Southern Europe is equal to 67 %: this means that their contribution is greater in proportion than the performance of similar enterprises in Northern Europe and other countries. In detail, it can be stated that both micro-enterprises and small enterprises of Southern European countries record the highest capacity to create added value compared to their counterparts in Europe. On the contrary, Eastern European countries record the lowest rates in both size categories. Focusing on the four examined countries, in 2012, an Italian enterprise produced an average value added of 168,000 EUR, which corresponds to nearly 54 % of the EU average added value. A better result was achieved by Slovakian enterprises since their average performance reached 96 % of the EU average. Hungary had the lowest average (28 %), although this figure was exceeded only a bit by Portuguese enterprises (35 %). Slightly different rankings emerge when considering the average amount of added value created by size category. The average added value created by micro-enterprises in Italy reached 52,000 EUR, followed by Slovakia (39,000 EUR), Portugal (27,000 EUR) and Hungary (17,000 EUR). Based on the average added value of small-sized enterprises, Italy is the first, followed by Portugal, Slovakia and Hungary. Also with reference to medium-sized enterprises Italy ranks first (it exceeded the EU average by 2 %), followed by Portugal, Slovakia and Hungary. Based on the average performance of corporations, the highest added value on average was generated in Italy. Portugal ranked second, followed by Hungary and Slovakia.

3.3 ICT Adoption Among Enterprises

When focusing on enterprises, ICT usage should be measured with reference to their IT infrastructure (hardware, network and software) which consists of all components that somehow play a role in overall IT and IT-enabled operations which allow an organization to deliver IT solutions and services to its employees, partners and/or customers. Thus, only through direct surveys addressed to enterprises it is possible to understand their ICT development level. Particularly important in contributing to added value creation is the software component which consists of numerous and different business information systems (IS) that can be adopted to support several business activities. IS can actually be connected to activities of strategic planning, management control and operational control [1] and designed to support different levels of managerial decision-making process. In details, an executive information system (EIS) is a type of management information system (MIS) that facilitates and supports senior executives information and decision-making needs. It provides easy access to internal and external information relevant to organizational goals. It is commonly considered a specialized form of decision support system (DSS). Management information systems (MIS) are distinct from other information systems because they are used to analyze and facilitate strategic and operational activities. Originally, the term MIS described applications providing managers with information about sales, inventories, and other data that would help in managing the enterprise. Over time, the term broadened to include: decision support systems, resource management and human resource management, enterprise resource planning (ERP), enterprise performance management (EPM), supply chain management (SCM), customer relationship management (CRM), project management and database retrieval applications. According to the traditional structure, MIS, DSS and EIS are based on a Transaction Processing system (TPS) which is a software system, or software/hardware combination, that supports the processing of individual, indivisible operations called transactions. CRM, SRM and SCM systems are basically designed to support decision-making at operational and tactical levels but it is inevitably necessary to have an underlying TPS system that addresses the daily tasks. Business Intelligence (BI) systems can include all sorts of decision support systems used at middle and senior management levels that appear as BI applications. BI systems are always based on some lower-level support systems, mostly on ERP systems. ERP and BI systems can also be found in a complex package. It is needed to emphasize that this categorization should not be regarded as a rule, it describes only the current major trends. There are instances showing that some systems also extend to other levels of decision-making, and general shifts between these levels are also possible due to the continuous development.

3.4 Research Design

To explore enterprises' IT infrastructure we conducted an empirical survey carried out by questionnaires. Questions were built taking into account the relevant literature as well as the results of some former empirical studies on the subject. The first part of the questionnaire contains questions about the company background information and issues related to hardware (number of workstations). Other questions focus on Internet usage habits, while the last and longest section is aimed at assessing the usage patterns of business information systems. Assuming that higher added value is related to more advanced IT infrastructure and considering that, as stated in previous paragraphs, Hungary records the lowest amounts for average added value creation in both micro, small and medium-sized enterprises and ranked second to last in the group of corporations, we hypothesize the following:

– Hungary either holds the last or the last but one position in the group of the studied countries in terms of both number of hardware devices used, frequency of using network infrastructure and business information systems implemented;
– Italy holds the first position, followed by Portugal, Slovakia and Hungary in terms of both number of hardware devices used, frequency of using network infrastructure and business information systems implemented.

The sample size for comparison was almost identical as 94 enterprises in Hungary, 35 enterprises in Portugal, 86 enterprises in Slovakia and 106 enterprises in Italy completed and returned the questionnaire by the set deadline. The sample of the responding enterprises cannot be considered as representative of the total population, so the results of the survey can be interpreted only within the scope of the responding companies. The evaluation of the received data and the representation of the results were assisted by the application of Excel 2007 and SPSS 16.0 statistical software package. Diagrams, tables and revealed correlations were compiled to interpret results.

4 The Correlation Between IDI and the Added Value

Correlation calculations are used to describe the direction and the strength of a linear relationship between variables. In our calculation, the correlation between two variables—the IDI of a country and the average added value created by enterprises—was examined. Depending on the individual countries, the values of IDI were between 5 and 8.5, the added value per enterprise was between 50,000 and 800,000 Euros. The correlation coefficient is 0.791, which indicates a strong positive relationship. The linear correlation coefficient is the square of the determinant coefficient, which explains the added value with the IDI by 61 %. The standard error of the estimate (SEE) helps determine the accuracy of the prediction. SEE shows the average standard deviation of the added value from the estimated values, which is a value of 1.39. The ANOVA table shows a similar division to variance analysis, based on the variance explained by each regression (817842.426), and non-explained variance (487849.245). Here, the significance of the f-test can also be read, which confirms the existence of the correlation (Sig. <0.05). In addition, it can also be observed by interpreting the t-test that the significance of the variable determining steepness is less than 5 %, therefore IDI has a real effect on added value. Based on the Unstandardized Coefficients, it is possible to read the formula of the regression line:

Added value = $-1010.976 + 196.45 * IDI$

It becomes clear that the member states of the European Union can be divided into four distinct groups. (1) Relatively high added value per enterprise with a comparably higher IT development level. This group of countries includes Austria, Germany, the United Kingdom and Ireland. (2) Relatively high added value per enterprise with a comparably lower IT development level. Denmark, the Netherlands, Finland, Sweden and France belong to this group. (3) Relatively low added value per enterprise with a comparably higher IT development level. Four countries can be found in this group, namely Slovakia, Cyprus, Romania and Bulgaria. (4) Relatively low added value with a comparably low IT development level. This is the most populous group, comprising Lithuania, Latvia, Estonia, Malta, Spain, Italy, Slovenia, Poland, Greece, the Czech Republic, Portugal and Hungary. Only Slovakia can be found above the regression line while Italy, Portugal and Hungary are located below it. It means that the average added value created by enterprises in these three countries is lower than the level of their ICT development. In contrast, the ICT development level of the enterprises operating in Slovakia is higher than the country's average added value.

5   The IT Infrastructure of Enterprises Operating in Italy, Portugal, Hungary and Slovakia

Typically, a standard IT infrastructure is distributed according to the following components: Hardware (servers, computers, data centers, switches, hubs and routers, etc.), Network (server-based network, Internet connectivity, firewall and security), Software (Business Information Systems, productivity applications and more) and Meatware (human users such as network administrators, developers, designers and generic end users with access to any IT appliance). Each component, except the last one, has been investigated through the empirical survey.

5.1   Number of Workstation and Use of Server-Based Networks

Results (as displayed in Table 1) from our primary research showed that Italian and Portuguese companies of all sizes record the highest number of workstations. The

Table 1 The average number of workstations (WS) and the frequency rate of server-based networks (N %)

Size/ Country	Micro-enterprise		Small-sized enterprise		Medium-sized enterprise		Corporation	
	WS	N %	WS	N %	WS	N %	WS	N %
Italy	5	52	28	94	241	94	1252	100
Portugal	5	67	33	100	145	100	1647	100
Hungary	3	30	7	52	55	93	1105	100
Slovakia	3	14	4	59	8	85	33	100

lowest number of workstations used by businesses was measured in Slovakia, although Hungary is not recording a big amount, lagging far behind the two Southern European countries.

The presence of server-based networks in large organizations is the same in all examined countries, while Portugal ranks quite high in all other size categories, followed by Italy, then Hungary and lastly by the Slovakian enterprises.

5.2 The Use of Business Information Systems

Integrated ERP systems are not made just for corporations. Based on our primary research, now more than 90 % of the Portuguese and Italian enterprises employing over 250 workers use ERP systems. This rate was almost 90 % in Slovakia and 60 % in Hungary in 2012. Based on our own research, SAP Business One, Libra6i, JD Edwards, Microsoft Dynamics NAV and Microsoft Dynamics AX were used by a quarter of the Italian microenterprises, two-thirds of small-sized enterprises and four-fifths of medium-sized enterprises. A favourable picture was shown by the Portuguese enterprises since three-quarters of small-sized enterprises and nine-tenth of medium-sized enterprises used ERP systems there.

In the field of MIS there are wide variations among the EU countries as well. Among the two Southern European countries examined in detail, a quarter of the Italian microenterprises used some sort of MIS systems. 16 % of those not using such systems reported that they were planning to introduce them. Based on our measurements, the Hungarian and Slovakian small-sized enterprises barely used MIS systems while the usage rate reached 60 and 57 % in Italy and Portugal, respectively. The use of MIS systems by the Hungarian medium-sized enterprises was more frequent, ranging up to 40 %. This was still only half of the data obtained from Italy but more than double of the usage frequency rate of MIS measured among the Slovakian medium-sized enterprises. The smallest difference was observed in the category of corporations. These systems were used by the corporations in the two Southern European countries with a frequency rate close to 90–100 % and 60–70 % in the two Eastern European countries.

The use of CRM by microenterprises was low in the studied countries because of the relatively small customer base. More than half of the small-sized enterprises in Portugal used this system. Much lower frequency rates were measured in Italy (23 %), Hungary (15 %) and Slovakia (9 %). More than a third of the Italian, Portuguese and Hungarian medium-sized enterprises applied some kind of CRM software. In this regard, Slovakia showed the poorest result with 17 %. More than half of the corporations used CRM systems in the surveyed countries in 2012. The data were outstanding in the case of Portugal where more than 80 % of the corporations used such systems.

More than a tenth of the Italian, Hungarian and Slovakian small-sized enterprises had some kind of SCM systems. The measured frequency rate was exactly twice as high in the case of the Italian medium-sized enterprises as among the small-sized ones there, that is 34 %. A quarter of the medium-sized enterprises in Hungary and less than a fifth of them in Slovakia used SCM systems. In all the surveyed countries at least 40 % of the corporations operate such systems. The highest frequency rate was measured in Portugal, where it reached 83 %.

6 Conclusions

At a country level, a significant relationship can be observed between the average added value generated by the enterprises in the EU and the general ICT development level. While the average added value created by Portuguese and Hungarian enterprises is lower, that of the Slovakian enterprises is higher compared to what they could achieve at their current ICT development level. Thus we can state that transition economies are not all equal. Actually, in terms of average added value created, Slovakian enterprises reach higher scores than their Hungarian counterparts in almost each business size category. With reference to company IT infrastructure, we can notice that country rankings emerged from survey results are quite in line with the ranking we could expect on the basis of average added value. Italian and Portuguese enterprises rank before Hungarian and Slovakian enterprises in terms of both the number of workstations and server-based network usage. The fallback of the Hungarian and Slovakian companies is the largest in the groups of micro and small-sized enterprises, while a since their frequency rate of using server-based networks was nearly half the rate experienced in the case of their Italian and Portuguese counterparts in comparison. In terms of the number of workstations, the gap between the studied Eastern European countries and the two Southern European countries is even larger. Half of the amount or even less could be observed in all size categories among the studied Eastern European countries than either in Italy or in Portugal. Also the higher adoption rate of business information systems among Italian enterprises emphasizes a relevant difference to their Hungarian and Slovakian peers. By examining the use of the highlighted business information systems more closely, it could be found that microenterprises both in Hungary and Slovakia hardly used or did not use any of those systems. The usage rate of business information systems by the Italian and Portuguese small-sized enterprises is three times higher at the level of tasks and ten times higher at an operational level than it could be found among the Hungarian and Slovakian enterprises belonging to the same size category. The use of business information systems among the Hungarian and Slovakian medium-sized enterprises was similar to that of the Portuguese ones at a tactical level, while a greater backlog of 30 % could be detected at the other levels. With reference to corporations differences in the use of business information systems lessen. Yet, a significant gap could be identified at a strategic level considering the corporations operating in these two countries. It is worthy to note that such variances in the penetration of business information systems dot not correspond to a different level of involvement by the top management. IT functions are supervised by different organizations according to both country and size. Most of the Italian and Hungarian microenterprises entrusted their executive, their Slovakian counterparts entrusted an employee working at a lower departmental level with this task. In Portugal, external service providers were responsible for IT functions. In the category of small-sized enterprises in Portugal and Hungary, the executive was the most commonly appointed person while an employee at a lower departmental level was preferred in Italy. In Slovakia mainly executives were chosen to coordinate the tasks in relation to IT. Regardless of the studied countries, IT managers or CIOs were generally in charge of the operation of IT functions in the categories of medium-sized enterprises and corporations.

This research was (partially) carried out in the framework of the Center of Excellence of Mechatronics and Logistics at the University of Miskolc.

References

1. Anthony, R.: Planning and Control Systems: A Framework for Analysis. Harvard Business Review (1965)
2. Aureli, S., Ciambotti, M., Giampaoli, D.: I sistemi informativi automatizzati a supporto dei processi di direzione aziendale. Ancora un ritardo cronico per le imprese? Controllo di Gestione, n. 6 (2012) (in Italian)
3. Bilbao-Osorio, B., Dutta, S., Geier, T., Lanvin, B.: The global information technology report 2013, The Networked Readiness Index 2013: Benchmarking ICT Uptake and Support for Growth and Jobs in a Hyperconnected World, 2013 World Economic Forum (2013)
4. Bonnell, V.E., Gold, T.B.: The new entrepreneurs of Europe and Asia: Patterns of business development in Russia, Eastern Europe, and China. Sharpe, New York (2002)
5. Brynjolfsson, E., Hitt, L.M.: Beyond computation: Information technology, organizational transformation and business performance. J. Econ. Perspect. 23–48 (2000)
6. Burt, E., Taylor, J.A.: Information and communication technologies: Reshaping voluntary organizations? Nonprofit Manag. Leadersh. 11(2), 131–143 (2003)
7. Caldeira, M.M., Ward, J.M.: Understanding the successful adoption and us of IS/IT in SMEs: An explanation from Portuguese manufacturing industries. Inf. Syst. J. 12(2), 121–152 (2002)

8. Cioppi, M., Savelli, E.: ICT e PMI. L'impatto delle nuove tecnologie sulla gestione aziendale delle piccole imprese, Genova: ASPI/INS-Edit (2006) (in Italian)
9. Colecchia, A., Schreyer, P.: ICT investment and economic growth in the 1990s: Is the United States a unique case? a comparative study of nine OECD Countries, OECD Science, Technology and Industry Working Papers, No. 2001/07, OECD Publishing (2001)
10. Csermely, A., Vincze, J.: Financing patterns in Hungary—as seen from balance sheets and from interviews. In: Colombo, E., Driffill, J. (ed.) The Role of Financial Markets in the Transition Process. Contributions to Economics, Physica-Verlag Heidelberg, pp. 199–225 (2003)
11. Davis, G.B., Olson, M.H.: Management information systems: Conceptual foundations, structure and development. McGraw Hill, New York (1985)
12. Dewan, S., Kraemer, K.L.: Information technology and productivity: Evidence from country-level data. Manage. Sci. 46(4), 548–562 (2000)
13. EBRD.: Transition Report 2013, European Bank for Reconstruction and Development: London. http://www.ebrd.com/downloads/research/transition/tr13.pdf (2013)
14. Enterprise and Industry.: SBA Fact Sheet, Austria, Belgium, Bulgaria, Cyprus, the Czeh Republic, Denmark, Estonia, Finland, France, Germany, Greece, Hungary, Ireland, Italy, Latvia, Lithuania, Luxemburg, Malta, Netherlands, Poland, Portugal, Romania, Slovakia, Slovenia, Spain, Sweden, United Kingdom (2012)
15. Haag, S., Cummings, M., McCubbrey, D.J.: Management Information Systems for the Information Age, McGraw Hill, Irwin, New York (2003)
16. Harindranath, G.: ICT in a transition economy: The case of Hungary. J. Glob. Inf. Technol. Manage. 11(4), 33–55 (2008)
17. Jalava, J., Pohjola, M.: Economic growth in the new economy: Evidence from advanced economies. Inf. Econ. Policy 14(2), 189–210 (2002)
18. Janke, F., Packova, M.: Impact of ICT investments on performance of companies in transition economies: evidence from Czech Republic, Hungary and Slovakia. Qual. Innov. Prosperity (Kvalita Inovacia Prosperita) 17(2), 9–21 (2013)
19. Kokles, M., Romanova, A.: Exploitation of information systems in Slovak enterprises. Ekonomicky Casopis 52(8), 1009–1026 (2004)
20. Koyame-Marsh, R.O.: The complexities of economic transition: Lessons from the Czech Republic and Slovakia. Int. J. Bus. Soc. Sci. 2(19), 71–85 (2011)
21. Kraemer, K.L., Dedrick, J.: Information technology and productivity: Results and policy implications of cross-country studies, Center for Research on Information Technology and Organizations. http://escholarship.org/uc/item/367812fd (2011)
22. Lucchetti, R., Sterlacchini, A.: The adoption of ICT among SMEs: Evidence from an Italian survey. Small Bus. Econ. 23(2), 151–168 (2004)
23. Oliner, S.D., Sichel, D.E.: The resurgence of growth in the late 1990s: Is information technology the story? (March 17, 2000). FEDS Working Paper No. 2000-20 (2000)
24. Oliner, S.D., Sichel, D.E.: Information technology and productivity: Where are we now and where are we going? Econ. Rev. Fed. Reserve Bank Atlanta Third Quarter 87(3), 15–44 (2002)
25. Piatkowski, M.: The new economy and economic growth in transition economies: The relevance of institutional infrastructure, WIDER Discussion Papers/World Institute for Development Economics (UNU-WIDER) 2002/62 (2003)
26. Samoilenko, S.: Contributing factors to information technology investment utilization in transition economies: An empirical investigation. Inf. Technol. Dev. 14(1), 52–75 (2008)
27. Samoilenko, S., Ngwenyama, O.: Understanding the human capital dimension of ICT and economic growth in transition economies. J. Glob. Inf. Technol. Manage. 14(1), 59–79 (2011)
28. Sasvari, P.: Usage habits of business information system in Hungary. Int. J. Eng. Innovative Technol. 2(8), 141–147 (2013)
29. Sasvari, P., Majoros, Z.: Comparison of the information technology development in Slovakia and Hungary. Int. J. Adv. Comput. Sci. Appl. 4(2), 59–64 (2013)

30. Venkatesh, V., Davis, F.D., Morris, M.G.: Dead or alive? technology adoption research. J. Assoc. Inf. Syst. **8**, 267–286 (2007)
31. Williams, M.D., Dwivedi, Y.K., Lal, B., Schwarz, A.: Contemporary trends and issues in IT adoption and diffusion research. J. Inf. Technol. **24**(1), 1–10 (2009)
32. World Bank, Unleashing Prosperity.: Productivity growth in Eastern Europe and the Former Soviet Union. Washington D.C, The World Bank (2008)

Management Discussion and Analysis in the US Financial Companies: A Data Mining Analysis

Carlo Caserio, Delio Panaro and Sara Trucco

Abstract This research aims to analyse how managers react to firm's financial conditions, in issuing the Management Discussion and Analysis (MD&A) and if MD&A content could be used to forecast firms' future financial performance. To do so, we appeal to text mining techniques such as natural language processing and sentiment analysis. The main assumption is that the MD&A content varies depending on financial and economic conditions companies are experiencing. The study is conducted on a sample of US listed financial companies which experienced, between 1995 and 2011, different financial conditions, namely: (1) companies which filed for Chap. 11, thus having a high risk of bankruptcy; (2) companies not filing for Chap. 11, but with a medium risk of bankruptcy according to their economic and financial performance ratios; (3) companies not filing for Chap. 11, with a healthy financial situation. Empirical results reveal some interesting findings regarding the association between the bankruptcy risk levels and the content of the MD&A. This research also provides useful statistical instruments in supporting the stakeholders to investigate the reliability of the MD&As, examining the language used by the companies (effect), as response to financial conditions (cause). Text mining analysis allows to reveal some information that would otherwise remain implicit or even hidden behind complex periods and sentences. Contrary to our expectations, results suggest that companies experiencing high risk of bankruptcy use more positive words than those with medium and low bankruptcy risk. Also, findings show that companies with medium and low bankruptcy risk make a more appropriate use of positive and negative words. Moreover, we found that negative words contained in MD&A are an useful indicator to forecast a worsening of the

C. Caserio (✉)
eCampus University, Novedrate (CO), Italy
e-mail: carlo.caserio@uniecampus.it

D. Panaro
iBe Tse Ltd., Rome, Italy
e-mail: d.panaro@be-tse.it

S. Trucco
Rome University of International Studies, Rome, Italy
e-mail: sara.trucco@unint.eu

© Springer International Publishing Switzerland 2016
D. Mancini et al. (eds.), *Strengthening Information and Control Systems*,
Lecture Notes in Information Systems and Organisation 14,
DOI 10.1007/978-3-319-26488-2_4

43

main financial ratios. Regarding to the future researches, this study provides the starting point for analysing the role of MD&A in supporting the independent auditors' reports. Recent studies show that audit firms often fail in predicting the bankruptcy risk of distressed companies and such an error could be due to the role of MD&A, as auditors may take it as a base for releasing their independent report.

Keywords Management's discussion and analysis · Bankruptcy risk · Text mining · Sentiment analysis · Financial companies

1 Literature Analysis

The Management's Discussion and Analysis (MD&A) is considered the most relevant document issued by managers, as it assesses the liquidity conditions of a company, along with its capital resources and operations. The MD&A firstly appeared in 1968 as an element of the Guides for Preparation and Filing of Registration Statements [1], but only starting from 1974, it became a mandatory accompanying document of annual report [2].

The mandatory nature of MD&A was imposed to make public and, above all, understandable the critical information about the predictable trends that may affect the future operations of the business [3]. Due to its role, MD&A is the most read and most relevant component among the financial information disclosed by the companies [4] and it is the document financial analysts rely on most frequently in the United States, when they prepare their reports [5, 6].

In the US context and according to SEC, the MD&A has three main objectives:

1. to provide a narrative explanation of a company's financial statements that enables investors to see the company through the eyes of management;
2. to enhance the overall financial disclosure and provide the context within which financial information should be analysed;
3. to provide information about the quality of, and potential variability of, a company's earnings and cash flow [7].

We focus on two main literature streams: (1) the quality and the fidelity of MD&A; (2) reliability of MD&A content to forecast future performance of a firm.

According to the first literature stream, the MD&A might not be as informative as intended. A frequent criticism that investors have advanced along the years against the MD&A is that it is often focused on numbers already disclosed in the financial statement, instead of on the future performance of the company and that, more in general, its quality and usefulness has declined in the recent years [8, 9]. Some scholars found out that most of the companies issuing MD&A paid much heavier attention to historical details, than to forecasts [10].

Even if the regulators have paid attention to improving the quality of MD&A, also in response to some financial scandals [11, 12], management's discretion remains a fact [8, 13–15]. We believe that this level of discretion might be even higher when a company is entering in a financial distress. On this topic, authors analysed the association between distress and disclosure, finding that the quality of MD&A disclosures is quite low because of the unethical behaviour of managers who insufficiently disclose items that would be of interest to investors. They also found that, on average, managers of distressed firms increase disclosure quality in the first years of distress [16]. Other studies lead to similar conclusions, showing that companies entering distress during a period of economic good times, may use on purpose a weak and inadequate disclosure as a means to make vague the poor prospects they have for recovery [17–19].

Authors which dealt with the association between financial distress and MD&A disclosure, took advantage from quality indexes consisting in scores provided by the personnel of SEC [20] or by the members of Toronto Society of Financial Analysts (TSFA) [21]. The critique role of discretion and interpretation, as results of the SEC guidelines, along with the opportunities for managers to influence investor's perceptions of future firm performance thanks to qualitative disclosures, led to a sensitive increase of the contributions regarding the textual analysis of such qualitative information.

The study of Huang et al. [22] offers an idea of which are the main disclosure medium analysed, the measure used for the qualitative characteristic and the outcome investigated. However, only a few studies based on a textual analysis are focused on the MD&A [3, 23–26].

According to the second literature stream, scholars show the existence of a growing interest in understanding *whether* and *how* the information *embedded* in the MD&As could be helpful for obtaining reliable forecasts on the economic and financial performances of the companies. In this regard, literature shows, quite clearly, that the content of MD&A assumes a great relevance for earnings forecasts. Lang and Lundholm [27], for example, using Financial Analysts Federation's (FAS's) ratings of the companies' disclosure as a proxy for the quality, found that the higher is the quality of the financial disclosure, the lower is the forecast error and dispersion. A follow-up analysis performed by Barron et al. [28] is focused on the quality of MD&A rather than on the global disclosure. They found that MD&A of highest rated firms are associated with less error and dispersion in analysts' earnings forecasts. Similar conclusions are obtained by a number of researches that analyse the quality of forecast in association with stock prices [29] and trading volume [30, 31]. However, the inclusion of the earnings forecasts in the MD&A can also result as a lever managers can use to give more emphasis to some aspects respect to others [32]. Nevertheless, in some cases, especially when the management's actions are difficult to anticipate by outsiders (e.g. when the firm's inventories are abnormally high, when there is an excess capacity or when the firm is experiencing a loss), management's forecasts contained in the MD&A are more reliable than those provided by analysts [33].

Our approach is to use text-mining tools to extrapolate useful information from MD&A that are subsequently used in classical regression analyses. First aim of our research is to let emerge whether and how the content of MD&As undergoes any changes according to the different business conditions that companies are experiencing. Secondly, we investigate whether the content of the MD&A could provide a reliable basis to forecast future financial performance.

2 Research Design

Starting from the preliminary consideration that the sector of financial companies is the most significant given its impacts on a wide range of stakeholders and even on the economic system as a whole, we noted that a quite low attention has been paid by scholars so far.

We, therefore, conducted the study on financial US-listed firms as the US is still considered the premier market and financial center and also because the US is where frauds, scandals and collapses have the biggest resonance, thus it deserves greater attention from regulators. We took as a reference the listed companies for two main reasons: (1) the higher impact they have on the stakeholders respect to non-listed companies and (2) data issued by listed companies are subject to higher publicity. Moreover, given the role of financial companies in the economic system, they receive higher attention by governments and regulators, consequently, they are expected to disclose information more thoroughly than industrial firms.

Given the high relevance reckoned to the US-listed financial institutions, the related MD&As are crucial as well. For this reason they deserve, more than other documents, a deep analysis able to reveal whether MD&A content varies according to the performance situation of the company. This aim is consistent with other recent contributions that investigated whether managers use discretion to hype the company beyond the level justified by financial ratios or to mask poor future financial performance [22].

Since literature agrees on these points, it cannot be neglected the relevance of MD&A issued by financial companies in financial distress.

We expect companies with higher level of bankruptcy risk to disclose in the MD&As more negative information than those disclosed by companies with low bankruptcy risk.

On these suppositions, we posit the first research question:

- *RQ1: Does the MD&A content vary according to financial conditions the company is experiencing?*

Furthermore, the content of MD&A could be considered a basis on which try to forecast the future financial performance of the companies.

As shown in the previous paragraph of this research, several attempts have been made by scholars so far to investigate the effects of MD&A content in earnings forecast [28–33]. Therefore, in this perspective, the analysis of the MD&A content is suitable to answer our second research question:

- *RQ2: Is the content of the MD&A useful to forecast future financial conditions of a company?*

3   Sample Selection

We focus the analysis on three samples of US listed financial companies, characterized by a different distress level.

In order to split the three samples according to the bankruptcy risk, we take advantage from the Chap. 11. Chapter 11 is a chapter of Title 11 of the United States Bankruptcy Code which allows companies to reorganise their debts under the US bankruptcy laws. Thus, we use the filing for Chap. 11 as a proxy of bankruptcy risk.

As first step, we collected 996 US-listed companies that filed for Chap. 11 between 2002 and 2011 from the Edgar SEC database. Among these, we extracted only the 60 belonging to the financial sector. For each one, using Thomson Reuters Datastream, we extracted the classical accounting performance ratios used for financial statement analysis, excluding companies for which there are no data available. We ended up with a list of 42 companies that, according to our proxy, have a High Risk of Bankruptcy (HRB group).

As second step, we randomly picked up 156 US financial companies which did not file for Chap. 11. According to the values of financial ratios, we then selectsed, from the sample of 156, two smaller samples of companies: (1) a group of 42 with the worst financial situation; (2) a group of 42 with the best financial situation. We assigned to the first sample a Medium Risk of Bankruptcy (MRB group) and to the second a Low Risk of Bankruptcy (LRB group). The MRB group is thus composed of firms that are not *healthy* but neither so prejudicial to need to file for Chap. 11, whereas the LRB group is composed of firms with *healthy* financial conditions.

For both two samples we extract the same classical accounting performance ratios collected for HRB firms.

For each firm we extracted, from the open SEC Edgar Database, the annual report (10-K or 10 KSB) from 1995 to 2011. According to the literature and the professionals [7, 26], the MD&A can be found in the item 7 named Management's Discussion and Analysis of Financial Condition and Results of Operations), in the item 7a named Quantitative and Qualitative Disclosures about Market Risks and in the succeeding item named Forward Looking Statements. For our analysis we thus captured the portion of the filing beginning with Item 7 (or Sect. 7) and ending with Item 8 (or Sect. 8)—Financial Statements.

SEC filings are useful within our research as they are quite standardized in the format, even if the word choice, the length and the tone across filings can significantly vary.

Following the literature recommendations [24, 26], we use the dictionary created by Loughran and McDonald [34] for textual analysis of MD&A and 10-Ks in general (word lists are available at http://www.nd.edu/~mcdonald/Word_Lists. html). In particular, Loughran and McDonald split the whole set of words into six semantic fields: (1) negative words; (2) positive words; (3) uncertainty words; (4) litigious words; (5) modal words strong; and (6) modal words weak. This classification scheme is thus used to measure the tone change in the MD&A sections as shown in the next paragraph.

4 Data Collection and Pre-processing

To collect data we appealed to some web crawling techniques. MD&As collection
has been carried out crawling EDGAR SEC database using the URLLIB2 library
embedded in the Python programming language. We download all the MD&As and
stored them in a plain text file. The starting list is composed of 2142 MD&As
referring to 126 companies. Each MD&A is related to the time period going from
1995 to 2011.

Data pre-processing is targeted to reduce words heterogeneity, to remove useless
words and to build synthetic and meaningful variables to be used in the statistical
analysis phase.

As first step, we *cleaned* MD&As removing stop words using the stopwords
package embedded in the NLTK package for Python [35].

Starting from the cleaned set of words, we tokenized each word through the
NLTK package [36] and stemmed them using the Porter stemmer [37].

Tokenization process consists in breaking a stream of text up into words,
phrases, or other meaningful elements called tokens whereas stemming is the
process for reducing inflected words to their root form.

For each MD&A, we stored:

- the total amount of words;
- the amount of positive words;
- the amount of negative words;
- the amount of uncertain words;
- the amount of litigious words;
- the amount of strong modal words;
- the amount of weak modal words.

The choice of above mentioned semantic fields and of the set of words belonging
to each of these, has been made according to the Loughran and McDonald Financial
Sentiment Dictionaries [34].

For some companies it has not been possible to retrieve the MD&A. The
resulting dataset is composed of 596 rows, concerning 101 financial corporations.
More in detail, the dataset of HRB companies is composed of 144 rows, concerning
30 companies; the dataset of MRB firms is composed of 224 rows, concerning 36
companies and the dataset of LRB firms is composed of 230 rows, concerning 35
companies.

5 Statistical Analysis

Firstly, we verify the existence of a relationship between the total amount of words
present in a MD&A and the size of a firm, measured through the net sales or
revenues, in order to preliminary investigate if the MD&A length varies according
to firms' features.

To answer our RQ1, we perform a regression analysis for each semantic variable: negative words, positive words, uncertainty words, litigious words, modal words strong.

We exclude the modal words weak, as data collection and preprocessing phase revealed the absence of this kind of words in our three samples of firms. As independent variables, we consider the following financial ratios, because they are mostly correlated to the issuance of a Going Concern Opinion: Return on Assets (ROA), Return on Equity (ROE), Return on Investment (ROI), Return on Sales (ROS) and Cash Flow/Total Assets [38].

To avoid issues due to multicollinearity we perform a regression for each financial index above mentioned.

Our first regression model is built as follows:

$y = x\beta + \varepsilon$

where

- y = the dependent variable is a vector containing each semantic variable listed above. Each indicator measures the number of each semantic variable divided by the total number of words in the MD&A from 1995 to 2011.
- x is a vector containing alternatively: (1) ROI: return on investment between 1995 and 2011; (2) ROE: return on equity from 1995 to 2011; (3) ROA: return on assets from 1995 to 2011; (4) ROS: return on sales from 1995 to 2011; and (5) CASH FLOW: the sum of net income and all non-cash charges or credits/net sales or revenues from 1995 to 2011.

In order to reduce data heterogeneity present in our sample, we split the whole dataset in three smaller sets according to risk level: HRB, MRB and LRB and we conduct the same analysis above mentioned.

To test how and if MD&A's content could be useful to forecast firms' performance (RQ2), we carry out a regression analysis in which dependent variables are financial ratios at time t, whereas independent variables are semantic variables listed above referring to time t−1. Our second regression model is built as follows:

$y(t) = \beta 0 + \beta 1$ Negative$(t-1) + \beta 2$ Positive$(t-1) + \beta 3$ Uncertainty$(t-1) + \beta 4$ Litigious$(t-1) + \beta 5$ Modal Words Strong$(t-1) + \varepsilon$

where

- y = the dependent variable is a vector containing each financial ratio listed above. Each indicator measures the performance from 1995 to 2011.
- Negative: vector containing ratios of negative words present in the MD&A.
- Positive: vector containing ratios of positive words present in the MD&A.
- Uncertainty: vector containing ratios of words which denote uncertainty in the MD&A.
- Litigious: vector containing ratios of words which denote litigious in the MD&A.
- Modal Words Strong: vector containing ratios of strong modal words in the MD&A.

6   Empirical Findings

Firstly we verify the existence of a relationship between the total amount of words present in a MD&A (dependent variable) and the size of the firm, measured through the net sales or revenues (independent variable) and we find a significant and positive correlation between these two variables at $p < 0001$ (β: 0.0005).

The results of the first regression analysis for the whole set of firms are reported in Table 1.

Table 1 Results of the first regression analysis of the whole dataset

Dependent variable	βROI	βROE	βROA	βROS	βCF
Negative	−0.026***	−3.02E-05***	−0.028***	−1.99E-05***	−4.73E-06***
Positive	−0.002	−1.99E-06	−0.002	−1.02E-06	8.37E-08
Uncertainty	−0.009**	−8.24E-06*	−0.008**	−6.13E-06**	−3.39E-06***
Litigious	−0.004	2.26E-06	0.001	−7.97E-06**	−8.11E-07
Modal words strong	−0.000	−5.69E-07*	−9.86E-05	8.04E-08	5.58E-08

*, **, *** indicate a significance degree between 0.10 and 0.05; between 0.05 and 0.01; and between 0.01 and 0, respectively

Results demonstrate a strong correlation: (1) between the ratio of negative words present in the MD&A and the financial conditions of firms; (2) between the ratio of uncertain words and the financial ratios. These results mean that if the financial conditions of a company worsen, the negative words and uncertain words in the MD&A increase and vice versa (β of each regression is always significant and negative).

Furthermore, results show that the ratio of litigious words in the MD&A is correlated to ROS (β is negative and significant; −6.13E-06). Even if the other financial ratios are not linked to litigious words, this result is coherent with the other results above mentioned.

Nothing can be said about the relationship between financial conditions and positive words, as any β for these regressions is significant.

Finally results regarding modal words strong seem particularly surprising, as the ratio of this kind of words in the MD&A seems to be linked to the ROE, even if β is negative and significant (β: −5.69E-07). This means that the amount of modal words strong increase when the ROE decreases; this kind of result deserves further investigations.

In order to test previous findings, we reduce data heterogeneity present in our sample and carry out deep investigations, splitting the whole dataset in three smaller sets namely HRB, MRB and LRB and testing the same regression model above mentioned.

The results of the regression analysis for HRB group are shown in Table 2.

Table 2 Results of the regression analysis of the HRB group of firms

Dependent variable	βROI	βROE	βROA	βROS	βCF
Negative	−0.053***	−8.61E-05***	−0.052***	−4.52E-05***	−3.97E-06**
Positive	−0.011***	−5.38E-06	−0.006**	−5.70E-06*	3.93E-08
Uncertainty	−0.012	−3.39E-05**	−0.020**	−1.75E-05**	−3.42E-06***
Litigious	0.002	−5.84E-06	0.002	5.08E-06	2.29E-07
Modal words strong	2.06E-05	3.82E-07	0.000	1.04E-06**	6.51E-08

*, **, *** indicate a significance degree between 0.10 and 0.05; between 0.05 and 0.01; and between 0.01 and 0, respectively

The correlation between length of the MD&A and size of HRB firms results significant and positive at $p < 0.001$ (β: 0.001).

Regression analysis of HRB group of firms generally confirms the results of the analysis conducted on the whole dataset, highlighting some peculiarities. In particular, as in the whole dataset, we find a strong correlation between the ratio of negative words present in the MD&A and the financial conditions of a firm (β of each regression is always significant and negative, as in the whole dataset).

Furthermore, as in the whole dataset, results show a strong correlation between uncertain words and financial ratios, as just ROI is not linked to this kind of words (other βs are significant and negative).

Nothing can be said about the relationships between litigious words and financial conditions of firms.

Contrary to the whole dataset analysed above, result shows that the amount of modal words strong seems to be significantly correlated only to ROS. β is positive and significant (β: 1.04E-06) and it means that modal words strong increase when ROS increases.

Unexpectedly, the ratio of positive words seems to be negatively correlated to some financial ratios (ROI, ROA and ROS). This means that positive words in HRB generally increase whereas the financial conditions worsen and vice versa. This result could suggest that, in strong financial distress situations, managers try to reassure stakeholders emphasizing firm's positive aspects.

The results of the regression analysis for MRB group are reported in Table 3. The correlation between length of the MD&A and size of MRB firms results significant and positive at $p < 0.001$ (β: 0.004).

Regression analysis of MRB group of firms also confirms the results obtained on the whole dataset, highlighting some peculiarities. As in the whole dataset and in the HRB group of firms, we find a strong correlation between the ratio of negative words used in the MD&A and the financial conditions of the firms (β of each regression is always significant and negative).

Table 3 Results of the regression analysis of the MRB group of firms

Dependent variable	βROI	βROE	βROA	βROS	βCF
Negative	−1059.10*	−1.95E-05***	−0.018***	−1.47E-05***	−7.78E-06**
Positive	−0.006	−1.85E-06	−0.001	−1.71E-07	2.58E-07
Uncertainty	−0.006	−1.85E-06	0.002	−3.87E-06	−2.26E-06
Litigious	−0.013	4.54E-06	0.005	−1.04E-05**	−6.97E-06**
Modal words strong	−0.000	−5.24E-07	7.67E-05	−9.74E-08	−6.003E-09

*, **, *** indicate a significance degree between 0.10 and 0.05; between 0.05 and 0.01; and between 0.01 and 0, respectively

Nothing can be said about the relationships between: (1) positive words and financial conditions of firm; (2) uncertain words and financial conditions and (3) modal words strong and financial conditions.

Regarding litigious words, results highlight that the ratio of this kind of words in the MD&A is linked to ROS and CF (Cash Flow) (both βs are negative and significant).

Finally, the results of the regression analysis for LRB group are reported in Table 4.

Table 4 Results of the regression analysis of the LRB group of firms

Dependent variable	βROI	βROE	βROA	βROS	βCF
Negative	−0.005	−6.17E-05*	−0.009	−5.30E-05	6.81E-05**
Positive	0.003	2.045E-05	0.003	3.15E-05	2.54E-05**
Uncertainty	−0.004	−4.45E-05*	−0.008	−4.41E-05	4.75E-05**
Litigious	−0.005	−4.36E-05	−0.012	−5.35E-05	−2.85E-05
Modal words strong	−0.000	−1.02E-05***	−0.001**	−4.81E-06	−3.77E-06

*, **, *** indicate a significance degree between 0.10 and 0.05; between 0.05 and 0.01; and between 0.01 and 0, respectively

The correlation between the length of the MD&A and the size of LRB firms results positive and not significant (β: 2.23).

The regression analysis of LRB group of firms highlights different trends compared to the ones concerning other sets.

In detail, we do not find a general correlation between the ratio of negative words in MD&A and the financial conditions of the firm; only for one ratio (ROE) we find a significant and negative correlation. Surprisingly, negative words ratio is positively correlated to CF. This could be due to the strong heterogeneity which still affects LRB sample. This trend is confirmed by the analysis of uncertain words, as β of ROE is negative and significant, whereas β of CF is significant and positive. The analysis shows a correlation between the ratio of positive words and CF (β is positive and significant). This result means that if CF of a company worsen, the positive words in the MD&As increase and vice versa.

We do not find any relationships between the ratio of litigious words and firm's financial conditions.

Moreover, we find that the ratio of modal words strong in the MD&A increases when ROE and ROI decrease and vice versa (both βs are significant and negative). This finding could seem particularly surprising but it could be due to the fact that healthy firms do not use strong modal words in their MD&As, as they could consider positive words and financial ratios adequate enough to demonstrate to stakeholders their good financial conditions. This reverse trend is particularly explicit considering uncertain words, as results suggest that these words increase if ROE decreases (β: −4.45E-05) and increases if CF decreases (β: 4.75E-05).

The results of the first regression analysis show that firms financial conditions strongly influence the ratio of words denoting negativity and uncertainty whereas the use of positive words seems not to be affected by firms health.

The results of the second regression analysis for the whole dataset of firms are reported in Table 5.

Table 5 Results of the second regression analysis of the whole dataset of firms

Dependent variable (t)	β(t−1) Negative	β(t−1) Positive	β(t−1) Uncertain	β(t−1) Litigious	β(t−1) Modal words strong	R^2 %
ROI	−0.99***	2.18**	0.23	0.31	−1.25	1.6
ROE	−1010.65***	1508.54	−181.66	554.94	−7353.49	2.5
ROA	−1.03***	2.05**	−0.34	0.42	−0.19	2.6
ROS	−2583.94***	4767.91***	−55.96	−101.50	11,796.6	4.6
CASH FLOW	−3722.53**	11,361.9***	−4679.34**	887.92	35,190.0	2.7

*, **, *** indicate a significance degree between 0.10 and 0.05; between 0.05 and 0.01; and between 0.01 and 0, respectively

This second regression analysis allows us to answer our RQ2. In detail, we find that the ratio of negative words could be really useful to forecast financial conditions of a company (β(t−1) of each regression is always significant and negative).

Even the ratio of positive words could be considered a good indicator to forecast financial ratios, with the exception of ROE whose β is not statistically significant, differently from the other ratios, all significant and positive.

According to our model, litigious words and modal words strong are not useful to predict future financial condition, whereas uncertain words is significant just in one case (CF).

7 Conclusions

This study, through an analysis of MD&A content, reveals some interesting findings regarding if and how managers react to firms financial conditions. Our results show that only some aspects of the MD&A varies depending on the financial conditions the company is experiencing.

Apart from the LRB subsample, we find that MD&A's length is correlated to firm size, providing a promising first weak evidence on correlation between firm's status and MD&A's content. The first phase of our analysis allowed us to answer our RQ1—*Does the MD&A content vary according to financial conditions the company is experiencing?*

The analysis conducted on the whole dataset, shows, as expected, that the ratio of negative and uncertain words used in the MD&A are negatively correlated with firm's financial conditions. No correlation emerged, instead, between the ratio of positive words and firm's financial conditions. Splitting the whole database in three groups, according to the level of the bankruptcy risk, we carried out a deeper investigation, which confirmed that healthy companies tend to use fewer negative words than companies with medium and high risk of bankruptcy. This evidence could suggest that managers do not try to hide financial distress.

The analysis on HRB subset of firms confirmed the trend of the whole dataset, highlighting some peculiar features. In particular, interesting considerations could arise from the analysis of signs of β for the regression in which the dependent variable is the ratio of positive words. βs are significant and negative and thus, in the HRB sample, a worsening of firm's financial conditions corresponds to an increase in the ratio of positive words in the MD&A. This result seems to suggest that managers try to bend the truth introducing more positive words than those needed for giving a fair view of the situation. This behavior is probably held to reassure stakeholder. Companies experiencing a high risk of bankruptcy have probably more financial requirements and this could lead managers to appear optimistic for the future, trying to be attractive despite the problematical current conditions.

Results show that healthy companies tend to use positive words in a proper way compared with companies having medium and high risk of bankruptcy.

Peculiar considerations could arise from the analysis of the MRB and LRB groups of companies. Empirical findings from MRB companies confirm the general trend regarding the negative words and show an increase in the ratio of litigious words, when firms' financial conditions worsen. The analysis of LRB group of firms reveals that firms tend to have more positive words if CF increases, confirming the relevance of this ratio, especially during financial crisis. However, LRB group highlights a counterintuitive behaviour with regard to the correlation between CF and the use of negative, uncertain and strong modal words: the results show that an increase in CF gives rise to an increase of negative, uncertain and modal words strong. Perhaps, in companies with a low risk of bankruptcy, managers behave in the sake of the prudence, avoiding to overestimate the financial results.

The second phase of our analysis allowed us to answer the RQ2—*Is the content of the MD&A useful to forecast future financial conditions of a company?* On the basis of our results, it emerged that the analysis of negative and positive words could represent a good proxy useful to forecast future financial performances of the companies, confirming that the content of the MD&A is usually coherent with the real health condition of the firm.

According to our model, litigious words and modal words strong are not useful to predict financial conditions, whereas uncertain words are significantly correlated only to CF.

The analysis presented in this research confirmed, apart from some exceptions, the reliability of the content of the MD&As (effect), as response to the firm's financial conditions (cause).

For this reason the use of negative language by distressed companies has to be interpreted as a reliable indicator of negative financial condition, even if a strategic use of discretion could have been expected. Positive correlation between financial distress and negative words contained in the MD&A is confirmed by the analyses on MRB and LRB samples.

Possible distortions in LRB firms analysis could be related to the casual method of extraction that we used to collect healthy financial institutions. This could mean that this subsample is characterized by firms that are heavily heterogenic.

To verify the robustness of the results, it could be helpful to extend the sample to other countries and to other industrial sectors.

Other insights provided by this research are related to the possible association between the MD&A and the audit opinion. Recent studies demonstrated that auditing firms often fail in predicting the bankruptcy risk of distressed companies [39, 40]. A possible explanation for this error could be due to the role of MD&A, as auditors may base their independent report on the content of MD&As. In this context, our study represents only a preliminary step that should be followed up through a more in-depth textual analysis of MD&A along with a comparison with auditors' failure. Tone analysis might not be sufficient to discover all the knowledge embedded in MD&As, hence further researches have to be carried out to investigate if there is an association between the failure of auditors in predicting bankruptcy and the MD&A content.

References

1. Securities Act Release 33-4936 (Dec 9, 1968)
2. Securities Act Release IC-8175 (Jan 10, 1974)
3. Li, F.: The information content of forward-looking statements in corporate filings—a naïve bayesian machine learning approach. J. Acc. Res. **48**(5), 1049–1102 (2010)
4. Tavcar, L.R.: Make the MD&A more readable. CPA J. Online (1998). http://nysscpa.org/cpajournal/1998/0198/newsViews/0198NV7.htm 03 June 2014
5. Knutson, P.H.: Financial Reporting in the 1990s and Beyond. Association for Investment Management and Research, Charlottesville, VA (1993)

6. Rogers, R.K., Grant, J.: Content analysis of information cited in reports of sell-side financial analysts. J. Finan. Statement Anal. **3**, 17–30 (1983)
7. Security Exchange Commission.: Interpretation: Commission Guidance Regarding Management's Discussion and Analysis of Financial Condition and Results of Operations; Rule (2003)
8. Sutton, S., Arnold, V., Bedard, J.C., Phillips, J.R.: Enhancing and structuring the MD&A to aid investors when using interactive data. J. Inf. Syst. **26**(2), 167–188 (2012)
9. Brown, S.V., Tucker, J.W.: Large-sample evidence on firms' year-over-year MD&A modifications. J. Acc. Res. **49**, 309–346 (2011)
10. Pava, M.L., Epstein, M.J.: How good is MD&A as an investment tool? J. Accountancy **175**, 51–53 (1993)
11. Securities Exchange Commission.: Commission Statement about Management's Discussion and Analysis of Financial Condition and Results of Operations, Release Nos. 33-8056; 34-45321; FR-61 (2003a)
12. Securities Exchange Commission: Interpretation: Commission Guidance Regarding Management's Discussion and Analysis of Financial Condition and Results of Operations. 17 CFR Parts 211, 231, and 241. Release Nos. 33–8350, 34–48960, and FR-72. Washington, D.C.: SEC (2003b)
13. Cohen, J.R., Gaynor, L.M., Holder-Webb, L.L., Montague, N.: Management's discussion and analysis: Implication for audit practice and research. Curr. Issues Auditing **2**(2), A26–A35 (2008)
14. Meiers, D.H.: The MD&A challenge: The difficulty of crafting a quality disclosure. J. Accountancy **201**(1), 59–66 (2006)
15. Verrecchia, R.E.: Discretionary disclosure. J. Account. Econ. **5**, 179–194 (1983)
16. Holder-Webb, L.L., Cohen, J.R.: The association between disclosure, distress and failure. J. Bus. Ethics **75**, 301–314 (2007)
17. Graham, J.R., Harvey, C.R., Rajgopal, S.: The economic implications of corporate financial reporting. J. Account. Econ. **40**(1–3), 3–73 (2005)
18. Desai, H., Hogan, C.E., Wilkins, M.S.: The reputational penalty for aggressive accounting: Earnings restatement and management turnover. Acc. Rev. **81**(1), 83–112 (2006)
19. Kothari, S.P., Wysocki, P.D., Shu, S.: Do managers withhold bad news? J. Acc. Res. **47**(1), 241–276 (2006)
20. Feldman, R., Govindaraj, S., Livnat, J., Segal, B.: The incremental information content of tone change in management's discussion and analysis. Working Paper. Electronic copy available at: http://ssrn.com/abstract=1126962 (2008)
21. Clarkson, P.C., Kao, J.L., Richardson, G.D.: Evidence that management discussion and analysis (MD&A) is a part of firm's overall package. Contemp. Acc. Res. **16**(1), 111–134 (1999)
22. Huang, X., Teoh, S.H., Zhang, Y.: Tone management. Working Paper. Electronic copy available at http://ssrn.com/abstract=1960376 (2011)
23. Li, F.: Annual report readability, current earnings, and earning persistence. J. Account. Econ. **45**(2/3), 221–247 (2008)
24. Feldman, R., Govindaraj, S., Livnat, J., Segal, B.: Management's tone change, post earnings announcement drift and accruals. Rev. Acc. Stud. **15**, 915–953 (2010)
25. Hales, J., Kuang, X.J., Venkataraman, S.: Who believes the hype? An experimental examination of how language affects investor judgments. J. Account. Res. **49**, 223–255 (2011)
26. Davis, A.K., Tama-Sweet, I.: Managers' use of language across alternative disclosure outlets: Earnings press releases versus MD&A. Contemp. Account. Res. **29**(3), 804–837 (2012)
27. Lang, M., Lundholm, R.: Corporate disclosure policy and analyst behaviour. Acc. Rev. **71**(4), 467–492 (1996)
28. Barron, E.E., Kile, C.O., O'Keefe, T.B.: MD&A quality as measured by the SEC and analysts' earnings forecasts. Contemp. Account. Res. **16**(1), 75–109 (1999)
29. L'Her, J., Suret, J.: Consensus, dispersion and security prices. Contemp. Account. Res. **13** (Spring), 209–228 (1996)

30. Bamber, L.S., Barron, O., Stober, T.: Trading volume and different aspects of disagreement coincident with earnings announcements. Acc. Rev. **72**(October), 575–597 (1997)
31. Ajinkya, B., Atiase, R., Gift, M.: Volume of trading and the dispersion in financial analysts' earnings forecasts. Acc. Rev. **66**(2), 389–401 (1991)
32. Clarkson, P.C., Kao, J.L., Richardson, G.D.: The voluntary inclusion of forecasts in the MD&A section of annual reports. Contemp. Account. Res. **11**(1–II), 423–450 (1994)
33. Hutton, A.P., Lee, F.L., Shu, S.Z.: Do managers always know better? the relative accuracy of management and analyst forecasts. J. Acc. Res. **50**(5), 1217–1244 (2012)
34. Loughran, T., McDonald, B.: When is a liability not a liability? textual analysis, dictionaries, and 10Ks. J. Finan **66**(1), 35–64 (2011)
35. Bird, S., Klein, E., Loper E.: Natural Language Processing with Python, O'Reilly Media, Inc. (2009)
36. Bird, S.: NLTK: The Natural Language Toolkit. In: Proceedings of the COLING/ACL on Interactive presentation sessions. Association for Computational Linguistics (2006)
37. Porter, M.: Snowball: A Language for Stemming Algorithms (2001)
38. Caserio, C., Panaro, D., Trucco, S.: A Statistical Analysis of Reliability of Audit Opinions as Bankruptcy Predictors. Discussion Papers del Dipartimento di Scienze Economiche— Università di Pisa, (http://www-dse.ec.unipi.it/ricerca/discussion-papers.htm) n. 2014/174 (2014)
39. Hodges, C., Cluskey Jr, G.R., Lin, B.: Analysing bankruptcy predictors using time series data. J. Account. Finance Res. **13**(1), 159–168 (2005)
40. Malgwi, C.A., Emenyonu, E.N.: Audit effectiveness preceding Cankruptcy in UK financial institutions. Int. J. Account. Auditing Perform. Eval. **1**(4), 503–518 (2004)

The Adequacy of Information Systems for Supporting the Asset Quality Review Process in Banks. Evidence from an Italian Case Study

Elena Bruno, Giuseppina Iacoviello and Arianna Lazzini

Abstract This chapter analyzes the role of the Information System (IS) in the Asset Quality Review process (AQR) for asset evaluation in a small Italian bank, whose main activity is credit intermediation (Mehta and Manhas in J Serv Res 5(2), 2006). 'Information Technology (IT) is a critical component in creating value in the banking sector. It provides decision-makers with an efficient means of reporting information about risk, profitability and preceding conditions for a loan' (Huaiq et al. in Monit Syst 16(2), 2011). IT is basic for supporting Risk Management (RM) in the decision-making process and aiding performance evaluation. Through a case study, we highlight the possibility of IS being able to support this new integrated process of credit monitoring, providing increasingly reliable real-time data, that are available on demand, and facilitating the development of global knowledge and new reporting tools, as well as the collaboration and integration between the areas of risk and business operating processes (Al-Laith in Int Manage Rev 8(1), 2012). The study focuses on the process of active monitoring of the entire credit portfolio, aimed at guiding the best migration between risk classes (Malinconico in Il credit risk management del portafoglio prestiti. FrancoAngeli, Milano, 2013) (Bouteille and Pushner in The handbook of credit risk management: originating, assessing, and managing credit exposures. Wiley Finance, New York, 2012). This is no longer understood as a sequence of stages, but as a set of integrated activities, in which the quality of information becomes a major determinant of the outcome (Bennardo et al. in J Internet Banking Commer 16(2), 2011). The study shows that the characteristics of the specific business make it necessary to take into account several aspects such as: variety of education and culture of the staff; functional

E. Bruno · G. Iacoviello (✉)
Department of Economics and Management, University of Pisa, Pisa, Italy
e-mail: giuseppina.iacoviello@unipi.it

E. Bruno
e-mail: elena.bruno@unipi.it

A. Lazzini
Department of Communication & Economics, University of Modena and Reggio Emilia, Modena, Italy
e-mail: arianna.lazzini@unimore.it

© Springer International Publishing Switzerland 2016
D. Mancini et al. (eds.), *Strengthening Information and Control Systems*,
Lecture Notes in Information Systems and Organisation 14,
DOI 10.1007/978-3-319-26488-2_5

relationships; and further appropriate technology resources. All these features affect the conception, development and deployment of IS solutions to be adopted in order to achieve the business objectives and in particular to improve asset quality, as mentioned above.

Keywords Information system · Asset quality review · Credit monitoring process · Risk management

1 Introduction

Some of the recent European Union directives, recommendations and reforms of domestic legislation emphasize the role of the Risk Management (RM) and the IS in the process of producing financial reporting to Asset Quality Review (AQR), to verify 'the proper conduct of performance monitoring on individual loan transaction'.

Thus, the regulations contained in the fifteenth update of the Bank of Italy Circular n. 263 of 27.12.2006 (Circ/263), calls for what we might define as 'revolutionary' innovations in banks, the aim of which is to introduce into the functioning of the company as a whole the culture of risks, in terms of the identification of the same and the establishment of their limits; the terms of definition of the roles of the control functions and of the contents of the information flows, and so on. The current organization of banking activities can be defined IT driven, that is centered on the use of IT resources. In particular, the Finance area merits consideration in the implementation of IT structures in order to speed up the execution of the processes, the necessary high degree of reliability of which should moreover be emphasized. The new technologies facilitate the preventive analysis of risks, continuous monitoring and the promptness of corrective measures. Financial innovation, the expansion of activities of banks and their intermediaries on a global scale, the significant increase in the volume of activities have been achieved without generating an uncontrollable increase in the overall instability of the market, by virtue of the strong support offered by the new technologies to the decision-making processes involved in control.

Combining the legal requirements regarding RM systems with the benefits offered by the Information System (IS), this chapter analyses the contribution of IS to the AQR process and considers how this process could guarantee the maintenance of the high quality of the loan portfolio, the only guarantee for the achievement of satisfactory business performance for creating value for shareholders.

The case study presented in this work is a good experimental model because the bank considered is one of the oldest savings banks in Italy and has maintained a strong presence in the region of Tuscany in support of its social and economic development with remarkable credit intermediation operations. The assessment of credit monitoring requires better information, improved management tools, and the constant use of innovation. For these reasons, over little more than a year, banks have adopted a rating system with a high strategic value. It consists in systems in which the automatic evaluations used, in the phase of granting credit facilities, can be modified, in the credit monitoring phase, by experts in the sector applying the technique of 'override', which allows the integration of the hard information produced by the Data Mining system with the soft information, which is not easily standardized.

The choice of the case examined is determined by its specific features such as, orientation towards traditional banking business, its push to expand in the region, and last but not least, the recent implementation of a system of rating for the retail segment.

In this context, the research questions are the following:

1. In what way can the recent regulatory changes to the risk management function in relation to the new integrated process of credit monitoring contribute to a reduction of the impairment of the credit portfolio quality?
2. How can IS contribute to the credit monitoring for the purpose of early warning (real time) deterioration of credit quality?

Using a case study method can yield initial answers to these questions and indicate the possible benefits for banks deriving from the implementation of an effective information system able to support loan performance monitoring process (i.e., efficiency, better decision-making, and cost savings) and their stakeholders (i.e., more reliable financial reporting).

The remainder of the paper proceeds as follows. Section 2 provides an analytical review of the literature, in particular Sect. 2.1 examines contributions regarding the implementation of the integrated IS solution and its managerial, organizational and accounting impacts; Sect. 2.1 analyses significant studies on the relation between credit risk management and asset quality from a regulatory and operational perspective. Section 3 provides a description of the research method. In Sect. 4 we present the empirical research, through a description of the case examined: the empirical results underline weaknesses and strengths of the IT solution and its pivotal impact emerging from interviews. Our conclusions are presented in the last section.

2 Literature Review

The literature examined focuses on the impacts of IS technology on the prevention of impairment of loan portfolio quality in a general context without considering specific small banks: most of the contributions refer to the IS in large banks and more recently to smaller banks [7, 8]. A few contributions focus on the implementation of advanced IT solutions in small banks to contribute to loan portfolio management with a view to improving asset quality [9, 10].

2.1 The Role of Information Systems in Banking Industry

Information and Communication Technology (ICT) has played an important role in the reorganization of the Italian banking system in terms of the collection and management of information. If ICT was initially applied to the accounting and administrative activities of the headquarters, it was then instrumental in enabling decentralization of information and responsibility at the local level [11].

Among the main advantages relating to the implementation of ICTs in Italian banks are: the slimming down of the chain of corporate control, the introduction of new services, cost containment, but above all the availability of digital information and the possibility to access it locally and not only from the headquarters of the bank [12]. In this direction the ability to manage not only quantitative, but also qualitative, information is particularly relevant. This is coherent with recent legislative changes and is an important part of the information processed by the banks, especially for small and medium enterprises (SME) [13]. The assumption of proper technologies and of a sophisticated information system can be considered a key factor in providing the banking sector with a real source of strength in the present market [14, 15].

The banking information system can be defined as a set of people, procedures, and tools designed to implement the collection, processing, exchange and archiving of data in order to obtain an organized flow of information that can be used to plan, execute, and control the business [16, 17].

From a strategic point of view, a safe and efficient information system makes it possible to exploit the opportunities offered by technology to expand and improve products and services offered to customers, to enhance the quality of work processes, to promote dematerialization of securities, to reduce costs also through the virtualization of banking services.

From an operational point of view, an information system enables managers to have detailed, relevant and up to date information for taking timely decisions and for the proper implementation of the process of risk management advocated by the new regulations. In a context where the banking business is increasingly dependent on new technologies, information security in terms of defense against attacks and continuity of service plays an important role in preventing, reducing and o controlling operational risk.

The information system has, in addition, the task of recording, storing and correctly representing facts and events relevant to the purposes provided for by law and by internal and external regulations (compliance). Through an efficient information system it is possible to speed up the transmission of messages relating to transfers of funds between banks; to implement an efficient flow of data and information between the branches and the central offices; to reprocess and reuse data concerning the various operations and for different purposes; to provide customers with an even wider range of products-computer services, particularly in the area of self-service banking.

Today banks require complete and reliable information and integration between different applications, data base and documents. In this perspective a comprehensive and integrated Information system able to capture all customer data, risk management and transaction information including trade and foreign exchange information is fundamental for managing loan portfolios proactively in order to minimize losses and earn an acceptable level of return for shareholders [18, 19].

In the customer analysis a substantial number of parameters are necessary. Qualitative evaluations, historical and not, such as industry scenarios and a supply chain analysis, are today required to be joined to standard information. It is clear that the presence of an integrated information system able to provide a dashboard for real time monitoring with alerting parameters is nowadays critical for banks.

In this direction a critical role can be played by Enterprise Resource Systems (ERP) [20, 21]. The implementation of ERP may bring significant benefits, making it easier to manage data and information among the various areas of the same organization minimizing time and streamlining the processes [22, 23].

ERP systems and more generally Information and Communication Technologies (ICTs) are a powerful tool for supporting information needs and, providing additional information, since they foster the efficiency of all processes. The need for sophisticated risk management systems becomes urgent for banks, meaning they need to be faster and based on a 'relational' logic [24] in order to ensure new information flows and more accurate input, process and output variable controls. Today it is a widely accepted opinion that a robust information system is critical to improving risk management. Because inadequate data can lead to mistakes in decision-making in a context in which corporate executives are asked to vouch for the accuracy of their financial statements and the quality of internal controls, a further step in the modernization of the banking sector is the introduction of technologies relating to business intelligence through which further, important changes in the approach to data analysis can be achieved. Indeed, if in the past the software houses tried to predict and define the information needs of managers already in the design phase, today's information systems allow the exploration of the heritage of the available data, avoiding for the user problems of regrouping and rationalization of information resulting from their dispersion in different platforms and in large archives. These systems basically make it possible to analyze data without the need to formulate a priori hypotheses and to retrieve the knowledge necessary to understand and anticipate the most complex phenomena.

2.2 The Optimization of Information for the Evaluation of Asset Quality

The fifteenth update of the Bank of Italy Circular n. 263 of 27.12.2006, entitled 'New regulations for the prudential supervision of banks', defining a set of rules, among other things, to strengthen systems of RM shown by recent empirical

evidence to be highly vulnerable, introduces important innovations in the monitoring of credit quality, especially for the treatment of migration risk [25]. Such
monitoring should be supported by technology and by information that are adequate
for the needs of the business, according to the principle of proportionality, so dear
to the national authorities [26].

Previous studies [27, 28] have concluded that there is a need for effective
internal control that keeps pace with developments in the IT environment. The use
of IT will have a direct impact on internal control work [3]. The impact of IT on the
efficiency of control does not differ from the traditional objectives of the internal
control systems although there are data security and safety risks [29]. Indeed, when
the information used by financial institutions is often entirely IT generated, managed and controlled, the confidentiality, availability and reliability of financial
information are crucial [30].

It is obvious that the banking IS is reduced to two subsystems: the operating
system and the directional system. These two sub-systems, while being highly
integrated, serve different purposes. The purpose of the office is the administration
of essential information for the strategic management of the bank. The monitoring
of business has always been an intrinsic part of the organized credit process. The
production of goods or services is always bolstered by organizational provisions for
measuring, monitoring and re-evaluating the process. The monitoring of organized
activities was mainly visual and manual until the progressive introduction of
computer technology into business operations. This principle is particularly
important for the IT function within a financial services organization. IT is often
implemented to manage, control and report credit risk, market risk and other types
of core business risk. "However, the IT applications and infrastructure elements are
still within the operational risk domain, regardless of their specific purpose. As an
example, the failure of a credit risk measurement application is an IT failure and,
therefore, a systems failure in the sense of operational risk" [31] (Fig. 1).

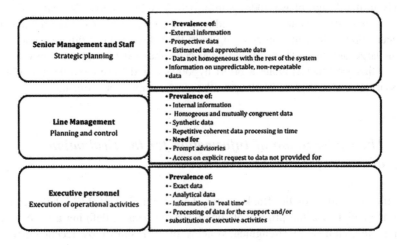

Fig. 1 Characteristics of the information support requested

The stages of monitoring and recovery of the credit process will be overseen by the BUs and the RM, although each will continue to maintain its distinctive expertise, respectively, for the functions at the first and second level. However, in the case of different assessments this will depend upon the opinion of the CRO; a new rule that should not be interpreted as a solution to the discrepancy between evaluations of the loan portfolio, but rather as a stimulus to a virtuous dialectic between the functions in question, aimed at sharing preventive tools and models proposed for controlling the quality of credit.

Proper management of these steps requires a regular flow of double-way information between the business units and the RM; and qualitative, quantifiable and processable data.

In the process of integration of the credit scores, the quantitative, qualitative and performance information must be combined with each other in order to formulate an overall judgement corresponding to the real profile of clients' risk of default. Some studies [32–35] show that the models that use soft information offer better results in the evaluation of creditworthiness than models based exclusively on information of a quantitative kind. Other studies [36, 37] relating to the behavior of Italian banks in the use of hard and soft information show that of the criteria for integration of the rating methods, most of the national banks adopt the override method, with the exception of those of larger dimensions which instead resort to statistical techniques of integration of information.

The quantitative models are potentially efficient if certain conditions are present: the existence and availability of balance sheets in space and time; quotation of the businesses and the possibility of defining a set of variable that make it possible to develop a predictive model of the probability of default. These represent the core of the process of determination and attribution of the rating, whose evaluations feed the systems of scoring [38] which constitute the basis of the process of evaluation of customers' probability of default.

However, for many Italian enterprises, because small in dimension, the above-mentioned conditions do not exist, necessitating therefore the integration of qualitative and quantitative variables in the models of credit risk management and monitoring. The most commonly used methods are based on linear scoring functions [39], on logistic regression [40] and on the method of classification trees [41, 42].

The main objective of the function of performance monitoring is the identification of positions in the past due to which a redefinition of the rating is required. This function is supervised by Business Units (BUs) and by specialized figures of RM (i.e. CRO, Relationship Manager, Monitoring Officer), and is supported by IS technology. This process needs the new information which provides a general judgment of the strength of an industry or a segment of the loan portfolio, and are incorporated and transformed into input parameters to be included in the optimization models. A significant contribution in terms of improving the quality of information and processes to supporting reporting activities is offered ultimately by the IS [43]. It is indeed unlikely that the function of IS is a stranger to strategic activities such as those aimed at controlling the quality of credit by consolidating the information heritage and making accessible to most individuals on the inside (local and central) the amount of diversified information which is useful in decision-making and in the making of strategic choices. The logic set out above expresses a systemic view of the credit process that is read not as a sequence of steps, but as a set of interrelated activities that take shape as a pattern of relations between the parties (subjects and procedures), and in this scheme the quality of the information in the circle becomes the major determinant of the expected result.

3   Methodology

The aim of this work is to analyze the contribution of the IS on the AQR process of credit monitoring, highlighting its implications, through a qualitative case study methodology, focusing on one bank.

The work has been formulated on the basis of the following hypotheses:

1. The process of AQR needs to adopt additional tools to the traditional ones that allow the RM to perceive the 'migration risk' of the loan portfolio, paying greater attention to the qualitative composition of the receivables.
2. Information systems are a priority in the strategic management of asset quality.

   They may allow:

- the impasse that is generated in the global, differentiated, non-linear and non-formalized information management resulting from the close-ratio between the local area and the client;
- the handling of 'positions' for homogeneous groups;
- parameterization of the objectives and thus the subsequent measurement and evaluation of performance;
- the timely availability of reliable information.

The choice of the case examined is determined by its specific features such as, orientation towards traditional banking business, its push to expand in the region, and, last but not least, the recent implementation of a system of rating for the retail segment. This allows the bank to have a more advanced management of risk of counterparty default using econometric models developed in collaboration with an external consulting company which completes the process of revision of the rating model developed about three years ago. These features of the operating model require taking into account several aspects: variety of education and culture of the staff, functional relationships, as well as appropriate technology resources.

4 Empirical Research

4.1 Case Study: Cassa di Risparmio di San Miniato (CARISMI)

It is a small size banking group consisting of the Holding Company (Carismi) and the Service Company. It has the traditional system model of corporate governance (Fig. 2):

4.2 Description of Credit Monitoring and IS Application to the AQR Process

The process of Credit Monitoring (CM) replaces a former architecture based on a highly diversified range of custom applications developed over the years without a unified vision. The process of verification of loan performance monitoring is carried out by the Monitoring and Problem Loan Management (MPLM) and the RM, on the basis of the mapping of control activities to be carried out within the scope of responsibilities of control for first-and second-level. Firstly, the function of RM becomes a second-level function only in the post-crisis period. Previously it was part of the control function of management and as such did not have the ability to report directly to top management and information flowed into the Asset and Liability Management Committee. From the 'insurance' of risk there has been a

Fig. 2 Governance and control system of holding group

switch to the management of risk and the subsequent growth of the information flow from Risk Management to the Board of directors and other corporate bodies.

The starting point of our research was an analysis of the credit processes in order to understand whether the bank is effecting a correct migration between risk classes in the credit process; the aim is to demonstrate whether it is possible to reach the ultimate objective of the highest quality of the credit portfolio, keeping under control all the phases involved in the process and, for each, to highlight those key variables which indicate a progressive worsening of the creditworthiness. This makes it possible to respond quickly by eliminating the anomalies identified.

The monitoring of credit is based on the classification of positions as 'performing loans' and 'non-performing loans—NPLs'. In the course of the use of credit, the position of the client can shift to an 'anomalous' state due to the occurrence of new events. The knowledge of these events is linked to the bank's ability to intercept and to prepare the tools (including organizational aspects), to systematically monitor positions, in order to bring out the 'anomalies' responsible for the deterioration of credit quality.

MPLM and RM are responsible for the monitoring of loan performance. What is the perimeter of the operations of each, since they are control functions respectively of first and second level? How can they contribute to the implementation of an efficient IS to contain the deterioration in credit quality?

We will try to verify these questions through our case study.

The Carismi loan portfolio is split into two main categories of credits: performing and NPLs. The first class includes positions that are performing and positions that are showing signs of being in trouble The other class of credit includes NPLs (Cfr. Fig. 3).

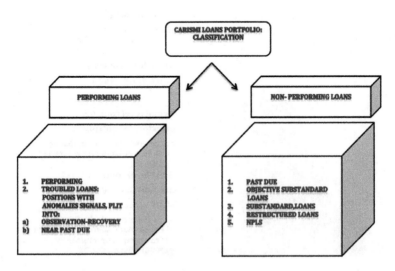

Fig. 3 Carismi loan portfolio: categories of credits

Carismi, in accordance with Cir/263, has developed credit monitoring tools shared by the organization, in order to make the control mechanism of the deterioration of credit quality more objective. Of course, the process of asset quality review cannot totally exclude the qualitative elements of the customer relationship, which represents the core variable in the management of the credit for which, at least for the foreseeable future, the quantification and standardization of information is neither necessary nor possible. And this is a difference between small and large banks; the latter need quantitative information which is necessary for the development of forms of remote monitoring as well as statistical tools useful for the identification of anomalies; in addition, they need detailed data; all of this justifies the need for the standardization of information. The smaller banks, such as the one in our case study, with close links with the local area, establishes credit relationships also on qualitative elements of customer relationships that do not fit in the IS due to the complexity of the data and the cost associated with information processes. Such information of a qualitative nature, fundamental for decisions concerning migration of debt positions between risk classes, not being standard, cannot always be made available to the whole business structure. The qualitative information heritage is held by divisional managers and therefore by the MPLM function, which in turn liaises with that of the RM for the performance monitoring of credit risk. On the basis of the instructions of Circ/263, the criterion of integration of the rating methods adopted by Carismi is that of override; such a criterion, as is well known, can determine upgrading or downgrading of the rating: in the first case, the ameliorative proposals are subjected to a precise evaluation procedure; vice versa, in the case of downgrading the evaluation is automatic.

In order to ensure that the deterioration of the loan portfolio is detected promptly, the bank should undertake a periodic review of the receivables (i.e. every six months, annually) and a verification of the quality of the loans whenever those who control them receive indications of a significant decline relative to the portfolio or part of it.

The monitoring system of the bank should be based on a reporting system that is capable of measuring the previously identified indicators, as shown below (Table 1).

Thus, the management of the positions can be automatic or pre-set by those in charge of the monitoring process.

In particular, the first credit position class (Performing loans) regards the exposure of enterprises that do not present anomalies or have abnormalities requiring a timely revision of the credit line and the continuous monitoring of movement to establish whether, within three months, it is possible to continue to maintain the in bonis position or if it is necessary to downgrade.

In the second credit position class (Non-Performing loans—NPLs), the classification of substandard loans can be automatic or pre-set by the MPLM. The former regards objective substandard loans. The Service Credit Monitoring can downgrade the positions manually, when the anomalies found are detrimental to the successful completion of the financing position. Therefore, in cases of substandard banking

Table 1 Segmentation of CARISMI loans portfolio

Credit position	Definition	Early warning	Method of downgrading	Frequency of the checks
Performing loans	1. In bonis 2. Troubled loans: positions with anomalies signals, split into:			
	(a) Observation-recovery	(a) Remaining over 90 days in this range	(a) Manually	(a) Monthly
	(b) Near past due	(b) Remaining over 90 days in this range and exceeded 5 % of used on the loan	(b) Manually	(b) Monthly
NPLs	(a) Past due	(a) Exceeded 10 % of used on the loan	(a) Automatic	(a) Quarterly
	(b) Objective substandard loans	(b) Loans over 100.000€ and remaining over 60 days in this range; loans under 100.000€ and remaining over 120 days in this range	(b) Automatic	(b) Quarterly
	(c) Substandard loans	(c) Remaining over 18 months in this range	(c) Manually	(c) Quarterly
	(d) Restructured loans	(d) Changes in the original terms of the loan	(d) Manually	(d) Quarterly
	(e) NPLs	(e) Discrepancy between adjusted doubtful loans blacklist of central risk	(e) Manually	(e) Monthly

carried out automatically within the procedure, the Credit Monitoring Service decides the downgrading.

The management of objective substandard loans, the third sub-class of NPLs, the treatment of which is the same as that of substandard loans, consists of the preparation of plans for the restructuring of the debt, also in part, or the repayment of the outstanding debt. Where the requirements are not met, the conditions occur for the classification of non-performing loans. This type of monitoring is therefore not carried out at the last stage of the credit process, where it has to be decided 'when' and 'how' to establish procedures to recover the credit, but rather concerns all stages of the credit process. As such, this could lead to a virtuous cycle that would in turn lead to an increase in the quality of the loan portfolio.

If the conceptual framework at the macro level (fifteenth update of the Bank of Italy Circ/263) is recognized, then at the micro level (territorial unit of analysis) common factors can be identified; they will be calculated with shared indicators so as to capture the specificity of the context. This contributes to the identification of different, but comparable, systems of measurement.

Table 1 indicates that in Carismi some controls can be effectively carried out automatically and others manually, with respect to the observation-recovery positions and past due training of troubled loans. In the last column, we indicate the frequency of the checks.

The monitoring system should be based on a reporting system that is capable of measuring the previously identified indicators. The purpose of reporting within IS is to provide analytical documentation on meaningful activities. Such disclosures should be as up-to-date and correct as possible and therefore should not generate inconsistent interpretations.

After the above activities have been completed, the aim is to redesign the IT system. In this way, for "every point in time", it can identify the contribution to RM of the operating results in all phases of the process, taking into account deviations, the causes of variations, and the impact on the NPLs.

The bank must consider the following questions:

- What database (DB) should be used?
  In our case study, the bank uses a transactional database that can, in turn, be used to develop an analytical DB or ERP system, possibly supplemented by external data sources and processes;
- What tools provide the information?
  The continuous monitoring of credit processes requires a group to use the reports prepared by the transactional database as well as new forms of communication through reports, direct conversation with customers, qualitative questionnaires. Data can be extracted from the mass; these extractions can be highlighted where there are exceptions to the norm; in this case there is a phase of the analysis of the reasons for these differences.
- What systems for guaranteeing security and reliability should be used for the data?
  Data security is a significant challenge: more information generates more value for those who use it, but confidential data also generate risks and have legal implications. The role of continuous monitoring is to ensure the reliability of the data; the monitoring of credit must be supplemented by data validation mechanisms that can provide an adequate level of privacy.
  Carismi has adopted an ERP solution; however it relies on a management reporting system that is based on database processing according to the information needs of the individual management areas. Since the questionnaire contains mainly qualitative information, the IS has a marginal role.
  The ratios and the results of choices cannot be extrapolated because the analyses are made on a judgmental basis and also aim to include examples of good practice.

Carismi deals with each case on its own merits rather than applying general rigid rules: this is because the projects selected for monitoring are established not on a statistical basis, but rather on a relational capital bases.

The definition of the rules implies that the data be:

- complete, it must be possible, for example, to export them from the branches on-line and off-line and integrate and aggregate them with other qualitative information and disseminate them over the net;
- primary, digital assets must be presented in a granular so that they can be integrated and combined with other data in digital format;
- timely, users must be enabled to access and use data on the network quickly and promptly;
- accessible and available for both the first level control and for the second-level control;
- reusable, to create new resources;
- permanent, to generate value.

In essence, the refinement of control will be followed by the need for an information system, essentially making the action of risk management more effective.

As other studies have shown [44], the consequences of the expanding role of IT tasks and base technology will be that the bank will have to regularly implement and manage complex and expensive IT systems at an integrated level of organization. This will include the planning of company resources (ERP) and global collaboration platforms. The bank has an IS in full out-sourcing (in accordance with the rule of Circ./263).

5   Conclusion

In addressing the contribution of IS to the AQR process in asset quality control we have focused on two main issues:

(a) the new provisions of the Bank of Italy regarding Internal Control Systems (compliant with Cir/263, 2013) and the increase in the responsibility of a Risk Management System for the actual functioning of risk control to guarantee the asset quality of the loan portfolio;
(b) the importance of IS as a support of the AQR process and its potential benefits for supporting the RM to identify promptly the deterioration of asset quality.

Overall, our case study on Carismi highlights the role of RM and IS in supporting the credit monitoring for the prevention of impairment of asset quality. Looking ahead, a regular exchange of information between the BUs and the risk control function could potentially benefit the implementation of a monitoring activity. This would not be limited to the management of non-performing loans, but would support managers in the overall control of migration between risk classes. The balancing of roles will tend to promote a dialectic between the two functions of first and second level, which will share ex-ante the evaluation criteria of receivables ('tools'), and which will be used by the business unit managers in the review process of asset quality. In this sense, the issue of monitoring the quality of credit by the RM function probably points to the area of greatest innovation introduced by the new regulations.

The case study confirms that the AQR process could help to reduce the deterioration of the asset quality of financial statements to the extent that it is able to activate a careful analysis of migration between risk classes. An examination of the mechanisms through which migration between risk classes changes the margins in lending highlights the benefits arising from monitoring from a risk control perspective. For these purposes the following are relevant: (1) allocative efficiency, defined as the capacity for diversification of the loan portfolio, which could achieve a reduction in the risk of deterioration of the joint debts; (2) the revision of the rating and the value of collateral; (3) the timeliness and effectiveness of recovery of NPLs.

Currently, IS is not a strategic priority; the information available is not structured within a system but it is useful for the so-called 'phase two' of asset quality review (AQR). Our second hypothesis was rejected, but in the future IS could be necessary for supporting risk management in the decision making-process and in aiding performance evaluation.

As this research is in an initial phase, this subject will require further analysis. Indeed, this work, contributes to an initial discussion of the potential implementation of AQR processes in small banks given the Italian legal framework; it discusses the control management tools implemented in small banks and their possible benefits, as well as how a culture of continuous credit monitoring and performance measurement can be generated within Carismi; it also provides evidence of the possible benefits to the bank's performance and thus encourages government policies that would incentivize the use of new IT tools by small banks in the management and control processes of AQR.

References

1. Mehta V., Manhas P.S.: Leveraging information systems tools, security and on-line usage in banking and insurance sector. J. Serv. Res. **5**(2) (2006)
2. Wang, H., Mylopoulos, J., Liao, S.: Intelligent agents and financial risk. Monit. Syst. JIBC. **16** (2) (2011)
3. Al-Laith, A.A.G.: Adaptation of the Internal control systems with the use of information technology and its effects on the financial statements reliability: an applied study on commercial banks. Int. Manage. Rev. **8**(1), 12 (2012)
4. Malinconico, A.: Il credit risk management del portafoglio prestiti. Da Basilea 1 a Basilea 3. FrancoAngeli, Milano (2013)

5. Bouteille, S., Pushner, D.C.: The handbook of credit risk management: originating, assessing, and managing credit exposures. Wiley Finance, New York (2012)
6. Bennardo, A., Pagano, M., Piccolo, P.: Multiple-bank lending, creditor rights and information sharing. J. Internet Banking Commer. **16**(2) (2011)
7. Seese, D., Weinhardet, C., Schlottman, F.: Handbook on information technology. Finance. Springer, New York (2008)
8. Gupta, U.G., Collins, W.: The impact of information systems on the efficiency of banks: an empirical investigation. Ind. Manage. Data Syst. **97**, 10–16 (1997)
9. Egloff, D., Leippold, M., Vannini, P.: A simple model of credit contagion. J. Banking Finance **31**, 2475–2492 (2007)
10. Streff K.: An information security management system model for small and medium-sized financial institutions. Issues Inf. Syst. **10**(2) (2009)
11. Berger, A.: The economic effects of technological progress: evidence from the banking industry. J. Money Credit Banking **35**(2), 141–176 (2003)
12. Brynjolfsson, E,. Hitt, L.M.: Beyond computation: information technology, organizational transformation and business performance. J. Econ. Perspect. (2000)
13. Ho, S.J., Mallick, S.K.: The impact of information technology on the banking industry. J. Oper. Res. Soc. **61**(2), 211–221 (2010)
14. Ferran C., M.L Lenard: An object oriented approach to banking information systems (1997)
15. Davenport, T.H., Short, J.E.: Information technology and business process design. Oper. Manage. **3** (1990)
16. Resti, A., Sironi, A.: Risk management and shareholders' value in banking: from risk measurement models to capital allocation policies. Wiley and Sons, New York (2007)
17. Petzer, D.J.: Risk, risk management and regulation in the banking industry. Routledge, London (2012)
18. Davenport, T.H., Harris, J., Cantrell, S.: The return of enterprise solutions: the director's cut. Accenture, Cambridge (2002)
19. Colgate, M.: Marketing and marketing information system sophistication in retail banking. Serv Ind J **20**(1), 139–152 (2000)
20. Davenport, T.H.: Mission critical: realizing the promise of enterprise systems. Harvard Business School Press, Boston (2000)
21. Davenport, T.H.: Putting the enterprise into the enterprise system. Harvard Bus. Rev. **76**, 121 (1998)
22. Simon, E.: Integrating ERP into organizations: organizational changes and side-effects. Int. Bus. Rev **5**(2) (2012)
23. Soh, C., Kien, S., Tay-Yap, J.: Cultural fits and misfits: is ERP a universal solution? Commun. ACM **43**(4), 47–51 (2000)
24. Mancini, D.: L'azienda-rete e le decisioni di partnership: il ruolo del sistema informativo relazionale. Management control, Franco Angeli (2011)
25. Banca d'Italia: Nuove disposizioni di vigilanza prudenziale per le banche. Circolare 263, Roma (2013)
26. Iannotta, G., Nocera, G., Sironi, A.: The impact of government ownership on bank risk. J. Financ. Intermediation (22) (2013)
27. Halandy, L., Ajeeb, A., Ghabban, A.A.: Role of internal control under the electronic accounting information system-applied study on a sample of the Kurdistan Banks-Iraq. Human Sci. Mag. **45**, 1–39 (2009)
28. Hamdan, A., Abzakh, M.: The (E-Auditing) and its effect on persuasiveness of evidences: evidence from Bahrain. Paper presented to European, Mediterranean & Middle East Conference on Information Systems, Abu Dhabi, (2010)
29. Schaad, A., Moffett, J., Jacob, J.: The role based access control system of a European bank: a case study and discussion. ACM, New York (2001)
30. Pavel, N., Unchiasu, S.F.: Implications of the operational risk practices applied in the banking sector on the information systems area. Account. Manage. Inf. Syst. **12**(1) (2013)

31. IT Governance Institute: IT control objectives for Basel II. The importance of governance and risk management for compliance. USA Printer (2010)
32. Berger, A., Frame, S.: Small business credit scoring and credit availability. J. Small Bus. Manage. **45**(1), 5–22 (2007)
33. Berger, A., Udell, G.F.: Small business credit availability and relationship lending: the importance of bank organizational structure. Econ. J. (2002)
34. Goodbillon-Camus, B., Godlewski, C.J.: Credit risk management in banks: hard information, soft information and manipulation. Universitè Robert Schumann, Strasbourg Cedex (2005)
35. Tadanori, Y., Takayoshi, N.: Soft information management effects on lending credit terms in Japan. Working paper, (2011)
36. De la Torre, A., Peria M.S.M., Schmukler, S.M.: Bank involvement with SMEs: beyond relationship lending. Policy Research Working Paper Series, The World Bank (2008)
37. Tarantola, A.M.: Banche e imprese: opportunità e sfide alla luce di Basilea 2. Working paper (2007)
38. Altman, E.I.: Financial ratios, discriminant analysis and the prediction of corporate bankruptcy. J. Finance **23**(4), 589–609 (1968)
39. Mayers, J.H., Forgy, E.W.: Development of numerical credit evaluation systems. J. Am. Stat. Assoc. **50** (1963)
40. Wiginton, J.C.: A note on the comparison of logit and discriminant models of consumer credit behaviour. J. Financ. Quant. Anal. **15**, 757 (1980)
41. Makowski, P.: Credit scoring branches out. Credit Management, november, (1985)
42. Coffman, J.Y., Darsie, J.S.: Collection scoring. Effective tool for determinanting collection priorities. The Credit World (75) (1986)
43. Altman, E.I., Sabato, G., Wilson, N.: The value of non financial information in SME risk management. J. Credit Risk **6**(2) (2010)
44. Montoya, M., Massey, A.P., Khatri, V.: Connecting IT services operations to services marketing practices. J. Manage. Inf. Syst. **26**(4), 65–85 (2010)

Kernel of a DSS for the Evaluation of the Founding Team of a University-Based Spin Off

Clara Bassano, Giuseppe D'Aniello, Matteo Gaeta, Mirko Perano and Luigi Rarità

Abstract This work focuses on a University-based Spin Off (USO) with consequent review of the traditional university mission on the need/opportunity to give more to Knowledge. Europe, Italian government and other institutions fund spin-offs through announcements, in which the evaluation method for merits still shows limitations, due to a light presence of Italian excellence. The work, starting from the Service Science Management Engineering and Design (SSMD+D), proposes a review of the literature about demographic factors in the founding team, but more generally of human capital in spin-offs in order to create value. According to Visintin and Pittino (see Visintin and Pittino in Technovation 34: 31–43, 2014), the paper aims to design a kernel of a fuzzy logic based DSS to evaluate ex-ante the likely success of the founding team of a USO. Academic spin-offs of the University of Salerno are useful to test the DSS.

Keywords University-based spin off (USO) · Creation and co-creation value · Service science management engineering and design (SSMD+D) · Decision support system (DSS) · Fuzzy logic · Problem solving · Decision making

C. Bassano
Dipartimento Di Studi Aziendali E Quantitativi, University Parthenope of Naples,
Via Generale Parisi, 13 (Palazzo Pakanowki), 80132 Naples, Italy
e-mail: clara.bassano@uniparthenope.it

G. D'Aniello · M. Gaeta · M. Perano · L. Rarità (✉)
Dipartimento Di Ingegneria Dell'Informazione, Ingegneria Elettrica E Matematica Applicata,
University of Salerno, Via Giovanni Paolo II, 132, 84084, Fisciano, SA, Italy
e-mail: lrarita@unisa.it

G. D'Aniello
e-mail: gidaniello@unisa.it

M. Gaeta
e-mail: mgaeta@unisa.it

M. Perano
e-mail: mperano@unisa.it

© Springer International Publishing Switzerland 2016
D. Mancini et al. (eds.), *Strengthening Information and Control Systems*,
Lecture Notes in Information Systems and Organisation 14,
DOI 10.1007/978-3-319-26488-2_6

1 Introduction

The Italian universities are living the so–called continuous change, reacting, as public administrations, with different timing than the private sector. The two traditional "missions" of research and training in universities, according to global trends and recent Italian regulatory changes, are converging to a "third mission", which consists of the development and sale of academic Knowledge, which derives from basic, industrial and experimental research. From the opportunities in research funding, through the cooperation due to an appropriate relational endowment, a process diffuses downstream on stakeholders and territories, starting from the value co-creation process and according to the Service Science Management Engineering and Design (SSMD+D), or *Service Science* for short (see [17], [21]). In fact, SSME+D offers a new university education model. It aims to develop transversal business skills to provide to young humanities, scientific, technical and economic faculties' students with an integrated set of key business skills. One will focus on the valued skills of creativity/innovation, international business vision and the digitization of business languages and processes, as distinctive traits of current and future entrepreneurial operations.

This strategic aim assumes the T-Shaped approach as a methodological foundation and foresees an innovative, adaptive entrepreneurial vocational profile with two structural dimensions that are fundamental for the systemic participated role of value co-creation and qualification of an organization's value proposition:

- The degree of professional expertise (know–how), or the specialist knowledge (in symbolism: the vertical line of the letter "T").
- The degree of openness and inter-professional or inter-organizational harmony (knowledge and qualities/attitudes), i.e. cognitive variety that qualifies a person's systemic competence and adaptability in a corporate structure (in symbolism: horizontal line of the letter "T").

By adopting the SSME+D with respect to profiles with new vocational skills required for the viability of the business systems, we intend to hold up a cultural change in the conception of "being an entrepreneur" and "entrepreneurial behaviour", training and outlining a profile of innovative, adaptive actor, as a person with a strong and timely professional specialization able to adapt and integrate in different environments, contributing to micro and macro social and economic growth processes. By this means, the competence based approach focuses on the educational process to develop proactive skills—thus, leadership, innovative management, delegation, analysis, communication, evaluation, etc., so as to form a guidance tool (dashboard), i.e. a set of ingredients to metabolize and acquire as an interpretative formula of an entrepreneurial role based on personal attitudes—, is coherent with the aforementioned T-Shaped profile proposed by the framework of the SSME+D.

The University thus becomes "entrepreneurial university", creating more value not only in terms of Knowledge but also of innovation, economic development and employment opportunities via the creation of spin-off companies (see [11] for a general dissertation).

Though a unique formal definition, recognized by the community (see [2]), does not exist, we assume that a spin-off is "[...] *a firm operating in high-tech sectors constituted by (at least) a professor/researcher or a PhD student/contractor/student, who has carried out many years of research on a specific topic, object of creation of the same firm*" (see [18]).

Starting from 2000, spin-offs, even in form of start-up companies or consortia for technology transfer (see [7]), leaded substantial benefits in terms of funding of various nature (chambers of commerce, regional, ministerial, European funds, and so on). These funds are useful for the creation, management of spin-offs or dedicated to specific tasks for the development of their products/services, based on the so-called "triple helix" model (see [4], [22]). The total amount of funds, made available by various agencies, is consistent. For example, in order to promote spin-offs in 2013, the Campania Region has finances available (about € 70 m) under the fund Campania POR FSE 2007–2013. Indeed, we have still to understand the true effectiveness of these funds in terms of produced results, although this evaluation is not complex. The measure of this efficacy, in fact, is achieved via a model useful to detect the gaps between the actually obtained financial results (final balance), and the expected ones (detectable in the business plan useful to gain access to funds). The question of the funding efficacy does not come only from the mortality data of spin-offs in Italy during the first years of life (a physiological phenomenon that, however, improved in last years, see [8]), but also from the lack of meaningful successful cases. Then, it follows the problem of understanding, before evaluation, which and how previous evaluative tools were used for spin-offs in order to grant benefits/funding. The evaluation of candidate spin-offs, nowadays, is essentially due to the ability of analysis and vision of expert committees. Indeed, this approach does not seem still suitable to provide reliable results. In this historical period, the critical factor is not only due to the funding dispersion, but also to the opportunity cost that the community supports to finance a bad practice, which will divert funds to other spin-offs with a higher chance of success. The opportunity cost does not refer only to the loan granted capital, but is the result of a combination of further positive elements of growth. This leads to a sizable efficacy problem in the funds management, which weighs on the community and limits an effective development of individual firms, individual sectors and, overall, the economic growth and employment in the country.

According to the classification by Piccaluga (see [1]), as for the university research, a spin-off is considered. The University-based Spin-Off (USO) is defined as "[...] a company that has both the university among the founding members or at least one academic year (full, associate and/or assistant professor, PhD student, research fellow) among the founders" (see [6]). Through empirical studies, qualified authors offer an interesting insight into the nature of the relationships among Entrepreneurs (Es) and Academics (As), Public Entity Research (PER) and Venture Capitalists (VC). In [10], authors provide a contribution, which tends to set up such relationships via a taxonomy of spin-offs from public research. Actually, a fruitful relationship between Es (spin-offs) and VC is still not existent (see [20]) in Italy.

The theoretical framework of this work is based on: a categorization of spin-off proposals by Piccaluga (see [1]), the nature of the relationships by Heirman and Clarysse (see [10]) and the methodological approach with the identification of the variables by Visintin and Pittino (see [25]). Starting from this last work, an inductive reasoning about the elements, which characterize a spin-off (*the human capital* and *the founding team*), is considered. Nowadays, all the described concepts represent an important heritage of Knowledge, which is still unconsidered. This is mainly due to the subjectivity of expert committees for the scientific evaluation and to a high amount of different schools of thought. The latter, indeed, focus on the business plan, technology ideas and economical—financial capacities. Such aspects are often neglected and do not consider the characteristics of the founders in terms of registry, experiences, attitudes and personality.

In this work, we propose a new methodology in which some results, known in literature and concerning the founding team, become objective and characterize the construction of a modern Decision Support System (DSS), as occurs in systems like, for instance, the ones based on text categorization (see [9]) or experience rule-based systems (see [19]). The idea deals with design and implementation of a first kernel of a fuzzy logic based DSS, useful to evaluate the success chances of a generic USO through elaborations of a set of indicators, as described by Visintin and Pittino (see [25]). The basic assumption is the following: "There is a correlation between the heterogeneity of the founding team in its demographic aspects and the USO performances".

The paper is structured as follows. Section 2 describes the problem of human capital and the dashboard of indicators for problem solving. In Sect. 3, a fuzzy DSS for USOs is presented, and research results are considered. Section 4 analyzes other results due to a preliminary prototype of the DSS. The paper ends with Conclusions in Sect. 5.

2   Human Capital, Founding Team for the Creation of USOs and Dashboard of Indicators

The theoretical framework of this work is the known dynamic capability (see [24]) of the organization to adapt itself and respond effectively to the continuous and sudden changes in the environment, with the aim of keeping sustainable competitive advantages for its own survival. Beside the organizational, relational and economical financial assets, human capital is the one useful to create value and represents a part of the intellectual capital, together with the relational and the structural one (see [23]).

From the analysis of the literature, with a focus on what motivates people to set up spin-off (including non-university), it follows that personal factors, such as the experiential background, often lead back to the most well-known theory of needs and motivation proposed by Maslow (see [14]). In support of this hypothesis, we have the contributions of other authors who, as for the motivations, highlight also the age, education, work experience, the individual background and the family one.

As for human capital, the creation of a start-up usually considers two different approaches. The first one is the "jack-of-all-trades": individuals with a wide range of skills are more likely to become entrepreneurs; therefore, a single should head the company. The second, on which this work relies, concerns the "production team", namely individuals should specialize on specific tasks. This means that, for a common aim, most individuals with multiple specializations are useful to cover the greatest number of expertise areas. The two approaches are better investigated by Müller (see [15]), who shows that, as for the survival of spin-offs, crucial factors for the creation of value are: the team size, the aspects for the combination of scientists/researchers and entrepreneurs with a greater business orientation, the specialized or generalized disciplinary background (the team rather than the individual).

Another interesting research result by Mustar, Wright and Clarysse (see [16]) shows ten entrepreneurial spin-offs, with teams having employees of the Technology Transfer offices of universities in different stages of development. The authors prove the assumption that teams, which own functional differences but common experiences, are more efficient. As for the formation of the founding team, Wright, Clarysse and Mustar propose a dichotomous classification of the constituent team members, according to their orientation: flexible versus control and their internal orientation versus the external one. From this research, it follows that a team, which combines either the flexibility or the external orientation, tends to be "innovative" in terms of a high degree of creativity and vision. On the other hand, team members with a high degree of external orientation and a control tend to be oriented towards the objectives.

Therefore, in the USO, a harmonious balance between commercial and scientific orientation is required, as well as an effective intersection between academic research and industry. Such phenomena represent two sides of the same coin and contribute to achieve better performances and dynamic competitive advantages for the creation of value. This leads to the motivation that guides to the design of the first kernel of a DSS from the founding team, with future extensions for members competences (see [12]). Visintin and Pittino (see [25]) defined a model with a dashboard of indicators with dependent/independent variables and tested it by a hierarchical regression model. The indicators analyse the heterogeneity of the founding team in its demographic profile in terms of profile differentiation: academic/non-academic, team size, different academic status of members, common expertise background of members, historical membership into the same project team or research group, similar previous work experience before the start-up of spin-off. The indicators are useful to evaluate the demographic composition of the top management of an academic spin-off, with the aim of evaluating the scientific and business impact of orientation on performance.

The borrowed indicators are the following:

V1. *Profile Differentiation (PD)*: differentiation among the members of the academic and non-academic entrepreneurial team. It is a function of the percentage of members belonging to the two subgroups. The higher is the degree of representation of the two categories of members, the higher is the balance between research and commercial orientation, hence reducing the risk of harmful effects of separation. Finally, notice that PD is computed via the absolute value of the difference between the two percentages, subtracting then 1 to such absolute value.

V2. *Team Size (TS)*: index measured as the total number of members of the entrepreneurial team.

V3. *Diversity in Academic Status (DAS)*: status classification of the academic members based on their position, distinguished as full professor, associate professor, assistant professor/lecturer, post doc/researcher, PhD student. DAS is measured within the academics sub-group, computing the Blau index: $1 - \sum p_i^2$, where p_i is the proportion of academics of each category.

V4. *Common Disciplinary Background (CDB)*: degree to which the two groups have similar disciplinary background in terms of specialization of education. In this sense, the homogeneity of subgroups members reduces the categorizations and promotes the cooperative interaction. CDB is defined as $P_{common\ disciplinary\ background}/P_{tot}$. Notice that $P_{common\ disciplinary\ background}$ is the number of pairs of members in which: (1) a member belongs to the academic group and the other one to the non-academic group and (2) they both have a common demographic attribute as the same disciplinary specialization. Finally, P_{tot} is the number of all possible pairs consisting of an academic member and a non-academic one.

V5. *Similarity in Work Experience (SWE)*: degree to which the two subgroups have similar working experiences. For instance, this happens in USO when academic and non-academic members had previous managerial or entrepreneurial experiences. In this case, the homogeneity makes the communication easier and more frequent among members and improves the effectiveness of the mutual control. On the contrary, when there is distance between members of the two subgroups, the integration becomes more difficult. SWE is defined as $P_{similarity\ in\ work\ experience}/P_{tot}$. Indeed, P_{tot} follows the previous definition. $P_{similarity\ in\ work\ experience}$ is the number of pairs of members in which: (1) a member belongs to the academic group and the other one to the non-academic group and (2) they both have a common demographic attribute such as the experience of similar work (for instance as a manager, entrepreneur, and so on).

V6. *Common Past Membership (CPM)*: it represents another important dimension that facilitates the integration. Notice that the members of the founding team (academic ones or others) with a previous history of group interactions have often a higher level of mutual trust, as well as similar priorities and opinions. CPM is defined as $P_{common\ past\ membership}/P_{tot}$. As always, P_{tot} obeys the previous definition, while $P_{common\ past\ membership}$ is the number of pairs of

Table 1 Indicators for society 1

Company	V1 (PD)	V2 (TS)	V3 (DAS)	V4 (CDB)	V5 (SWE)	V6 (CPM)
Society 1	0.34	6	0.72	0	0.6	0.8

members in which: (1) a member belongs to the academic group and the other one to the non-academic group and (2) they both have a common demographic attribute as a past membership in the same research team and/or the same project.

We make an example to clarify the meaning of each indicator. Consider a company, to which we refer as Society 1.

Society 1 has a team with six members, whose five ones are academic. Precisely, the academic members are a full professor, an associate professor, two researchers and a research assistant. The five academic members belong to engineering fields and, in the past, three of them worked as technicians. The non-academic member is classified as technician and entrepreneur. Moreover, three academic members worked with the non-academic member within a research project.

The values of the indicators are in Table 1.

3 A Fuzzy DSS for the Performances of USOs

The proposed Decision Support System (DSS) is designed via the Fuzzy Logic Theory (see [3, 26]). Fuzzy Logic (FL) is a suitable tool to deal with uncertain issues, subjective evaluations and problems with a high-dynamics behaviour.

FL combines either language or human intelligence through mathematics of fuzzy membership functions and provides a formal framework to represent and reason with vague, uncertain, and imperfect information (see [5]). As a result, the decision-making process consists of a better model of human assessment and judgement. The DSS process is in Fig. 1. The user inserts data of the founding team of the USO by answering a questionnaire (1). The questionnaire is analysed (2) in order to compute the six indicators (3) described in Sect. 2. Then, the fuzzy system evaluates the USO (4, 5 and 6) and the user obtains the results.

In detail, a general FL system consists of the following modules (Fig. 1):

1. *Fuzzification*: the transformation of a crisp set into a fuzzy one by membership functions.
2. *Inference engine and Rule base*: the inference engine processes the fuzzified input via the Rule base elements (rules).
3. *Defuzzification*: the fuzzy inference output is a fuzzy set obtained by compositions of output of each rule. The fuzzy output has to be transformed into a crisp value by the defuzzier via a membership function, in order to be useful in the real world.

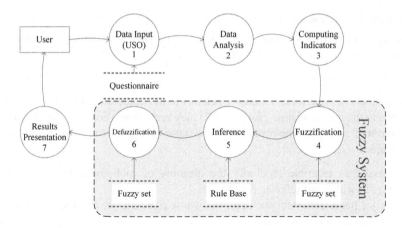

Fig. 1 DFD of the fuzzy DSS

The first step for a fuzzy DSS design is the identification of input and output variables. The system has six input variables (that correspond to the six indicators analysed in Sect. 2) and one output variable (the evaluation of the founding team). Moreover, the membership functions of all variables have to be designed. Finally, it is necessary to define the rules for the inference engine.

In cases where it is not possible to identify or compute all the described indicators (e.g., for the lack of data about the spin-offs), it is needed to slightly modify the proposed system.

In particular, the set of rules for the inference engine are lightly different with respect to the ones describes as follows. This is due to the fact that each parameter affects the evaluation of the team in different ways, and it may have some dependencies with respect to the other parameters.

As a result, when an indicator is missing, nothing can be asserted about its value and so a different rule that associates the remaining indicators with the evaluation have to be defined.

3.1 Input Variables of the Fuzzy DSS

This subsection describes the six input variables of the DSS and the corresponding membership functions, whose ranges have been defined considering the following characteristics: suitable values for some parameters as suggested by the scientific literature, see [25]; tuning of the parameters using the dataset characteristics. Indeed, little variations of the chosen values do not imply consequent meaningful modifications in the output, as we are dealing with fuzzy logic.

PD index: it suggests that the higher is the profile differentiation among academic and non-academic members, the higher are the performances of the USO

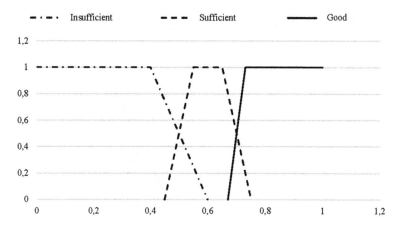

Fig. 2 Membership functions for the PD index

Table 2 Fuzzy sets for the PD index

Input	Fuzzy set	Range
PD	Insufficient	[0, 0.5[
	Sufficient	[0.5, 0.7[
	Good	[0.7, 1]

(especially as for the employment growth and the sales increase). This input variable has three fuzzy sets: *"Insufficient"*, *"Sufficient"* and *"Good"*. Their membership functions are trapezoidal. Figure 2 shows the membership functions for PD, while their fuzzy sets are in Table 2.

TS index: a team of a USO should have less than nine team members and it would be suitable to have small teams rather than large ones (see [25]). Generally, a core team should consist of a project manager with experience, a business manager, an enterprise information manager and a lead developer or a technical architect. As a result, the optimal size of a team consists of 3, 4 or 5 members, and it should never be composed of more than 7 members. This variable has three fuzzy sets: *"Insufficient"*, *"Sufficient"*, *"Good"*. A TS of 7 members or more is *Insufficient*; a TS of one member is *Sufficient* whereas a *TS* among 2 and 6 members is considered *Good*. Figure 3 shows the membership functions for TS while their fuzzy sets are in Table 3.

DAS index: it has a negative effect on the performances of the USO. The higher is the diversity, the lower are the performances of the USO. Such a phenomenon occurs as a high diversity in the academic status usually leads to disparity in the authority, in the research skills and in the position of each member within the social ladder. The fuzzy sets of DAS (Table 4) are *"Good"*, *"Sufficient"* and *"Insufficient"*, and the correspondent membership functions are trapezoidal (Fig. 4).

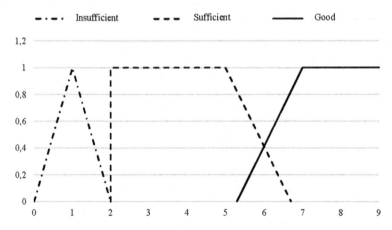

Fig. 3 Membership functions for the TS index

Table 3 Fuzzy sets for the TS index

Input	Fuzzy set	Range
TS	Insufficient	[7, 8, 9, ...[
	Sufficient	[1]
	Good	[2, 3, 4. 5, 6]

Table 4 Fuzzy sets for the DAS index

Input	Fuzzy set	Range
DAS	Good	[0, 0.4]
	Sufficient	]0.4, 0.6]
	Insufficient	]0.6, 1]

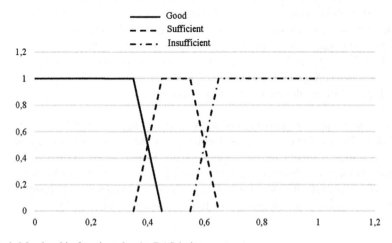

Fig. 4 Membership functions for the DAS index

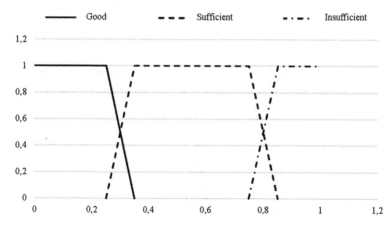

Fig. 5 Membership functions for the CDB index

Input	Fuzzy set	Range
CDB	Insufficient	[0, 0.3]
	Sufficient	]0.3, 0.8[
	Good	[0.8, 1]

Table 5 Fuzzy sets for the CDB index

CDB index: such input variable has three fuzzy sets: "*Insufficient*", "*Sufficient*" and "*Good*". Their membership functions are trapezoidal, as shown in Fig. 5, while Table 5 reports the range for the fuzzy sets.

SWE index: as for this index, when the founding team members had similar work experiences in the past, the communication among them is more effective and frequent, leading to better performances of the USO. The SWE input variable has three fuzzy sets: "*Insufficient*", "*Sufficient*", "*Good*" (see Table 6 for their range) and membership functions of trapezoidal type, see Fig. 6.

CPM index: this index has the same characteristics of SWE. Indeed, if the team members have been in the same team in the past, the performances of the USO is generally better. Notice that CPM has the same three fuzzy sets and the same membership functions of SWE (Table 6 and Fig. 6).

Input	Fuzzy set	Range
SWE, CPM	Insufficient	[0, 0.3[
	Sufficient	[0.3, 0.5[
	Good	[0.5, 1]

Table 6 Fuzzy sets for SWE and CPM indices

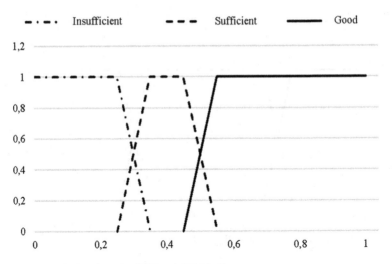

Fig. 6 Membership functions for SWE and CPM indices

3.2 Output Variable of the Fuzzy DSS

The aim of the system is to evaluate the founding team according to the performance of the USO. The output variable, namely Team Evaluation (TE), is a percentage value. When it increases, the team performances become better. This output value has three fuzzy sets: "*Not Recommended*", "*Recommended*" and "*Good*". Figure 7 represents the membership functions while Table 7 shows the corresponding fuzzy sets.

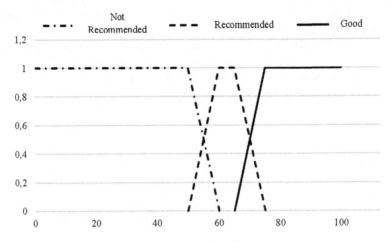

Fig. 7 Membership functions for the output variable TE

Table 7 Fuzzy sets for the variable TE

Output	Fuzzy set	Range
TE	Not Recommended	[0, 60]
	Recommended	]60, 75]
	Good	]75, 100]

Rule	IF	Input Variables						THEN	Output Variables
		PD	**TS**	**DAS**	**CDB**	**SWE**	**CPM**		**Team Evaluation**
1		Insufficient	Insufficient	Insufficient	Insufficient	Insufficient	Insufficient		Not Recommended
3		Insufficient	Insufficient	Insufficient	Insufficient	Sufficient	Good		Not Recommended
12		Insufficient	Insufficient	Sufficient	Good	Good	Good		Not Recommended

Fig. 8 DFD of the fuzzy DSS

3.3 Fuzzy Rule Base

In what follows, we assume that all six indicators are fundamental in order to study the system dynamics. In this case, the rule base consists of 729 rules, given by an unordered selection of $k = 6$ variables with $n = 3$ values ($n^k = 3^6 = 729$). These rules allow establishing the founding team performances by exploiting the input variables described in previous sections.

According to Mamdani and Assilian (see [13]), fuzzy inference and Rule Base use rules, structured as follows: *IF* X is A *AND* Y is B, *THEN* Z = C. For instance, a rule for the proposed system is *IF* PD = Good *AND* TS = Sufficient *AND* DAS = Good *AND* CDB = Good *AND* SWE = Sufficient *AND* CPM = Good, *THEN* TE = Good.

Such rules are obtained according to either the dataset characteristics or the opinions of experts, as for the Spin-Off foundation. Indeed, each indicator, which appears inside the antecedent of the various rules, has a weight, as described in [25]. Notice that the importance of each weight is embedded within the rules themselves. For example, rule 12 in Fig. 8 shows that, for insufficient PD and TS, the Team Evaluation is always Not Recommended even if the other input variables are sufficient or good. This is a consequence of the analysis in [25] and of the system characteristics, and does not depend on the variables separately.

Figure 8 shows some of the 729 rules of the Rule Base.

4 A Preliminary Evaluation

In order to evaluate the proposed Fuzzy DSS, we have developed a prototype through Microsoft.Net Framework. A first experimentation considers five real USOs of the University of Salerno. The necessary data have been obtained via questionnaires, administered to one of the members of each USO. As an example, we describe two representative case study among the analyzed five ones. The results of the questionnaires are the following. *USO#1* has a team of six members, five of which are academic members: one full professor, one assistant professor, two researchers, and one post doc. All academic members have an engineering background, while the non-academic one is a business manager. Furthermore, three academic members worked in a same research project in the past. *USO#2* has three members. Two of them are non-academic ones with a common disciplinary background in business studies, while the other one is a full professor who worked with another member in a research project before the establishment of the Spin-Off. Starting from this data, the system is able to compute the value of the six indicators, as shown in Table 8.

Table 9 shows the results of the fuzzification process for USO#1 and USO#2. Each cell represents the membership degree of each variable for each fuzzy set.

Figure 9 shows the fuzzy logic rules used for the two case studies. Specifically, rules number 1 and 2 are used for USO#1 whereas the other ones are used for USO#2.

The output of the fuzzy inference is in Fig. 10. The final result is obtained combining, via the Mamdani model for inference mechanism (see [13]), the output of each of the above rules.

Table 8 Crisp data for the two case studies of USOs

USO	Sales trend	PD	TS	DAS	CDB	SWE	CPM
#1	Irrelevant, < 50 k €	0.34	6	0.72	0	0.6	0.8
#2	/	0.66	3	0	0	0	0.5

Table 9 Fuzzification of input variables for USO#1 and USO#2

	PD		TS		DAS		CDB		SWE		CPM	
USO	#1	#2	#1	#2	#1	#2	#1	#2	#1	#2	#1	#2
I	1	0	0.5	0	1	0	1	1	0	1	0	0
S	0	1	0.5	0	0	0	0	0	0	0	0	0.5
G	0	0	0	1	0	1	0	0	1	0	1	0.5

Rule	IF	Input Variables						THEN	Output Variables
		PD	TS	DAS	CDB	SWE	CPM		Team Evaluation
1		Insufficient	Good	Insufficient	Insufficient	Good	Good		Recommended
2		Insufficient	Sufficient	Insufficient	Insufficient	Good	Good		Not Recommended
3		Sufficient	Good	Good	Insufficient	Insufficient	Sufficient		Recommended
4		Sufficient	Good	Good	Insufficient	Insufficient	Good		Good

Fig. 9 Used fuzzy logic rules

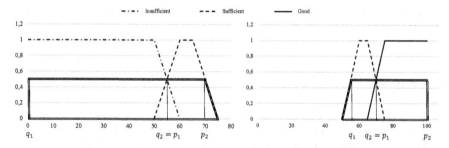

Fig. 10 Fuzzy sets for the variable TE. *Left* USO#1; *Right* USO#2

Table 10 Expert—based evaluation of DSS

USO	#1	#2	#3	#4	#5
Experts	Neutral	Positive	Negative	Negative	Negative
DSS output	NR	Good	NR	NR	NR

For the defuzzification process, the weighed mean technique is used. The result for the *USO#1* is $z = 45$ % (which means that the founding team is not recommended) and $z = 73.75$ % for the *USO#2*, namely the founding team is good. These results have been compared to the opinions of experts in the evaluation of USOs of the Italian MIUR. Their opinions and the system output are in Table 10. It is possible to notice a high matching degree among expert opinions and DSS outputs. In particular, if the DSS has a "Good" output, the experts give a positive evaluation. Obviously, the contrary happens in case of a "Not Recommended" (NR) DSS output, while the only exception occurs for USO#1 as the expert does not give a valid opinion.

5 Conclusions

Starting from [25], a kernel of indicators, useful to estimate the performances of USOs, has been defined. These indicators have been used as input of a fuzzy DSS that evaluates the performances of the USOs in order to limit the subjectivity in evaluations and help the user in dealing with non-analytical factors. A preliminary expert-based experimentation, which involved well-known USOs of the University of Salerno, has provided encouraging results. As for future works, we will focus on: an extension of the set of indicators by considering other factors, such as the age of members, their competencies, personality, behaviours, past experiences in other Spin-Offs, and so on; a wider experimentation, which involves a high number of USOs and experts.

Acknowledgments The authors wish to thank Eng. Angela Mastrogiacomo for her assistance in obtaining the results of this paper.

References

1. Conti, G., Granieri, M., Piccaluga, A.: Le imprese spin—off della ricerca pubblica. La gestione del trasferimento tecnologico. Strategie, Modelli e Strumenti. Springer, Milano (2011)
2. Degroof, J.J., Roberts, E.: Overcoming weak entrepreneurial infrastructures for academic spin-off ventures. Working Paper Series, MITIPC – 04 – 005, MIT (2004)
3. Di Martino, F., Loia, V., Sessa, S.: Fuzzy transforms method in prediction data analysis. Fuzzy Sets and Syst. **180**(1), 146–163 (2011)
4. Etzkowitz, H.A., Leydesdorff, L.: The dynamic of innovation: from National systems and "Mode 2" to a triple Helix of university—industry—government relations. Res. Policy **29**(2), 109–123 (2000)
5. Fakhry, H.: A fuzzy logic based decision support system for business situation assessment and e-Business models selection. Commun. IIMA **10**(4), 61–76 (2011)
6. Fini, R., Grimaldi, R., Santoni, S.: Complements or substitutes? The role of universities and local context in supporting the creation of academic spin-offs. Res. Policy **40**, 1113–1127 (2011)
7. Gaeta, M., Piscopo, R.: A case of successful technology transfer in southern Italy, in the ICT: the pole of excellence in learning and knowledge. In: D'Atri, A., et al. (eds.) Information technology and innovation trends in organizations, pp. 301–309. Springer Physica Verlag, Berlin (2011)
8. Gaeta, M., Perano, M., Piscopo, R.: Hypothesis for a new model to support the public research ICT spin-offs, In: Proceedings of ITAIS 2013, pp. 1–8 (2013)
9. Gentili, G.L., Marinilli, M., Micarelli, A., Sciarrone, F.: Text categorization in an intelligent agent for filtering information. Int. J. Pattern Recogn. Artif. Intell. **15**(3), 527–549 (2001)
10. Heirman, A., Clarysse, B.: How and why do research—based start—ups differ at founding? A resource-based configuration perspective. J. Technol. Transf. **29**(3–4), 247–268 (2004)
11. Knockaert, M., Spithoven, A., Clarysse, B.: The innovation paradox explored: what is impeding the creation of ICT spin—offs. Technol. Anal. Strateg. Manage. **22**(4), 479–493 (2010)
12. Loia, V., De Maio, C., Fenza, G., Orciuoli, F., Senatore, S.: An enhanced approach to improve enterprise competency management, In: 2010 IEEE World Congress on Computational Intelligence, WCCI (2010)
13. Mamdani, E.H.: An experiment in linguistic synthesis with a fuzzy logic controller. Int. J. Man Mach. Stud. **7**(1), 1–13 (1975)
14. Maslow, A.H.: Motivation and personality. Harper, New York (1954)
15. Müller, B.: Human capital and successful academic spin-off, Discussion paper No. 06–081, ZEW Center for European Economic Research, November (2006)
16. Mustar, P., Wright, M., Clarysse, B.: University spin-off firms: lessons from ten years of experience in Europe. Sci. Public Policy **35**, 67–80 (2008)
17. Payne, A., Storbacka, K., Frow, P.: Managing the co-creation of value. J. Acad. Market. Sci. **36**(1), 83–96 (2008)
18. Piccaluga, A., Balderi C.: Consistenza ed Evoluzione delle Imprese Spin-Off della Ricerca Pubblica in Italia. Rapporto di Ricerca, Scuola Superiore di Sant'Anna (2006)
19. Ruiz, P.P., Foguem, B.K., Grabot, B.: Generating knowledge in maintenance from experience feedback. Knowl.-Based Syst. **68**, 4–20 (2014)
20. Salvador, E.: Il finanziamento delle imprese spin-off della ricerca in Italia. Piccola Impresa/Small Bus. **1**, 75–106 (2007)

21. Spohrer, J., Maglio, P.: The emergence of service science: toward systematic service innovations to accelerate co-creation of value. Prod. Oper. Manage. **17**(3), 238–246 (2008)
22. Spohrer, J., Siano, A., Piciocchi, P., Bassano, C.: Reframing innovation: service science and Governance. In: Advances of the human side of service engineering. Proceedings of the Second International Conference on the Human Side of Service Engineering. Krakow, July 19th–23th (2014)
23. Stewart, T.: Intellectual capital: the new wealth of organization. Doubleday, New York (1997)
24. Teece, J.D., Pisano, G., Shuen, A.: Dynamic capabilities and strategic management. Strateg. Manage. J. **18**(7), 509–533 (1997)
25. Visintin, F., Pittino, D.: Founding team composition and early performance of university-based spin-off companies. Technovation **34**(1), 31–43 (2014)
26. Zadeh, L.: A computational approach to fuzzy quantifiers in natural language. Comput. Math Appl. **9**, 149–184 (1983)

Performance Measurement of Advertising Actions: Can Web-Metrics Improve Management Control Processes?

Nicola G. Castellano and Roberto Del Gobbo

Abstract The aim of the paper is to describe, through a preliminary case study, how to measure the outcomes of a traditional advertising campaign through web-metrics, which are usually adopted to evaluate the success of the company communication via the Internet. The results clearly show that web-metrics (compared to traditional thought-recall/listing measures), allow wider and multi-faceted insights about the customer response to advertising. Furthermore, web-metrics overcome the traditional measures in terms of timeliness of information, and for what concern the time and costs needed for data gathering and elaboration.

Keywords Performance measures · Web metrics · Effectiveness of advertising campaign · Brand awareness

1 Introduction

The effectiveness of a management control systems depends, as first, on how clear the strategy is formulated and depicted in all the most important key success factors, and the consequent management control actions needed to achieve the desired performance.

A sound performance measurement system (PMS) must be aligned to strategy and must consider all the measures that allow to verify whether the desired result is accomplished through managers' actions.

The design of a PMS, therefore, requires the selection of suitable measures that allow to quantify all the several strategic factors and management actions involved in the achievement of strategy. The managers involved in the PMS design could face

N.G. Castellano (✉) · R. Del Gobbo
Department of Economics and Law, University of Macerata, Macerata, Italy
e-mail: nicola.castellano@unimc.it

R. Del Gobbo
e-mail: roberto.delgobbo@unimc.it

© Springer International Publishing Switzerland 2016
D. Mancini et al. (eds.), *Strengthening Information and Control Systems*,
Lecture Notes in Information Systems and Organisation 14,
DOI 10.1007/978-3-319-26488-2_7

problems of data availability and accuracy, especially when they need measures expressing the outcomes achieved in terms of market response to company's efforts.

The present paper intends to focus on the measures employed to assess the outcomes produced through an advertising campaign based on TV commercials. Our main intent is to compare the accuracy and significance of traditional measures, with the web metrics.

Web-metrics allow to effectively measure the customers' interaction with the company, as a proxy of their cognitive response, developed after being exposed to the TV advertising (ads hereafter). In particular, the web-metrics provide insights about the response function of customers, expressed in terms of connections and navigation of the company website.

Usually the success of an advertising campaign is measured by capturing the customers' perceptions through surveys. These kind of measures may be biased by the fact that the consumers' opinions are collected on the initiative of the company that invites the customers to join the survey and to answer its questions.

On the contrary interactive media allow to assess the intensity of the interaction between the company and its customers from both the sides of the relation.

The employment of web measures as a proxy for the measurement of the success of an advertising campaign on TV represents a novelty. Generally, the web-metrics are used as a mean to evaluate the performance of web-advertising, web-communication and the interaction effectiveness between a company and its customers [1].

The results of the case study described in the following sections enhance the extant literature showing that web-metrics can integrate and complete the traditional measures, as they can provide new and interesting insights about the reactions of the customers. The results obtained could be useful also for managers involved in the company strategic planning and in the design of PMS in order to identify more effective and reliable connections between company strategy and consequent expected outcomes.

The paper is structured as follows: in the next section we describe the extant literature about advertising measures, then we discuss in deep the web measures adopted in the case study. In Sect. 4 the main findings are discussed, and in the last section some concluding considerations and directions for further research are commented.

2 Literature Review

Generally speaking, company's expectations about the outcomes produced by advertising expenses might be roughly summarized as an influence on customers' behavior that results in a sales enhancement [2].

The relation "advertising expenses-sales improvements" does represent a big challenge in marketing literature which, over time, has been overlooked for two main reasons: (1) strong difficulties arise when trying to define the period of time during which sales improvements can reasonably be influenced by the advertising effort, and (2) generally, it is considered easier and more effective to analyze the changes in customers' attitudes and perceptions induced by the advertising, rather than focusing on the direct effects produced on sales, considering that advertising is only one of the plentiful variables that are likely to impact on sales [3].

According to Stewart [4], the outcomes of advertising can be analyzed only by considering the assumptions underlying the response function, i.e. the model which is supposed to give raise to the response function and to the measures employed to quantify the response.

Two basic models are generally considered by extant studies on learning theory: the replacement model and the accumulation model [5]. The former presumes that the increasing exposure to ads allows to replace incorrect with correct responses, while the latter conversely assumes that correct responses increase with exposure, but compete with incorrect (or undesired) responses.

The adoption of a replacement model should require absolute measures of correct responses, since they which are assumed to replace the incorrect ones, as consequence of increasing exposure to ads. Conversely the accumulation model assumes that the probability of a given response is a function of the strength of the desired response, in connection with the strengths associated to all the competing responses; for that reason relative measures are considered more accurate.

The correct recognition is one of the measures commonly used to assess the success of an advertisement policy. It is calculated employing a hit rate and a false-alarm rate, derived from psychophysics and other fields of study of experimental psychology [6]. The hit rate expresses the number of the right targets chosen by a respondent above the total number of targets presented, while the false-alarm indicates the number of distractors which have been mistakenly chosen by the respondent, above the total number of distractors presented. The false-alarm rate provides indications about the accuracy of the recognition. Leigh and Menon [6] in their study compare these indicators with six alternative measures derived from the threshold/choice theory and from the signal/detection theory and, notwithstanding the strong differences in basic assumptions and formulas employed, surprisingly they find a significant convergence in the results provided by the set of alternative measures considered. Conversely, almost all of the measures show significant difficulties in their calculation, and several of them are based on propositions that are, or may be in some cases, false, or whose validity is difficult to be tested.

Recent studies suggest the employment of measures based on the assumptions that people react mentally to the ads, and their reaction (namely cognitive response) maybe considered a significant determinant of the change in the consumers' attitude [7].

The main critics moved to the traditional thought-listing measures relate to the biases concerned with the introspection needed to collect the data. The respondent might be unwilling or unable to answer, or his original thoughts might be conditioned or modified as consequence of new thoughts and experiences occurred after the exposure to the ads.

Neither the measures of cognitive response are free of criticism, since the reactions of the respondent may not occur, or different persons may reveal different kinds of reaction. Nevertheless, according to several authors cognitive measures are supposed to provide a clearer causal relation about advertising and its determinants, because they are less influenced by other factors.

Huang and Hutchinson [7] show that traditional thought-listing measures may fail in capturing specific cognitive responses known to affect attitudes, and that traditional valence-weighted measures of cognitive response predict some, but not all, of the systematic variation in attitudes across people. Furthermore, their results evidence that the measures proposed (thought recognition and belief verification) provide a greater predictive power and that implicit cognitive measures may be more effective when people are unable to access to their thoughts and when they should provide non-verbal responses. The measures are "implicit" when allow to assess reactions or thoughts that are unconscious or not easily consciously controlled.

According to Stewart [4], measures such as thought-recall or recognition are affected by historical and environmental factors. The formers relate to the history of the previous exposures to the same ads, or to the same campaign or to different campaigns of the same product, or to different campaigns of competitive products. Environmental factors relate to the customer knowledge about the product or brand and its personal attitudes and intentions. The combination of these factors may impact on the customer's learning process, through phenomena known as pro-active or retro-active inhibition.

Pro-active inhibition assumes that the higher is the intensity of the exposure to several ads, the lower is the ability of the customer to retain information content from anyone ad, whereas retro-active inhibition assumes that things more recently learned interfere with recall of older material.

The measurement of advertising effectiveness should also consider the media used to deliver the message to customers. The several attempts to rank the different media in terms of effectiveness come to different results [8, 9], even if television is commonly considered as the most valuable source of advertising [10].

In particular television is more effective in catching the consumer attention and in stimulating the consequent purchasing action, whereas the Internet is considered a more valuable media for what concern the ability to satisfy the consumers' information needs [11].

In the definition of an advertising strategy, television and the Internet may allow synergies and interactions between a company and its customers.

For what concern the measurement of advertising effectiveness, the Internet provides great amounts of data, without requiring significant costs. Consequently a wide range of measures may be easily calculated, such as exposure/popularity, stickiness and quality of user relationships, usefulness of content, just to name a few [1].

To our knowledge, web-metrics are widely used to assess the effectiveness of web advertising [1, 12], but given that the effectiveness of an advertising campaign can be enhanced when television and the Internet are integrated, then our purpose in the present paper is to adopt web-metrics to measure the success of a TV advertising campaign. In particular the web-metrics should allow to isolate the interactions between the company and its customers which are likely to be triggered by the TV ads.

The web measures, in this context, may then provide a proxy of TV advertising effectiveness, and insights about the consequent customers' interactions with the company, by encompassing the above described limitations connected with the traditional thought-listing or thought-recall measures.

3   Web-Metrics

Web-metrics record and analyze web data for purposes of understanding and optimizing web usage [13]. They can be used to estimate whether users' goals are being achieved and to provide feedback to developers, managers, and other stakeholders about how people access and visit a particular website.

Web site metrics allow to determine the website performances, considering either the expectations of users and those of the managers [14].

Since web-metrics help a company to stay on the right track by fine-tuning and optimizing its website, they can serve as an effective support to strategic management [15].

Several different metrics have been developed to evaluate a website usage. Generally, the metrics, most commonly used within organizations can be grouped into 4 categories: traffic source metrics, user profiling metrics, navigation mode metrics, e-commerce metrics [16].

The most important metrics for each category are described below.

Traffic source metrics. The traffic source metrics allow to identify the traffic sources that drive visitors to the company website. Three main traffic source metrics are generally adopted:

- Direct traffic: users that visit the company website by typing URL into their browser.
- Referral traffic: users that visit the company website by clicking on a URL when visiting another website.
- Traffic from search engine: users that discover the company website by entering a keyword in a search engine (Google, Bing, Yahoo, etc.).

User profiling metrics. The user profiling metrics allow to discover the characteristics of users that visit the company website:

- Unique visitors: the uniquely identified clients that are generating page views or hits within a defined time period (e.g. day, week or month)
- New visitors: visitors that have not made any previous visit.
- Returning visitors: visitors that made at least one visit formerly. The period between the last and current visit, usually measured in days, is called visitor recency.

Navigation mode metrics. The navigation mode metrics allow to understand how users interact with the company website. The metrics most commonly measured are:

- Visits: the total number of sessions held by visitors on the company website, typically measured on a daily basis. One visit is made when a user visits the site and accesses a series of pages.
- Page views: the total number of HTML documents accessed by visitors on the company website. One page view occurs when a visitor views a web page during the visit.
- Average page views per visit: the total number of page views divided by the total number of visits during the same timeframe.
- Page/session duration: the number of seconds (minutes) during which a visitor stands in a single page (session), as he/she navigates through the company website.
- Bounce rate: the percentage of visitors who leave after viewing one page.
- Exit rates: the percentage of visitors who conclude the session after having visited a determined number of pages.

E-commerce metrics. The e-commerce metrics provide information on activities and sales performance through the website:

- Conversion rate: the percentage of visitors who end up buying from the company web store.
- Visits to purchase: the average number of visits it takes for a user to convert.
- Average order value: the average size of an order on the company web store.
- Number of orders: the total number of transactions through the company website.
- Cart abandonment rate: the percentage of users who start the checkout process but do not complete it.
- Checkout page completion percentage: the percentage of users who get to the checkout page and complete their purchase.
- Average number of days to repurchase: the average number of days it takes for a previous purchaser to come back and make a subsequent purchase.

The web-metrics allow then to measure the intensity and the success of the interactions between a company and its customers via the Internet. In that sense, they can be employed as performance measures, in order to set targets and measure the achievement of results.

The extant literature about performance measurement suggests that measures need to be aligned with the strategy. From this point of view, web-metrics can help to measure the success of the advertising efforts and particularly of an Internet advertising campaign, or the success of on-line sales, or the customer satisfaction about the information available on the company website.

In the case study described in the following section, an original adoption of web-metrics is proposed. In particular, web-metrics are adopted in order to evaluate the success of a traditional TV commercial campaign. Given that synergic connections and integration interactions between the Internet and the traditional media are documented by extant literature [11], web measures should allow to assess if and how the intensity of connections to a company website changes right after a TV commercial is broadcasted.

If so, the web measures could then catch up the customers' reactions to the TV commercial, providing new and interesting insights that would allow scholars and managers to draw more reliable relations between company commercial actions and expected outcomes.

4 Research Method and Findings

The case study concerns the TV advertising campaign launched by an Italian company operating in the kitchen furniture industry. The campaign was broadcasted in the TV "prime time" during January 2013.

Originally the company decided to measure the success of the TV advertising campaign by adopting a traditional set of thought-recall measures obtained through a telephone survey, aimed at evaluating how the brand awareness changed after the TV advertising campaign.

The survey involved two random samples of telephone users respondents in telephone interviews, one conducted before and after the launch of the ad campaign.

The samples were creating by using the Random Digit Dialling (RDD), that provides a representative probability sample of all telephone users, unlike telephone surveys which rely on registered telephone number lists or directories [14]. The two samples were obtained by employing the stratified sampling techniques. The stratification variables are the geographical area (the provinces), and the resident population in each province. The final samples were both composed of 384 units.

We performed a χ^2 test to verify the existence of statistically significant differences between the percentage of respondents that heard of, or recognized (without or with prompting) the company's brand before and after the launch of the ad campaign (see Table 1).

The results obtained do not show a significant change in brand awareness after the launch of the ad campaign: the p-value is higher than 0.05, therefore the null hypothesis of equality of the proportions in the two time instants cannot be rejected.

Some limitations may influence the reliability of findings in Table 1. Since the company produces and sells kitchen furniture (then "durable goods"), the level of commitment with the product becomes particularly relevant (i.e. the respondents should have been directly or indirectly involved in a purchasing experience or they should be involved in the future). The random sampling does not allow to assess this level of commitment ex ante, then the results could be significantly biased if a relevant portion of respondents is not interested in the product.

Table 1 Brand recall before and after advertising campaign

Brand recall	Before ad campaign (%)	After ad campaign (%)	df	χ^2	p-value
Yes	34.1	36.6	1	0.462	0.4968
No	65.9	63.4			

These limitations are reduced considerably by employing web-metrics, given that a sample is not required to be extracted. Web-metrics are calculated on data collected through the interaction between users and the company website. In other words, the website interaction represents an explicit expression of interest by the users, that self-select themselves, reducing the problems of representativeness.

According to recent figures (Iab Seminar Mobile and Advertising. Audiweb, July 2014), the 82.2 % of the Italian population between 18 and 74 years old can access to the Internet from anywhere, then the coverage bias can be considered not relevant.

Through web-metrics, the consumers' response to the ad campaign can be observed measuring the changes in their browsing behavior, as a proxy of involvement or interest triggered by the ad broadcast.

For some of the main web-metrics (described above) we calculated the average values in the month before the ad campaign, and we compared them with the average values during the campaign, and in the month after. We performed a t-test to assess the statistical significance of the differences: the null hypothesis which was tested for each web-metric is the equality of mean over time.

As shown in Table 2 the navigation mode metrics analyzed show a significant increase in the average value during the broadcast of ads.

It is worth noting that for what concern the durability of the impact produced by the ads, the average value of metrics after the end of the ad campaign remained higher than before.

We interpret this result as a confirmation of a substantial increase in brand recall: the p-value of t-test (<0.001) shows the significance of the results.

We also analyzed the traffic source metrics, that consider the different methods through which the company website has been accessed by viewers. Direct traffic, search engines, and referring sites are the alternative sources considered. More specifically, the direct traffic compared to accesses via search engines allow to understand whether the viewer kept in mind the website address and the brand name provided promoted during the ads.

For viewers who accessed the site via search engines is also possible to analyze the keywords employed in order to evaluate the brand awareness: during the broadcast of the ads the employment of the keywords "kitchens Lube" increased remarkably (see Table 3).

Table 2 Web metrics: monthly comparison before, during, and after ad campaign

	Mean (before)	Mean (during)	t	df	p-value	Mean (after)	t	df	p-value
Visits	1.949	4.344	−16.60	60	<0.001	4.166	−19.95	60	<0.001
Pageviews	11.346	26.395	−16.10	60	<0.001	25.068	−18.54	60	<0.001
New visitors	1.264	2.908	−14.95	60	<0.001	2.702	−18.92	60	<0.001
Daily unique visitors	1.703	3.804	−16.27	60	<0.001	3.623	−19.94	60	<0.001

Table 3 Traffic source metrics: monthly comparison before, during, and after ad campaign

	Mean (before)	Mean (during)	t	df	p-value	Mean (after)	t	df	p-value
Direct visits	540	1.064	−14.2	60	<0.001	1.045	−18.7	60	<0.001
Search engine	1.182	2.711	−15.6	60	<0.001	2.554	−18.1	60	<0.001
Keyword "kitchen Lube"	227	691	−14.6	60	<0.001	598	−15.9	60	<0.001
Keyword "LUBE"	214	481	−13.1	60	<0.001	430	−15.2	60	<0.001

Finally, also the metrics about the session length show a significant increase during and after the ad broadcasts (Table 4).

The case study clearly shows how wide is the spectrum of analysis provided by web-metrics, also when employed to measure the outcomes produced by an advertising campaign broadcasted on a traditional media. Thus, such set of measures can integrate and even further replace the traditional measures of advertising effectiveness.

It is worth to mention that web-metrics allow significant advantages in terms of time and costs savings for what concern the collection of data and their elaboration. All the measures presented in Tables 1, 2, 3 and 4 are calculated on the browser-based web analytics platform used by the company (ShinyStat©) that provides analyses and web data in real time. The annual fees (based on the number of monthly page views) are absolutely not significant. In terms of timeliness, the web-metrics are available few seconds after the ads broadcast and they allow a real-time monitoring, whereas survey-based measures can be calculated only with a certain delay that might represent an additional bias in the accuracy of results, as described above.

Table 4 Website engagement metrics: comparison month before, current month, month after ad campaign

	Mean (before)	Mean (during)	t	df	p-value	Mean (after)	t	df	p-value
Average page view	5.79	6.08	−2.8	60	0.007	5.65	1.7	60	0.098
Session duration (min)	6.04	6.37	−3.8	60	<0.001	6.27	−2.7	60	0.008

5 Conclusions

This paper shows how the web-metrics may provide an exhaustive and multi-faceted picture of how consumers behave in response to advertising.

The results show that web measures overcome traditional thought-listing/recall measures on several aspects.

In particular web measures allow to isolate the behaviors of "interested customers", those who react after or during the ads exposition by searching for additional information on the Internet.

The analysis of such behaviors provide managers with relevant information to be employed in several different directions. In particular they allow to create more accurate performance measurement systems, by considering the cause and effect relations between advertising campaigns and Internet interaction.

Furthermore, the results obtained enrich the extant literature about measurement of advertising effectiveness, since to our knowledge, web-metrics have never been adopted in the evaluation of a TV advertising campaign.

The goal-directed behavior, in the form of consumer involvement or interest, has long been recognized as an important determinant of consumer response to marketing campaigns [17]. The interaction with a company website could then become a valid proxy to measure the level of commitment triggered by the advertising and then a valid predictor of a subsequent response. Consumers are likely to interact when the product or service is of high importance to them, when they are convinced that this interaction will be beneficial to them (e.g., when the interaction is consistent with their goals). Web-metrics allow to capture and measure this interactions, and thus seem to be more effective in assessing the success of an advertising campaign.

As limitation of the study, we must underline that the single company analyzed in the case study, operating which operates in a context of durable goods, does not allow to generalize the results obtained. In a different context (such as for consumer goods), the customers might be differently influenced by the ads: considering the substantially higher frequency of purchases, and their interactions with the company websites, as consequence of the exposure to the ads, may change.

Thus, a possible direction for further research could be to test whether web-measures can be adopted as proxies of a TV advertising campaign effectiveness in multiple different operating environments.

References

1. Bhat, S., Bevans, M., Sengupta, S.: Measuring users' web activity to evaluate and enhance advertising effectiveness. J. Advertising XXXI(3), 97–106 (2002)
2. Schreiber, R.J., Appel, V.: Advertising evaluation using surrogate measures for sales. J. Advertising Res. 30(6), 27–31 (1991)

3. Pearce, M., Cunningham, S.M., Miller, A.: Appraising the Economic and Social Effects of Advertising. Marketing Science Institute, Cambridge Mass (1971)
4. Stewart, D.W.: Measures, methods and models in advertising research. J. Advertising Res. **29**, 54–60 (1989)
5. Mazur, J.E., Hastie, R.: Learning as accumulation: a reexamination of the learning curve. Psychol. Bull. **65**(6), 1256–1274 (1978)
6. Leigh, J.H., Menon, A.: A comparison of alternative recognition measures of advertising effectiveness. J. Advertising **15**(3), 4–12 (1986)
7. Huang, Y., Hutchinson, J.W.: Counting every thought: implicit measures of cognitive responses to advertising. J. Consum. Res. **35**, 98–118 (2008)
8. Shyam Sunder, S., Narayan, S., Obregon, R., Uppal, C.: Does web advertising work? Memory for print versus online media. Journalism Mass Commun. Q. **75**(4), 822–835 (1998)
9. Gallagher, K., Foster, K.D., Parsons, J.: The medium is not the message: advertising effectiveness and content evaluation in print and on the web. J. Advertising Res. **41**(4), 57–70 (2001)
10. Ducoffe, R.H.: Advertising value and advertising on the web. J. Advertising Res. **36**, 21–35 (1996)
11. Nagar, K.: Advertising effectiveness in different media: a comparison of web and television advertising. IIMB Manage. Rev. **21**, 245–260 (2009)
12. Palmer, J.W.: Web site usability, design, and performance metrics. Inf. Syst. Res. **13**(2), 151–167 (2002)
13. Clifton, B.: Advanced web metrics with google analytics. Wiley Publishing, New York (2010)
14. Khoo, M., Pagano, J., Washington, A.L., Recker, M., Palmer, B., Donahue, R.A.: Using web metrics to analyze digital libraries. In: Proceedings of the 8th ACM/IEEE-CS JCDL '08, pp. 375–384. New York (2008)
15. Hong, I.: A survey of web site success metrics used by internet-dependent organizations in Korea. Internet Res. **17**(3), 272–290 (2007)
16. Peterson, E.: Web analytics demystified: a Marketer's guide to understanding how your web site affects your business. Celilo Group Media and CafePress, New York (2004)
17. Waksberg, J.: Sampling methods for random digit dialing. J. Am. Stat. Assoc. **73**(361), 40–46 (1978)

Measurement and Control Challenges in the *Human Capital Management* for *Mentoring* Relationships System

Luisa Varriale and Assunta Di Vaio

Abstract The aim of this paper is to identify and describe possible measurement indicators for monitoring the performance within a mentoring relationships system. We propose to investigate which factors can provide an adequate assessment of mentoring recognized as one innovative and specific technique to support the human resources management policies within any organizations. We analyze mentoring programs applied in different organizational settings evidencing their main functions and application areas and trying to evidence if and how some specific factors can affect their effectiveness. Starting from these dimensions, we develop and analyze key performance indicators which can support the mentoring evaluation process. This is a theoretical study that, through a review of the literature on mentoring topic, allows us to identify and evidence a set of effective and successful key performance indicators. This study outlines some relevant key factors for generating and developing effective mentoring programs by systematizing and clarifying the main contributions on this topic and identifying new research perspectives.

Keywords Mentoring · Key performance indicators · Performance measurement · Mentoring effectiveness

1 Introduction

Mentoring is conceived as one innovative and specific technique in the learning and teaching processes, and, recently, many organizations tend to adopt this instrument within different application areas. Hence, mentoring is applied in many different

L. Varriale (✉) · A. Di Vaio
Parthenope University, Naples, Italy
e-mail: luisa.varriale@uniparthenope.it

A. Di Vaio
e-mail: susy.divaio@uniparthenope.it

© Springer International Publishing Switzerland 2016
D. Mancini et al. (eds.), *Strengthening Information and Control Systems*,
Lecture Notes in Information Systems and Organisation 14,
DOI 10.1007/978-3-319-26488-2_8

areas, including learning and training processes, socialization, diversity management, or work-life balance policies [1–7].

In the last decades, the global economy is deeply changed, also as a consequence of a wide financial crisis. In this scenario, characterized by high levels of competiveness and globalization, firms tend to search for more effective and efficient tools to manage their human resources recognized as crucial source of competitive advantage. Indeed, mentoring represents an innovative technique to support the human resource management policies within any organizations. Mentoring constitutes a relationship between two or more individuals, mentor and protégé: the former provides functions aimed to support the latter to develop his/her skills and competences in his/her personal and professional development.

Most studies on mentoring programs evidence the major outcomes associated mainly to the protégé in terms of career benefits (promotion, high job and career satisfaction, organisational commitment improvement, and high salaries) [2, 8–10]. Likewise, personal outcomes have been outlined by some authors in terms of increasing of self-esteem and self-efficacy for the protégé [2, 9, 11]. Despite the broad analysis of mentoring programs outcomes, scholars tend to pay less attention to the effectiveness of mentoring relationships within organizations and mostly to the key factors that can improve the performance of individuals involved and support the decision making process by the top management in the Human Capital Management.

This paper aims to investigate the mentoring relationships system, considering the formal mentoring programs, in order to identify the main factors that can make each mentoring relationship successful for the actors involved, such as protégé, mentor and enterprise (the organization promoter of the mentoring program). Then, subsequently, analysing each mentoring relationship identified in terms of outcomes, that is benefits received from the partners, we develop a set of key performance indicators to measure and control the effectiveness of mentoring process.

After a brief review of the literature on mentoring and its effectiveness related to performance measures, we describe and identify key performance indicators regarding mentoring relationships used to evidence in which way it is possible to improve the mentoring relationships in terms of related outcomes for the actors involved. In fact, mentoring programs can have several effects, positive or negative, also by depending on the specific personality traits of individuals or contextual factors. We found out that most organizations adopt successful mentoring programs to support their employees in their personal and professional development process (learning and teaching processes) and this study evidences some relevant key factors for generating and developing effective mentoring programs by systematizing and clarifying the main contributions on this topic and identifying new research perspectives.

The paper is organised as follows: Sect. 2 is focused on mentoring topic evidencing its function, outcomes, criticisms and perspectives of the related relationships. In Sect. 3 we analyse the measurement and control of a mentoring relationships system identifying key performance indicators starting from the main factors (demographic, personal and professional characteristics) that contribute to affect the effectiveness of mentoring. We draw some final considerations in Sect. 4.

2 Mentoring in the Human Capital Management

Individuals with different background, expertise, and seniority can significantly and deeply learn thanks to social interactions [12]. Mentoring is one important relationship that serves as a forum for personal learning [13].

Mentoring has ancient origins that go back to Greek mythology. Mentor was the old and good friend to whom Odysseus, Kingdom of Ithaca, before leaving for the war against Trojan, gave his son. Hence, as Homeric narrates, the concept of mentoring means "to entrust a young person in training and learning to an expert adult".

Numerous examples of mentoring have been provided from the history and cultural evolution, outlining that always the relationship with a more experienced and old individual becomes crucial for the development of young people in many settings, for example, the relationships between head expert-apprentice, doctor-medical students, teacher-student, and so on [14]. In any organizational context, mentoring is conceived as "a relationship where there are two individuals, a senior person (mentor) who, thanks to his/her advanced experience and knowledge and maturity, has the duty to guide, to advise, to suggest junior individual (protégé/mentee) in his/her professional and personal development"; it is an exclusive relationship "person to person" between protégé and mentor, there is a dyadic personal and constant relationship (one-to-one) [1, 3, 6, 15–18].

Last studies tend to conceive mentoring as a multiple developmental relationship phenomenon [7], in which a protégé can establish relationships with more than a mentor within organizational context [7, 19–21]; therefore, a protégé has not only one mentor, but he/she has multiple relationships with several and distinguished actors who has typical functions of mentoring within network of persons, establishing multiple simultaneous relationships. This developmental network perspective suggests that individuals are better served, if supported from a variety of mentors, who give more contributions in terms of perspectives, knowledge and skills [22].

Most studies on the topic have distinguished two main mentoring functions: career development support, including coaching, sponsoring advancement, providing challenging assignments, protecting protégés from adverse forces, and foresting positive visibility; psychosocial development support, involving such functions as personal support, friendship, acceptance, counselling, and role modeling [2]. Some authors consider these two mentorship factors of career development and psychosocial functions [18], others found role modeling to represent a third factor that is distinct from psychosocial support [3, 23]. However, mentor can provide all or only one of such functions [24].

Some authors associated positive outcomes, in terms of higher levels of job satisfaction and promotions, to mentoring within organizational settings, as an effective instrument in socialization process, training and learning process and career development [2, 6, 25].

Support, counselling, friendship are mainly related to psychosocial dimensions [1, 26]. According to Kram's mentor role theory, career functions help protégé "to learn the ropes" and mentor can facilitate his/her advance within organizational context.

In recent decades, mentoring initiatives are becoming more popular because of their goal, in fact, "programs with this aim now number well into the thousands and benefit from significant levels of governmental, corporate, and philanthropic support" [27: 647].

In the literature, mentoring has been recognized an effective instrument to support human resources management policies, in fact, mentoring is an innovative learning instrument [28] or instrument for organizational socialization of the staff [29]. According to this perspective, mentoring can play a different role within organizational context, and consequently the definition of mentoring programs needed and, sometimes, it is necessary to formalize the mentoring relationships. In this direction, some scholars distinguish formal or informal mentoring programs in terms of formality and length of the relationship, and purpose of the relationship meant like specific goals [2, 30–32]. Protégés can build their relationships with mentor also thanks to new technologies, for example, thanks to channel internet/e-mail [33–36]. In this case, depending on the choice of techniques or systems of communication, face-to-face or with other typologies, innovative typologies of mentoring programs have been developed, named e-mentoring, also electronic mentoring or mentoring online or telementoring. This new approach is still unknown because prior studies consider above all traditional mentoring (t-mentoring) schemes.

E-mentoring has been defined by Single and Mueller [37] as "a relationship that is established between a more senior individual (mentor) and a lesser skilled or experienced individual (protégé), primarily using electronic communications, and that is intended to develop and grow the skills, knowledge, confidence, and cultural understanding of the protégé to help him or her succeed, while also assisting in the development of the mentor" [37: 108]. Also, the authors Bierema and Merriam [33] conceive e-mentoring as "a computer mediated, mutually beneficial relationship between a mentor and a protégé which provides learning, advising, encouraging, promoting, and modeling, that is often boundaryless, egalitarian, and qualitatively different than face-to-face mentoring" [33: 212]. The traditional mentoring scheme is over in e-mentoring programs, because the relationship between mentor and protégé considers distance communication ways, internet, email, chat rooms, and so on, overcoming the traditional schema (t-mentoring). E-mentoring can overcome organizational or geographical barriers and can thus pair individuals or groups from organizations that may be totally dissimilar, consequently the career process is more effectively, especially for women [38, 39]. Five clear advantages of online mentoring can be identified: greater access, reduced costs, and equalization of status, decreased emphasis on demographics and a record of interactions. E-mentoring also allows flexibility with time and space since protégés and mentors do not have to be in the same place at the same time, thanks to the overcoming of geographic, space and time limitations, e-mentoring also facilitates the development of a professional network [40] by supporting the career process [41]. Otherwise, e-mentoring "is not a panacea, neither is it an inexpensive alternative to face-to-face mentoring" [42], although the main advantage is related to the cost effectiveness with high start-up costs but low operational costs [34].

Some studies evidence that e-mentoring has some key challenges, such as the likelihood of miscommunication, a slower development of relationships online, negative effects of computer malfunctions, issues of privacy and confidentiality [40]. However, the main negative outcomes of e-mentoring programs concern the lack of training and support for mentor and the lack of feedback.

Empirical evidence is still needed from schemes that exploit the full potential of computer-mediated-communication (CMC) [34, 35]. In this case, mentor and protégé can actively interact, in fact, the authors, Ensher et al. [34], examine online mentoring and computer-mediated communication. Tree different models can be identified and distinguished: CMC-Only, CMC-primary and CMC-supplemental, in terms of instruments used for mentoring relationship; they associate each form and specific activity of e-mentor (friendship, counseling, coaching, etc.) with a benefit/function of traditional mentoring [34].

With reference to the mentoring functions, as already outlined, the career development support concerns all actions aimed to promote protégés protecting and helping them to face any challenges, and supporting them in their advancement process at workplace. Furthermore, functions as personal support, friendship, acceptance, counselling, and role modelling are included in the mentors' psychosocial roles.

Mentoring programs have applied in several main organizational areas: learning and training processes; the main leadership theories; negative experiences; Work Life Conflict (WLF) management through mentoring; diversity management in terms of the composition of the relationship (gender, age, race, and so on) and the role of mentoring to manage diversity.

In this study we focus exclusively on formal mentoring in order to investigate its effectiveness, trying to measure and control the key factors for its successful development.

3   The Role of *Performance Measurement* and *Management Control* in the Mentoring Relationships System

Although the prevalent literature evidences and investigates mentoring as "multiple developmental relationships phenomenon" [7, 32], we focus on each one-to-one mentoring relationship established within any organizations. Crucial characteristics, known as key variables, have been identified within each one-to-one mentoring relationship into the mentoring relationships system, investigating exactly the interactions between the mentor and protégé involved in the mentoring relationships.

According to the prevalent studies on mentoring, we choose three different categories of variables that play a significant role in the creation and development of mentor-protégé relationships in the mentoring formal program, affecting mainly its effectiveness [10, 43–46]: demographic, psychosocial and professional characteristics as below (Table 1).

More specifically, the demographic variables (first group) consist of the following characteristics: age, country of origin, gender, race, socioeconomic status and educational level. In the prevalent literature on mentoring these dimensions are investigated as control variables in empirical studies, especially in comparing mentored-individuals and not-mentored individuals [6, 8, 47–49]; likewise, these variables are also considered in order to analyze how the benefits of mentoring change in the mentor-protégé interaction because of their different impact. For instance, in diversified mentoring relationships in which female-mentors interact with male-protégés there is a minor knowledge exchange, especially regarding the career developmental process, consequently career outcomes are less frequent compared to male-mentors/female-protégés relationships [3]. According to the Similarity-Attraction Theory [50–52], individuals tend to interact mainly and more frequently with people with similar country origins, same gender and race and

Table 1 Key variables in *one-to-one* mentoring relationships

Variables	Mentor	Protégé	Mentor-Protégé
Demographic characteristics (*1st group*)			
Age (range 10–15 years)			X
Country of origin			X
Gender			X
Race			X
Socioeconomic status			X
Educational level			X
Psychosocial characteristics (*2nd group*)			
Authenticity			X
Empathy			X
Motivation			X
Personality traits			X
Protégé's perception of mentor as significant adult		X	
Professional characteristics (*3rd group*)			
Seniority			X
Tenure	X		
Mentor's experience	X		
Mentor's expertise within the sector	X		

educational level; in this case, human resources within organizations with similar demographic characteristics are more able to share their expertise, knowledge and information regarding their personal and professional developmental process.

The second and third groups of key variables regard mainly the mentor-protégé interaction within the mentoring relationships, with the exception of the psychosocial variable "protégé's perception of mentor as significant adult" and three professional variables (tenure, mentor's experience and expertise within the sector); in fact, these variables concern more the mentor or protégé specific profile.

Starting from these variables, we identify some relevant outputs (that is the outcomes in the prevalent studies on mentoring) which affect the performance of each partner involved in the mentoring relationship investigated, such as mentor, protégé and the same enterprise that is the promoter of the formal mentoring program (Table 2). More specifically, drawing from the literature on mentoring, we have grouped the main factors investigated that mostly affect the outcomes of mentoring relationships; for instance, some studies have evidenced how diversified mentoring relationships (gender, race, educational level) can have different effects on the individuals involved in terms of career support, in fact, gender and race tend to negatively affect the professional development for female protégés in male-dominated occupations [23–26]; also, other authors have outlined how mentors with high experience can better provide the career support function, especially assuming the role of coach and sponsor for the protégés [26, 32, 43].

Starting from the identified variables, we focus on the related outputs, reworking and grouping together the main results outlined in the existing literature; in details, we distinguish personal, professional and organizational outcomes for all the partners involved, that is mentor, protégé and the same organization (enterprise). Hence, specific variables have been usually associated in the previous studies to some outputs, e.g. the "protégé's perception of mentor as significant adult" and "seniority" are usually linked to the reinforcement of the mentor's leadership.

In our analysis, some outcomes concern both mentor and protégé involved in the mentoring relationships, such as the increase of the self-efficacy and self-esteem; other outcomes concern only the protégé (the development of analytical skills,

Table 2 Outputs in *one-to-one* mentoring relationship

Outputs	Mentor	Protégé	Enterprise
Analytical skills		X	
New working method		X	
Organizational climate			X
Promotions		X	
Relational orientation			X
Self-efficacy	X	X	
Self-esteem	X	X	
Time management	X	X	X
Leadership reinforcement	X		

e.g. the capacity to collect and manage data processing; the adoption of new method working, e.g. the use of technologies as support at workplace; the obtaining promotions, e.g. the advancement within the enterprise at high organizational levels), instead, sometimes only the mentor is involved (the leadership reinforcement, e.g., the mentor acquires more visibility and power within organizational contexts). Regarding the enterprise, the table below shows the following outputs: the improvement of the organizational climate (e.g. the employees perceive the organization more oriented to their wellbeing and pay more attention to their work improving the general performance), the development and adoption of a relational orientation (e.g. the enterprise tends to facilitate the knowledge and information sharing within its structure focusing on the central role of its employees), and an effective time management (concerning also the protégé, e.g., the acquisition of right ways in terms of timing schedules to manage the phases of the production process).

In this context briefly described concerning the key variables and outputs within the mentoring relationships system, we distinguish the following sub-relationships within the mentoring process (Fig. 1): mentor-protégé relationship, enterprise-mentor relationship, protégé-mentor relationship and protégé-enterprise relationship. In each mentoring relationship we try to evidence the collection, processing and reporting of data and information. In the mentoring relationships system, enterprise-mentor relationship and mentor-protégé relationship represent two different direct relationship; while, protégé-enterprise and protégé-mentor relationships can be identified as indirect mentoring relationships. Both the direct mentoring relationships are characterized by the central role of mentor.

In the first direct mentoring relationship (mentor-protégé), that is the starting point of the mentoring process, the exchange between the two partners mostly concerns the elements regarding the mentor's knowledge and expertise.

In all the mentoring relationships identified, information and data collection usually occurs thanks to different channels of communication, such as in the mentor-protégé relationship by email, forum, chatrooms, face-to-face meetings, and so on. Otherwise, we evidence that the data collection is easier in e-mentoring programs, because of the support of technology especially in CMC-primary and CMC-only models; in this case, there is a specific platform that supports and

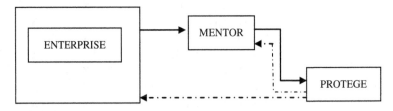

Fig. 1 Information management process in the mentoring relationships system. *Solid line* direct relationships system. *Dashed line* indirect relationships system

facilitates the information and data collection and transfer in the mentoring program.

However, the sharing of information, language codes, and software among all the partners involved in the relationships becomes a critical factor for their development [53], and this crucial role is also played in the mentoring relationships, although the data and information processing is often inadequate.

The information sharing might improve the performance of the partners within mentoring relationships. Data and information for the top management do not represent a very rigid rule for the enterprise system, but it supports them for a more effective and responsible governance of the firm [54].

Otherwise, because of the involvement of partners that differ for their roles and motivation, there is the high risk that they adopt opportunistic behaviors. First, because the program is introduced from the organization, in fact, the senior top management of enterprise develops and implements the mentoring program. Second, mentor and protégé can face some challenges because of their different background, gender, or race, which affect their behavior making them less available to share information, knowledge, and expertise.

Considering the literature on inter-organizational relationships, it has been outlined that "the exchange and sharing of information provide efficient coordination or cooperation in inter-organizational relationships" [55: 447] and it is also important to understand "if and how" the control mechanisms are useful to create a long term relationship system. Drawing from this outline and considering our described scenario, we argue that the mentoring relationships can develop more effectively thanks a clear exchange of data and information among the partners, making the relevant transition from the analysis of the overall relationship, that is the processes and activities inside the relationship, to the exam within the relationship, considering the specific partners involved in order to avoid opportunistic behaviors.

In the mentoring relationships identified in our study, it seems that data collected are not deeply transformed and shared, but they are directly considered to make the useful information needed for the development of the mentoring process. Instead, we can observe as final step in the mentoring process with its relationships system, the crucial role of the reporting. For instance, in the relationship between enterprise and mentor, and also between mentor and protégé, the mentor provides reports with different timing schedules (every 3–6–9–12 months) in which he/she outlines the main findings recorded by the protégé in terms of outcomes obtained, especially to evaluate the achievement of fixed and shared goals. These reports usually consist in paper documents, especially in t-mentoring programs, or in virtual files, detailed worksheets.

In this direction, it is necessary not only to observe phenomena related to the human resources management, but in order to encourage the development of human capital in its complexity, it might be appropriate to identify a set of indicators that allows, on one side, to measure the performance of the mentoring relationship and, on the other side, to control the efficiency and effectiveness of processes identified recognized as an expression of the Human Capital Management.

In the last step of our study, we propose some key performance indicators related to each partner involved in each one-to-one mentoring relationship in the broad mentoring relationships system.

Regarding the protégé, we identify the following key performance indicators:

(1) No. promotions obtained in t_1/No. promotions expected in t_1
(2) Hrs spent to the tasks performing/Hrs available for performing tasks
(3) Total work hours really provided in t_1/No. tasks to perform in t_1

The key indicator (1) measures the effectiveness of the mentoring program in terms of achievement of fixed goals, as promotions obtained by the protégé. In this case, such indicator can be clearly linked to the output "promotion", showing how much effective mentoring was for the protégé in terms of improvement of his/her career achieving advanced job positions. The indicator (2) explains the time management by the protégé, in terms of total hours available at work to perform general tasks compared to the hours specifically used for performing own tasks. Finally, the key indicator (3) shows the efficiency in terms of tasks performed by the protégé comparing to the total work hours in t_1. These two last indicators can be directly linked to the outputs for the protégé identified in the improvement of the time management and the adoption of new and more effective working method.

Regarding the mentor, we describe the key performance indicators as below:

(4) No. mentoring programs closed in t_1/No. mentoring programs planned in t_1
(5) Hrs for performing tasks in t_1/Hrs available to perform tasks in the mentoring program in t_1
(6) Hrs dedicated to the mentoring tasks performing in t_1/Hrs available to perform general work tasks in t_1

The key indicator (4) measures the effectiveness of the mentor in the relationship in terms of successful programs concluded at fixed time (t_1) compared to the planned mentoring programs. The mentioned indicator can be associated to the improvement of self-efficacy and self esteem for the mentor; in fact, because of the achievement of the planned goals with mentoring programs, mentors feel more satisfied and relevant in their role within organizations. The indicator (5) explains the time management, in terms of total hours available to work for mentor compared to the hours used for performing tasks related to the mentoring program. The key indicator (6) evidences the impact of the mentoring program tasks on the total work hours for mentor, and it measures the efficiency in time management for the mentor, assuming a value between 0 and 1. If this indicator is low, that is closer to 0, it means that the contribution of mentor to the relationship is higher, improving the performance.

About the enterprise we identify the following key performance indicators:

(7) Hrs to provide enterprise processes in t_1/No. mentoring programs closed in t_1
(8) No. outcomes (product/services) in t_1/Hrs off from the mentoring program in t_1
(9) No. outcomes (products/services) in t_1/Hrs spent for mentoring program in t_1

The key indicator (7) measures the efficiency of mentoring programs through the reduction of total hours needed to provide the processes within the organization. The indicator (7) is clearly linked to the output "time management", it means that in this case we evidence the capacity of the enterprise to better manage its processes including the mentoring programs. The indicators (8) and (9) explain the productivity of the mentoring programs in terms of the link between the hours off or spent in the mentoring programs and the total outcomes obtained. In this case, if the two values tend to increase, the mentoring program provides less positive effects for the enterprise. Also, these last two indicators can be linked to the development and adoption from the enterprise of a more relational orientation and improvement of its organizational climate thanks to the introduced mentoring programs.

These identified key performance indicators might represent an useful and adequate instrument for the senior top management in defining and implementing effective mentoring programs, which can overcome the limits related to general and abstract information characterizing enterprise activities. In this case, such indicators allow to plan and implement more effective mentoring programs improving the human resources involved in the same program, enriching them with new competences and skills that contribute to increase the main elements of recognition for the enterprise, such as, for example, the customer loyalty, the image within the market and also outside the firm [56].

4 Final Remarks

This paper contributes to the existing literature on mentoring providing a wider analysis perspective in which we aim to identify and investigate the main factors that can measure and evaluate the effectiveness of mentoring programs, giving important suggestions in the planning and implementation process.

Our study shows that in the mentoring relationships identified the partners pay still less attention to the transfer and exchange of data and information, even if we consider e-mentoring programs. Consequently, the adoption of key performance indicators can facilitate and support the planning process of mentoring programs making them more successful. The identified key performance indicators can both support the decision making process of the top management and evaluate the effects of the implementation of mentoring programs within firms.

This study shows that in the planning and implementation of mentoring programs, also e-mentoring, it could be necessary standardize the main aspects concerning the mentoring relationship, especially the exchange of knowledge and expertise in the relationship through appropriate mechanisms, such as information systems or digital platforms or easily shared worksheets; otherwise, the information and knowledge sharing among the partners does not represent the crucial condition so that there is an improvement of the performance.

The main limit of this paper concerns its theoretical nature, but it constitutes an interesting research starting point, in fact, in the future development of this study, the intention is to identify and measure the main variables in a wide research design on mentoring programs applied in specific organizational context, such as educational and consulting sectors. In the future, we aim to investigate the effectiveness of mentoring programs through the measurement and control of their relationships system, adopting the different and specific indicators related more clearly to the outputs of mentoring.

References

1. Kram, K.E.: Phases of the mentor relationship. Acad. Manage. J. **26**, 608 (1983)
2. Kram, K.E.: Mentoring of work: developmental relationships in organizational life. Scott, Foresman, Glenview (1985)
3. Scandura, T.A.: Mentorship and career mobility: an empirical investigation. J. Organ. Behav. **13**(2), 169–174 (1992)
4. Scandura, T.A.: Mentoring and organizational justice: an empirical investigation. J. Vocat. Behav. **51**(1), 58–69 (1997)
5. Scandura, T.A.: Dysfunctional mentoring relationships and outcomes. J. Manag. **24**(3), 449–467 (1998)
6. Fagenson, E.A.: The mentor advantage: perceived career/job experiences of protégés versus nonprotégés. J. Organ. Behav. **10**, 309 (1989)
7. Higgins, M.C., Kram, K.E.: Reconceptualizing mentoring at work: a developmental network perspective. Acad. Manage. Rev. **26**(2), 264 (2001)
8. Seibert, S.: The effectiveness of facilitated mentoring: a longitudinal quasi-experiment. J. Vocat. Behav. **54**(3), 483–502 (1999)
9. Day, R., Allen, T.D.: The relationship between career motivation and self-efficacy with protégé career success. J. Vocat. Behav. **64**(1), 72–91 (2004)
10. Allen, T.D., Eby, L.T., Poteet, M.L., Lentz, E., Lima, L.: Career benefits associated with mentoring for proteges: a meta-analysis. J. Appl. Psychol. **89**(1), 127–136 (2004)
11. Karcher, M.: Increases in academic connectedness and self-esteem among high school students who serve as cross-age peer mentors. Prof. Sch. Couns. **12**(4), 292–299 (2009)
12. Hayes, J., Allinson, C.W.: Cognitive style and the theory and practice of individual and collective learning in organizations. Hum. Relat. **51**(7), 847 (1998)
13. Kram, K.E.: A relational approach to career development. In Hall D., Associates (eds.) The Career is Dead-Long Live the Career, pp. 132–157. Jossey-Bass, San Francisco (1996)
14. Hunt, D.M., Michael, C.: Mentorship: a career training and development tool. Acad. Manag. Rev. **8**(3), 475–485 (1983)
15. Levinson, D.J., Darrow, C.N., Klein, E.B., Levinson, M.A., McKee, B.: Seasons of a man's life. Knopf, New York (1978)
16. Burke, R.J.: Mentors in organizations. Group Organ. Stud. **9**, 353 (1984)
17. Thomas, D.A., Kram, K.E.: Promoting career-enhancing relationships in organizations. The role of the human resource professional. Acad. Manage. J. **5**, 49 (1988)
18. Noe, R.A.: An investigation of the determinants of successful assigned mentoring relationships. Pers. Psychol. **41**(3), 457–479 (1988)
19. Kram, K.E., Hall, D.T.: Mentoring in a context of diversity and turbulence. In: Kossek, E.E., Lobel, S.A. (eds.) Managing Diversity: Human Resource Strategy for Transforming the Workplace, pp. 108–136. Blackwell, Cambridge (1996)
20. Higgins, M.C.: The more, the mentor? Multiple developmental relationships and work satisfaction. J. Manage. Dev. **19**, 277 (2000)

21. De Janasz, S.C., Sullivan, S.E.: Multiple mentoring in academe: developing the professorial network. J. Vocat. Behav. **64**(2), 263–283 (2004)
22. Varriale, L.: Mentoring and technology in the learning process: e-mentoring. In Organizational Change and Information Systems, pp. 371–379. Springer Berlin (2013)
23. Scandura, T.A., Ragins, B.R.: The effects of sex and gender role orientation on mentorship in male-dominated occupations. J. Vocat. Behav. **43**(3), 251–265 (1993)
24. Ragins, B.R., Cotton, J.L.: Mentor functions and outcomes: a comparison of men and women in formal and informal mentoring relationships. J. Appl. Psychol. **84**(4), 529 (1999)
25. Riley, S., Wrench, D.: Mentoring among women lawyers1. J. Appl. Soc. Psychol. **15**(5), 374–386 (1985)
26. Allen, T.D., Eby, L.T., Poteet, M.L., Lentz, E., Lima, L.: Career benefits associated with mentoring for proteges: a meta-analysis. J. Appl. Psychol. **89**(1), 127 (2004)
27. DuBois, D.L., Rhodes, J.E.: Introduction to the special issue: youth mentoring: bridging science with practice. J. Community Psychol. **34**(6), 647–655 (2006)
28. Boldizzoni, D., Nacamulli, R.C. (eds.): Oltre l'Aula. Strategie di Formazione nell'Economia della Conoscenza. Apogeo Editore (2004)
29. Kreitner, R., Kinicki, A.: Comportamento Organizzativo. In: Apogeo (ed.) (2004)
30. Zey, M.G.: Mentor programs: making the right moves. Pers. J. **64**, 53 (1985)
31. Ragins, B.R.: Barriers to mentoring: the female manager's Dilemma. Hum. Relat. **42**(1), 1–22 (1989)
32. Lankau, M.J., Scandura, T.A.: An investigation of personal learning in mentoring relationships: content, antecedents and consequences. Acad. Manage. J. **45**(4), 779 (2002)
33. Bierema, L.L., Merriam, S.B.: E-mentoring: using computer mediated communication to enhance the mentoring process. Innovative High. Edu. **26**, 211–227 (2002)
34. Ensher, E.A., Heun, C., Blanchard, A.: Online mentoring and computer-mediated communication: new directions in research. J. Vocat. Behav. **63**, 264 (2003)
35. Headlam-Wells, J., Gosland, J., Graig, J.: There's magic in the web: e-mentoring for women's career development. Career Dev. Int. **10**(6–7), 449 (2005)
36. McLoughlin, C., Brady, J., Lee, M.J., Russell, R.: Peer-to-peer: an e-mentoring approach to developing community, mutual engagement and professional identity for pre-service teachers. In: Australian Association for Research in Education Conference. (2007)
37. Single, P.B., Muller, C.B.: When email and mentoring unite: the implementation of a nationwide electronic mentoring program. In: Stromei L.K. (ed.) Creating Mentoring and Coaching Programs, pp. 107–122. American Society for Training and Development, Alexandria (2001)
38. Wadia-Fascetti, S., Leventman, P.G.: E-mentoring: a longitudinal approach to mentoring relationships for women pursuing technical careers. J. Eng. Educ. **89**(3), 295–300 (2000)
39. Mueller, S.: Electronic mentoring as an example for the use of information and communications technology in engineering education. Eur. J. Eng. Educ. **29**(1), 53–63 (2004)
40. Milne, J.: Personal computing: how can mentoring or coaching by e-mail help leaners get more out of e-learning. IT Training, January (2005)
41. De Janasz, S.C., Ensher, E.A., Heun, C.: virtual relationships and real benefits: using e-mentoring to connect business students with practicing managers. Mentoring Tutoring Partnership Learn. **16**(4), 394–411 (2008)
42. Single, P.B., Single, R.: E-mentoring for social equity: review of research to inform program development. Mentoring Tutoring Partnership in Learn. **13**(2), 301–320 (2005)
43. Hegstad, C.D., Wentling, R.M.: The development and maintenance of exemplary formal mentoring programs in fortune 500 companies. Hum. Resour. Dev. Q. **15**(4), 421–448 (2004)
44. Berk, R.A., Berg, J., Mortimer, R., Walton-Moss, B., Yeo, T.P.: Measuring the effectiveness of faculty mentoring relationships. Acad. Med. **80**(1), 66–71 (2005)
45. Underhill, C.M.: The effectiveness of mentoring programs in corporate settings: a meta-analytical review of the literature. J. Vocat. Behav. **68**(2), 292–307 (2006)
46. Deutsch, N.L., Spencer, R.: Capturing the magic: assessing the quality of youth mentoring relationships. New Dir. Youth Dev. **121**, 47–70 (2009)

47. Chao, G.T., Walz, P., Gardner, P.D.: Formal and informal mentorships: a comparison on mentoring functions and contrast with nonmentored counterparts. Pers. Psychol. **45**(3), 619–636 (1992)
48. Ragins, B.R., Cotton, J.L., Miller, J.S.: Marginal mentoring: the effects of type of mentor, quality of relationship, and program design on work and career attitudes. Acad. Manag. J. **43** (6), 1177–1194 (2000)
49. Eby, L.T., Allen, T.D., Evans, S.C., Ng, T., DuBois, D.L.: Does mentoring matter? A multidisciplinary meta-analysis comparing mentored and non-mentored individuals. J. Vocat. Behav. **72**(2), 254–267 (2008)
50. Byrne, D.E.: The attraction paradigm, vol. 11. Academic Press, New York (1971)
51. Baskett, G.D.: Interview decisions as determined by competency and attitude similarity. J. Appl. Psychol. **57**, 343–345 (1973)
52. Tsui, A.S., O'Reilly, C.A.: Beyond simple demographic effects: the importance of relational demography in superior-subordinate dyads. Acad. Manag. J. **32**(2), 402–423 (1989)
53. Mancini, D.: Il Sistema Informativo e di Controllo Relazionale per il Governo della Rete di Relazioni Collaborative d'Azienda, vol. 91. Giuffrè, Milano (2010)
54. Marchi, L.: I Sistemi Informative Aziendali. Giuffré, Milano (1993)
55. Choe, J.M.: Inter-organizational relationships and the flow of information through value chains. Inf. Manag. **45**, 444–450 (2008)
56. Bruni, G., Campedelli, B.: La Determinazione, il Controllo e la Rappresentazione del Valore delle Risorse Immateriali nell'Economia dell'Impresa. Sinergie, 30 (1993)

From Theory to Practice: First Adoption of Integrated Reporting by the Italian Public Utilities

Matteo Pozzoli and Benedetta Gesuele

Abstract Corporate reporting has been recently changed by the globalization of economies, crises, the adoption of new legislative acts and the growing demand for information. This significant change is due also to the evolution of the stakeholders' information needs, which are increasingly dedicated to non-financial information regarding, among other things, governance, strategy and the environmental policy. Integrated reporting has been framed and developed in response to those changes. It aims at providing readers with a better comprehension of the organization needed to create value over the short and the medium-long term, combining financial and non-financial information. The aim of this paper is to explore the quality of integrated reports (IRs), in terms of its interpretation of specific elements related by their essential characteristics. This research focuses its attention on the IRs published by Public Utilities (PUs) attending the Pilot Programme (PP) and having a public sector ownership.

Keywords Integrated report · Public utilities · Accountability · Public sector ownership

M. Pozzoli · B. Gesuele (✉)
Department of Law, Parthenope University, Naples, Italy
e-mail: benedetta.gesuele@uniparthenope.it

M. Pozzoli
e-mail: matteo.pozzoli@uniparthenope.it

© Springer International Publishing Switzerland 2016
D. Mancini et al. (eds.), *Strengthening Information and Control Systems*,
Lecture Notes in Information Systems and Organisation 14,
DOI 10.1007/978-3-319-26488-2_9

1 Introduction[1]

This paper aims at providing initial empirical considerations on the quality of the integrated reports (IRs) published by Public Utilities (PUs) attending the Pilot Programme (PP) and having a public sector ownership. This study proposes some first empirical consideration concerning the application of the guidelines enacted by the International Integrated Reporting Council (IIRC). The words used in the investigated reports and their consistency with the IIRC Framework are considered specific elements quality.

The PP is a project promoted and managed by the IIRC, which is the body intended to publish and disseminate worldwide the best practices on integrated reporting.

The IR is a recent form of external communication, which incorporates and combines financial and non-financial material information in order to support stakeholders in expressing their judgment on the organization's performance and its value creation [1, 2]. The IIRC launched a Pilot Programme Business in October 2011. There are 104 companies participating into this project, each operating in different parts in the globe, and working in heterogeneous sectors such as finance, manufactory, services, etc.

As far as the IRs' content is concerned, the Framework enacted by the IIRC states that the IR is "[...] a concise communication about how an organization's strategy, governance, performance and prospects, in the context of its external environment, lead to the creation of value over the short, medium and long term" [3, 4].

The IR is intended as the final step of a process of integrated thinking, which should orient the organizations to be accountable and legitimize their role by taking into consideration not only the maximization of profit, but also the realization of appropriate extra-financial performances. From this perspective, integrated reporting seems to be an appropriate instrument to illustrate the management of public sector entities as well [3].

As far as definition elements is concerned, it can be observed that PUs are used to furnishing public at large with essential services, such as water, electricity, natural gas, telephone service, and others. The investigated PUs are managed or controlled (directly or indirectly) by public sector agencies. This feature can lead to express further considerations on the governments sensibility about financial and nonfinancial external communication.

The elements which were addressed to opt for analyzing PUs attending the Pilot Program were: the appropriateness of the adoption of the integrated reporting by PUs, oriented not only to optimized their profit but also to pursue social aims and the relevancy of the sector.

---

[1]Even if this paper is the result of a joint research, paragraphs 1 and 2 can be attributed to M. Pozzoli, paragraphs 3 and 4, can be attributed to B. Gesuele. Paragraph 5 was jointly written by the Authors.

Furthermore, PUs should present a high level of disclosure because they are naturally oriented to satisfy a wide range of information needs; this implies that their stakeholders are extremely careful with regards to the extra-financial performance, the realized outcome and the impact produced on the community.

The investigated sector is extremely relevant worldwide on a financial and non-financial basis. The combination of the above-mentioned factors determines that many PUs have been pioneers in the adoption of the most sophisticated techniques of non-financial information and often represent a benchmark for other companies.

The research method is based on content analysis effected on the 2012 annual reports published by the eleven selected companies.

This paper contributes to the development of the literature providing scholars with evidence gathered from an empirical analysis of the first reports based on IIRC guidelines; it focuses upon the elements which have been stressed in those reports, the qualitative characteristics and the definition of consolidated practices and techniques.

In order to pursue this objective, the lay-out of this paper is as follows: the following Section reviews the literature related to analyses similar to the one here presented; Section three describes the research design applied to the proposed qualitative analysis; the subsequent illustrates the findings and the empirical data arisen from the research; the last Section introduces some conclusive observations, limits and proposals for future research.

2 Literature Review

The IR is a recent model of non-financial external communication and management system [5]. The idea to determine worldwide guidelines on integrated reporting was "formally" established in a period when the financial crisis exasperated the inability of financial information to meet the stakeholders' information needs [6]. From this perspective, scholars proposed a communication approach oriented to include information on financial and non-financial performance and prospective in the creation of value [7]. According to this, the literature is quite limited on this specific issue [2, 8, 9], even though the single items and aspects related to the adoption of the IIRC's guidelines (materiality, stakeholder relationships, strategy, etc.) arise from long and well-known debates [10].

Furthermore, the IIRC's Framework does not aspire to define a completely new model; it mostly starts from systemizing and combining perspectives, approaches, models and techniques already known to scholarship and practitioners. Specifically, many companies are trying to move from the technical requirements of the Global Reporting Initiative to the ones published by the IIRC [11].

The innovative idea consists in combining and disclosing the impact of financial and non-financial multiple capitals [8], without dividing them into separate and autonomous categories [1, 7, 12].

IRs are primarily oriented towards capital lenders. This does not imply that IRs cannot satisfy the information needs required by the primary audience of mission driven entities, such as PUs [13]. There are even today a set of case studies dedicated to the adoption of IIRC's guidelines by PUs [14–16].

The analysis of the content of the IRs cannot forget to take into consideration the reasons for which organizations decide to prepare an IR and apply the IIRC's guidelines.

It could be the case that companies decide to apply the IIRC's requirements only (or essentially) to declare this compliance and achieve a larger credibility in the community by adopting generally accepted standards and practices [17, 18]. Some pioneering studies conclude that, based on the neo-institutional theory, current IRs are substantially characterized by a high level of isomorphism and cosmetic behaviors [19] and that IRs are often not consistent with the generally accepted guidelines [20].

On the other hand, there are studies finding a relation between the practice of IR long-term oriented investor base [21] and financial performance [22]. Even though there is no evidence that IR supports economic decisions, these studies confer a "substantive" role to the integrated reporting and thinking; a body of literature has already provided similar results referring to sustainability disclosure and performance [22, 23]. Some authors focused their research on the analysis of sustainability reports published by PUs [24, 25]. In this context, Boschee [24] shows that PUs are firms characterized by a high level of disclosure. Similarly, other scholars [25], using content analysis, note that PUs have a significant depth of disclosure. Other studies [26], using content analysis as well, investigate risk disclosure included in the sustainability reports of the Italian PUs listed on the the Italian Stock Exchange.

2.1 Research Design

In the following section the methods used, the sample choice and the model to describe performance keyword.

2.2 The Sample Under Investigation

The aim of this paper is to explore the quality of IR, in terms of its interpretation of specific elements related by their essential characteristics. Specifically we would explore the relationship between the content and the length of reports and the usefulness of some crucial words. In other words, we would explore the level of accountability of IRs in the PUs participating into the IIRC's Pilot Programme business network which have public ownership. Doing so, our aim is to establish an

Table 1 The sample under investigation

Name	Country	Sector
Port Metro Vancouver	Canada	Port
New Zealand Post	New Zealand	Postal services
AES Brazil	Brazil	Utilities
EnBWEnergie Baden-Württemberg AG	Germany	Electricity
Coega Development Corporation	South Africa	Government
EnelS.p.A.	Italy	Electricity
eniS.p.A.	Italy	Oil and gas producers
FlughafenMünchen GmbH	Germany	Transportation services
Rosneft	Russian Federation	Oil & gas producers
N.V. Luchthaven Schiphol	Netherlands	Transportation services
Transnet	South Africa	Transportation services

understanding of the most important trends of current integrated reporting practices for these companies.

The sample chosen is composed by eleven companies, located in various countries, as Canada, New Zealand, Brazil, Germany, South Africa, Italy, Russian Federation and Netherlands (Table 1).

These companies belong to different sectors such as, electricity, oil and gas producers, transportations services. Notwithstanding, they can be included in the broader category of PUs. According to Epstein [27] a PU is: "an agency performing a service in which the public has a special interest sufficient to justify governmental regulatory control, along with the extension of legal privileges, but not governmental ownership or management of all the agency's activities". It is an organization that maintains the infrastructure for a public service as electricity, natural gas, transport and water.

Some companies, such as Terna, Enagas and CPFL Energia, which are part of the Pilot Programme, and can be considered belonging to the Public Utilities sector have been excluded because their annual reports are published only in their native languages; for this reason the applied methodology would not have produced comparable and consistent information.

2.3 Methodology to Investigate the Quality of Integrated Reporting

The methodology used in order to explore the study aim is the content analysis. Content analysis is a method of codifying the text (or content). It is considered "a research technique for making replicable and valid interferences from data according to their context" [28]. To implement this technique, we have chosen to use the online program "write word writers" with the aim of reducing human errors.

Fig. 1 Research design

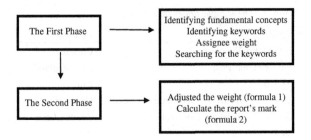

This technique is used according to the qualitative methodology. Document analysis has been carried out to search for the keywords relevant to express a judgment on the quality of the IRs published on the companies' websites.

The research design can be divided in two phases and in several steps (Fig. 1).

The first phase can be divided in four consequential steps: identifying fundamental concepts; identifying keywords; assigning weight to fundamental concepts; searching for the keywords in the reports in order to implement a qualitative approach of content analysis.

The second phase consists in individuating the report's mark in order to evaluate the keywords performance.

With the aim to study the topic chosen, it seemed suitable to identify a context of analysis that was already well established in literature. Doing so, the analysis identifies the fundamental concepts starting from the analysis of the Albert Luthuli centre for Yearbook 2013 [21]. These fundamental concepts are extracted from the Consultation Draft [22] of the international IR Framework and based on the study of previous literature [3, 4, 10, 27]. The research takes into account the quality of IRs published in 2013, evaluating their compliance with the content of the Consultation Draft. At this end, we chose fourteen fundamental concepts. For every fundamental concept we chose three keywords, identifying a list of forty-two keywords. The third step of our analysis was the identification of a certain weight for every fundamental concept. The total weight is one hundred (Table 2).

Applying the chosen methodology, we searched for the keywords in the reports with the help of an online programmer (fourth step).

Every relevant keyword was considered, even in its various grammatical forms (adjective, adverb and preposition, etc.).

In the second phase, we defined the report's mark in order to evaluate the keywords performance. Before determining a mark for every keyword, we decided to adjust the number of word in the reports (Formula 1). As a last step we used an equation to determine a report's mark (Formula 2) [21].

Table 2 Keywords

Fundamental concept	Keyword			Weight
The capitals				
Financial capital	Cash	Profit	Fund	4.2
Manufactured capital	Equipment	Ability	Asset	4.2
Human capital	Employee	Train	Productivity	4.2
Intellectual capital	Research	Knowledge	Brand	4.2
Social capital	Stakeholder	Society	Trust	4.2
Natural capital	Environment	Sustainable	Impact	4.2
The business model	Input	Convert	Product	10.4
Value creation	Convert	Growth	Enable	10.4
Guiding principles				
Strategic focus and future orientation	Vision	Direction	Resource	6.3
Connectivity of information	Link	Network	Between	10.4
Stakeholder responsiveness	Accountable	Responsible	Engage	10.4
Materiality and conciseness	Issue	Important	Focus	10.4
Reliability and completeness	Assurance	Include	Boundary	10.4
Consistency and comparability	Benchmark	Basis	Principle	6.3

3 Analysis

3.1 First Phase

During the first phase of the analysis we identified two types of fundamental concepts thanks to the Consultation Draft of the international IR Framework (and thus the capitals and guiding principles).

In the IR framework, the capitals comprise financial, manufactured, intellectual, human, social, relationship and natural elements that an organization uses and effects. Capitals are included in the framework as a benchmark for ensuring that groups consider all the forms of capital they use or effect, and because they can be considered as part of the theoretical underpinning for the concept of value.

Fundamental concepts are the organization's business model and the creation of value. The first can be considered the system of inputs, business activities, outputs and outcomes that aim to create value over the short, medium and long term; the second lies at the central and most important part of the report.

In this context, strategic focus and future orientation are related to the companies' ability to create value in the short, medium and long term; connectivity of information explores the relationship and dependencies between the organization's components that create value over time; stakeholder responsiveness describes the quality of the relationship between companies and their key stakeholders; materiality and conciseness mean that the report can be short and offer concise information; reliability and completeness indicate that the report needs to include both positive and negative information; consistency and comparability mean that the IR report has to give information comparable to the same information in the other companies. Lastly, using the on line program, we searched for the keywords and assigned a certain weight to each one.

3.2   Second Phase

Considering that the reports have different lengths (number of words), we chose to use a simple equation (Formula 1) to adjust the number of words by marking out keywords. This enabled us to have a better comparison. In this way, we have obtained a keyword-adjusted value. Starting from the analysis of the Albert Luthuli centre for Yearbook 2013 [20], the research uses the report with the least number of words as a benchmark, adjusting the number of words in the other investigated reports in order to normalize their length. In this way, the keyword chosen was directly comparable to a keyword mark in other reports.

$$\frac{Min\ ob\ Kw}{Max\ ob\ TotWordR} \times Min\ ob\ TotWordR \tag{1}$$

where

Min ob Kw	number of minimum observation for every keyword in every report
Max obTotWordR	maximum number of total words in the report
Min obTotWordR	minimum number of total words in the report

Then we used an equation to determine a report's mark for keywords (Formula 2), basing on the analysis of the Albert Luthuli centre for Yearbook 2013 [20], In our research, the mark calculated can be considered as the performance in terms of the measurement instrument; this performance is expressed as a percentage out of one hundred.

$$\frac{Adj\ value\ Kw - Min\ Adj\ value\ Kw}{Max\ Adj\ value\ Kw} \times WKw \tag{2}$$

where

Adj value KW	adjusted value for keyword (Formula 1)
Min Adj value Kw	minimum adjusted value keyword
Max Adj value Kw	maximum adjusted value keyword

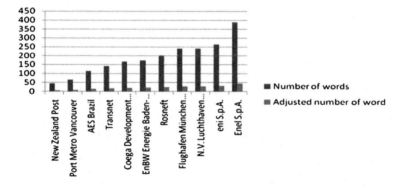

Fig. 2 The total number of words in the report: adjusted value versus not-adjusted value

For instance, in the Port Metro Vancouver (number of words 453), keywords related to the cash measurement point were observed 59 times. In order to calculate the number of Port Metro Vancouver report keywords on equal terms with the other report we performed the following calculation: (59/453) * 4.2.

On the basis of the Consultation Draft of the international IR Framework and in according to the analysis of the Albert Luthuli centre for Yearbook 2013 [20], that underlines the importance of conciseness in integrated reports, we started from the total number of words in the reports. For practical reasons we compared the adjusted and not-adjusted value, and we chose to consider the adjusted value (Fig. 2).

Another step was the outlining of the report's mark, first for keywords and then for the total mark of every report. Then, considering the importance of conciseness in integrated reporting, we compared the total keyword marks to the total adjusted number in the report.

The relationship between the number of words for report and total marks (adjusted measurement) suggests a relation between number of words and the performance of companies report under investigation measuring as marks.

The following figure shows the total number of words in every report and the total mark adjusted in order to explore the performance of companies' report. Companies that have public ownership are not able to respect the principle of conciseness; in other words, they are unable to report many important concepts in few words (Fig. 3).

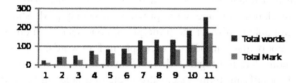

Fig. 3 Total words versus total marks

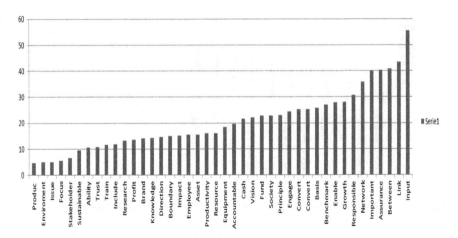

Fig. 4 Keywords performance

The other parts of the analysis include investigating the performance or mark for each keyword. Figure 4 illustrates that the chosen keyword has different marks and as far as there are different stretching areas. Thanks to this assumption, it is possible to identify in the analyzed reports different disclosure stretching areas.

In line with the previous literature review, the analysis of keyword performance shows that keywords such as stakeholder, sustainable and accountable are inconsistent with regard to guideline principles and accountability standards; their marks are fewer than other words' marks. Words like between, link and input seem to have the best performance and disclosure stretching area.

4 Discussion and Conclusions

The research report concludes by offering a view about one important topic: the quality of communication in the IR considering PUs attending the Pilot Programme (PP) and having a public sector ownership.

In our study, we explored the relationship between the content and the length of reports and the use of some keywords within them. In other words, we explored the level of accountability of IR for companies under investigation.

Our first consideration regards the length of the IR. The results of the analysis show that there is a relationship between the report length and the adjusted total marks. That correlation, in line with previous research [18], shows that these companies are not able to respect the principle of conciseness; in other words, they are not able to report many important concepts in few words.

Our second consideration regards the performance or mark for every keyword, with the aim of identifying more disclosure-stretching areas in the reports [7, 18].

The results show that keywords that have been used in corporate reports for a comparatively long time (such as cash, equipment, principle, productivity, fund and resource) have marks included in the mark average. This could be due to a relatively high level of consensus in the corporate reports.

The words that have the lowest marks are product, environment, issue, focus, stakeholder and sustainable. Taking these results and the characteristics of the sector into consideration implies a high level of incoherency.

Otherwise, the words input, link, between, assurance, important and network have the highest results; this shows openness to relations with the outside, that is, a symbolic adaptation to new ways and communication systems.

The analysis on keyword performance shows that several keywords such as stakeholder, sustainable and accountable can be considered inconsistent with regards to guideline principles and accountability standards; in fact, their marks are rather low.

According to previous literature, the analysis does not show strong discrepancies in marks between different fundamental concepts.

This research highlights some limitations. Firstly, the heterogeneity of the sample. The analysis has been conducted only on one annual report. In order to comprehend the development of the practice, it is necessary to repeat the research on an annual basis for a longer period, using the same keywords to determine the level of change for every mark.

At the same time, the study could add or include other fundamental concepts.

Lastly, this investigation used only two fundamental concepts. It would be appropriate, in order to express an exhaustive judgment on the quality of the investigated IRs, to explore other fundamental concepts as continent elements, preparation and presentation.

References

1. King, M.: Foreword to: IRCSA integrated reporting and the integrated report. Discussion paper, www.sustainabilitysa.org (2011)
2. Porter, M., Kramer, M.: Creating shared value: how to reinvent capitalism—and unleash a wave of innovation and growth. Harv. Bus. Rev. 89(1–2), 63–77 (2011)
3. IIRC: The international framework (2013)
4. IIRC/EY: Background paper for 'IR'. Value creation (2013)
5. Eccles, R.G., Krzus, M.P.A: Chronology of integrated reporting. Harvard Business School Accounting & Management Unit Case. Available at SSRN: http://ssrn.com/abstract=2025125 (2011)
6. Lev, B.: The end of accounting and what's next? Presentation at the Conference Oltre il Bilancio. L'informazione non Contabile verso il Reporting Integrato, Florence, (2013)
7. Dumitru, M., Giovan, M.E., Gorgan, C., Dumitru, V.F.: International integrated reporting framework: a case study in the software industry. AUASO 15(1), 24–39 (2013)
8. Eccles, R.G., Krzus, M.P.: One Report. Integrated of a Sustainable Strategy. Wiley, New Jersey (2010)

9. Churet, C., Eccles, R.G.: Integrated reporting, quality of management, and financial performance. J. Appl. Corp. Financ. **26**(1), 56–64 (2014)
10. GRI: G4 Sustainability Reporting Guidelines. Available at: https://www.globalreporting.org/reporting/g4/Pages/default.aspx (2013)
11. Painter-Morland, M.: Triple bottom-line reporting as social grammar: integrating corporate social responsibility and corporate codes of conduct. Bus. Ethics Eur. Rev. **15**(4), 352–364 (2006)
12. Eccles, R.G., Cheng, B., Saltzman, D.: The landscape of integrated reporting. In: Reflections and Next Steps, Harvard Business School, Cambridge (Mass.) (2010)
13. Bartocci, L. Picciaia, F.: Towards integrated reporting in the public sector. In: Busco, C., Frigo, M.L., Riccaboni, A., Quattrone, P. (eds.) Integrated reporting. Concepts and cases that redefine corporate accountability. Springer, Berlin, 191–204 (2013)
14. Parrot, K.: Integrated reporting, stakeholder engagement, and balanced investing at American electric power. J. Appl. Corp. Financ. **24**(2), 27–37 (2012)
15. Mio, C., Fusan, M.: The case of Enel. In: Busco, C., Frigo, M.L., Riccaboni, A., Quattrone, P. (eds.) Integrated Reporting. Concepts and Cases that Redefine Corporate Accountability. Springer, Berlin, 225–236 (2013)
16. King, M., Roberts, L.: Integrate: Doing Business in the 21st Century. Juta & Co., Ltd., Claremont (2013)
17. Dillard, J.F., Rigsby, J.T., Goodman, C.: The making and remaking of organizational context. Acc. Audit. Account. J. **17**(4), 506–542 (2004)
18. Di Maggio, P.J., Powell, W.W.: The iron cage revisited: institutional isomorphism and collective rationality in organizational fields. Am. Sociol. Rev. **48**(2), 147–160 (1983)
19. Wild, C., Staden Van, S.: Integrated reporting: initial analysis of early reporter an institutional theory approach. In: Proceeding Conference APIRA KOBE (2014)
20. Alcrl: IR yearbook 2013 current realities and future consideration (2013)
21. Serafeim, G.: The need for sector-specific materiality and sustainability reporting standards. J. Appl. Corp. Financ. **24**(2), 65–71 (2012)
22. Churet, C., Eccles, R.G.: Integrated reporting, quality of management, and financial performance. J. Appl. Corp. Financ. **26**(1), 56–64 (2014)
23. Dhaliwal, D., Li, O.Z., Tsang, A.H., Yang, Y.G.: Voluntary non-financial disclosure and the cost of equity capital: the case of corporate social responsibility reporting. Account. Rev. **86**(1), 59–100 (2011)
24. Boschee, P.: Investors pressfor climate risk disclosure. Energy Mark. **10**(5), 16–20 (2005)
25. Beretta, S., Bozzolan, S.: A framework for the analysis of firm risk communication. Int. J. Account. **39**(3), 265–288 (2004)
26. Aureli, S., Salvatori, F.: Perception of risk management practices through the reading of public corporate financial documents. In: III Financial Reporting Workshop, Naples, Italy (2012)
27. Epstein, L.: Political Parties in the American Mold. University of Wisconsin Press, Madison, WI (1986)
28. Krippendorff, K.: Content Analysis: An Introduction to Its Methodology, London Sage (1980)

Business Intelligence in Public Sector Organizations: A Case Study

Alessandro Spano and Benedetta Bellò

Abstract Information Technology (IT) makes it possible to manage the increased complexity that all businesses, both public and private, face. One of the consequences of the growing use of IT is the large quantity of data produced and stored. However, very often this data is not exploited to their full potential. An existing tool that can increase the benefits related to the availability of data, specifically for supporting the decision-making process, is Business Intelligence (BI). BI may be defined as "an integrated, company-specific, IT-based total approach for managerial decision support" (Kemper et al. Business intelligence and performance management: theory, systems, and industrial applications, Springer, U.K., pp. 3–12, 2013). We investigate the impact of BI on managers' behaviours. More specifically, the main aim of our research is to understand how the information provided by BI is used, what the perceived advantages and disadvantages are of its use and how the use of the BI module influences the managerial decision-making process.

Keywords Business intelligence · Public sector · Managerial decision-making process

1 Introduction

Information Technology (IT) makes it possible to manage the increasing complexity that all businesses, both public and private, face. One of the consequences of the growing use of IT is the large quantity of data produced and stored. Information

A. Spano (✉) · B. Bellò
Department of Economic and Business Sciences, University of Cagliari, Cagliari, Italy
e-mail: spano@unica.it

B. Bellò
e-mail: benedetta.bello@gmail.com

© Springer International Publishing Switzerland 2016   133
D. Mancini et al. (eds.), *Strengthening Information and Control Systems*,
Lecture Notes in Information Systems and Organisation 14,
DOI 10.1007/978-3-319-26488-2_10

Systems (ISs) provide the data and information necessary to manage an organization, be it public or private. In recent years, an increasing amount of money has been invested in this field [1].

An Enterprise Resource Planning (ERP) system is an advanced IS. It provides a comprehensive overview of the organization and a common database in which business transactions are recorded and stored [2]. Moreover, ERP systems help to reduce costs and improve inefficient processes [3].

Even though ERP systems are more popular in the private sector, they have been gaining acceptance in the public sector as well [4]. The majority of research regarding ERP implementation has focused on the private sector, with relatively little research conducted about public organizations, particularly regarding the impact on organizational processes and individual behaviour.

According to some scholars, there are no significant differences between private and public sector organizations with regards to ISs [5]. Other scholars hold a different viewpoint and believe that private and public organizations implement and manage ISs differently [6, 7]. With regards to ERP systems in particular, there has been a lack of research about ERP in public organizations and there is a need to focus on empirical research, to better understand how ERP systems may be implemented in the public sector and to investigate their impact on internal processes and individual behaviours [7].

ERP implementation involves changes to business processes [8–10], since these systems strongly support change management [4], supply chain management [11, 12] and organizational performance improvement [13].

However, very often information provided by an ERP system is not exploited to its full potential. One of the existing tools available that can increase the benefits related to the availability of data, specifically for supporting the decision-making process, is Business Intelligence (BI). BI can be defined as "an integrated, company-specific, IT-based total approach for managerial decision support" [14]. "BI is an ICT tool that allows its users to leverage the best use of their data, summarising and aggregating information" [15]. According to the UK National Audit Office, "When combined with effective systems for budgeting, planning, forecasting and optimisation, BI systems provide the means to navigate through and share management information across an organization and are key to informed decision-making in knowledge-intensive organizations" [16].

This paper reports on the implementation of BI in connection with an ERP system in an Italian public sector organization.

Using data from a set of semi-structured interviews, coupled with document analysis, we provide answers to the following research questions:

- How do managers use BI-related information?
- What are the perceived advantages and disadvantages of using a BI system?
- How can BI-related information influence managers' decision-making processes?

2   Business Intelligence

Rouhani et al. [17] note that "Business intelligence is the process of using information and analyzing them in order to support decision-making and using different methods helping organizations to forecast the behavior of competitors, suppliers, customers and environments to stay alive and survive in a global economy" [17]. BI is not a new concept. In 1976, Pearce argued that the main objective of BI was to support decision-making at different levels [18]. According to Nylund [19] BI was coined by Howard Dresner of the Gartner Group in 1989. In 1988, Tyson identified five different nuances of Intelligence: Customer Intelligence, Competitor Intelligence, Market Intelligence, Technological Intelligence, Product Intelligence and Environmental Intelligence [20]. BI systems play a fundamental role in providing managers with timely and easy-to-use information for both operational and strategic decision-making [21]. "BI systems combine operational data with analytical tools to present complex and competitive information to planners and decision makers. The objective is to improve the timeliness and quality of inputs to the decision process" [22]. BI is today used for decision support, executive information systems and management information systems [23]. Some authors suggest the need to integrate BI and knowledge management in order to improve decision-making and performance [24]. The effective use of BI systems requires specialized infrastructure, such as Online-Analytical Processing, data mining tools and specialized databases. In addition, BI Systems are often used where an ERP system has been previously implemented [25]. BI makes it possible to leverage the investments in data infrastructure, in particular ERP systems, and unlock the large value hidden in a firm's data resources [25, 26]. In addition, BI merges already-available ERP data with other data, proving executives with data from multiple sources [27].

The adoption of BI in the public sector is far behind that of the private sector [28]. Only one in five public sector organizations in the United States and Europe have already invested in BI, as opposed to two in five organizations in the private sector (excluding small companies) [29].

According to recent research, firms using BI systems experiment with improvements in the internal organizations, in the decision-making process and in cost improvement. Top managers are among those making the most extensive use of BI information [30]. With regards to the public sector, although the use of BI systems has increased, the potential market is significant and is estimated to approach €300–350 million [31].

BI systems allow for the redesigning of processes in a smarter way, not focusing on mere re-engineering, but instead on gathering, storing and using data consistently in line with the organization's vision, mission and culture. This process requires 'managerial capital,' i.e., the availability of skilled managers capable of exploiting the huge potentialities of advanced ISs [32]. BI systems may play a fundamental role in the public sector context, where service delivery often involves multiple organizations, implying the cooperation and integration of different ISs

[32]. The public sector is often characterized by a huge volume of data. In Italy, for example, the number of databases managed by public sector organizations is significant (almost 1400 (DigitPA)). In this context, BI systems are fundamental to making this data accessible and usable. The strategic value of BI systems is important, rather than the technological value, since BI Systems should be accelerators or catalysts of the innovation process [31].

3   Research Context

In the Italian context, there are limited instances of the use of advanced IT systems by regional governments. A few notable exceptions are represented by the Emilia Romagna Region and the Sardinia Region. There are also other regions that are experimenting with the implementation of BI systems: Lombardy, Umbria, Marche (for the health sector only), Veneto and the Autonomous Province of Trento. Since 2001, Emilia Romagna has adopted a BI platform composed of a Staging Area and a Data Warehouse [31]. This platform makes it possible to simultaneously query different information systems, sort data from different databases and share these data among employees. The Sardinian Region introduced in 2007 an ERP system called SIBAR (translated as the Regional Government Basic Information System) in order to support managerial and accounting assignments. Previous research has highlighted the main features of SIBAR, focusing on both the implementation process and the impact of its introduction on organizational process and individual employees [33–35]. With SIBAR, the Sardinian Regional Government has adopted one of the most advanced information systems in Italy.

This system allows for rapid and reliable online data management; moreover, it minimizes the waste of paper through the digitization of documents and it creates a common database for the entire regional government. SIBAR is composed of several modules: (1) SB (Basic System: document and work flow management, protocol system and other general functions, (2) SCI (Integrated Accounting System: accounting and monitoring, for managing financial and accounting data and (3) human resources (HR) management.

In 2012, a BI module was added to the existing ERP system, called Business Objects (BO). BO plays a central role in producing information for operative and strategic decision-making; it combines operational data with analytical tools to present complex and competitive information to planners and decision makers such as managers and politicians. The objective of BO is to improve the timeliness and quality of inputs to the decision-making process. The BO module analyzes data and prepares them for use by different stakeholders, according to modern aesthetic and functional standards, through the use of specific dashboards and reports. For instance, users can visualize the information in a numerical or graphic way, and choose different methods of data representation (histograms, diagrams, pie charts, etc.). Moreover, it provides summarised information but it leaves the customers with the possibility of searching through the original data in more depth and it offers them a personalized layout. In other words, BO produces high-quality dashboards and reports based on data pre-collated by other systems.

The two main reasons for introducing the BO module were:

1. To provide managers with functional dashboards that can be used in the decision-making process; dashboards are visually homogeneous and recognizable (internal aim: standardization);
2. To provide different stakeholders (citizens, regional cabinet members and councillors, private firms and the National Court of Accounts) with data related to how the Regional Government spends money (external aim: transparency).

In fact, before the introduction of the ERP system, it was thought that the reports it could generate would have been sufficient to support managers in their decision-making process. However, the standard reports were too specific and obtaining additional reports was too expensive since each adjustment to the existing ERP is very costly. As a consequence, the implementation of a BO module was decided upon, since it should be capable of producing more reports in a more flexible way at a lower cost. The original aim was that the BO functions would have been used not just by regional managers, but also by other stakeholders. Therefore, the idea was quite innovative, and consisted of providing civil servants as well as politicians and citizens with the same data and information (with different levels of analysis), increasing transparency and reducing complexity in data management and analysis. In addition, a few licenses were given to the regional section of the National Court of Accounts, which is in charge of auditing and controlling regional expenditures. Even though the provision of BO information to individual citizens has not been implemented yet, each regional manager and councilor has access to BO. The implementation of the BO module for managers had two fundamental aims. Given that not all regional managers have a standard ERP license, the first aim for introducing a BO module was to provide these individuals with the information needed to support the decision-making process. The second aim was related to managers who have an ERP licence. In this case, the BO module should speed up the process of obtaining necessary information by providing advanced and timely dashboards that can be easily accessed at one's convenience.

4 Methodology

We present the case study of an Italian region that in 2007 had introduced an ERP system. In 2012, this same region added a new module, called BO as a module of BI. A case study allows for the exploration and understanding of complex issues and can be considered to be a robust research method, particularly when a holistic, in-depth investigation is required, as is this case with Sardinia, one of the first regions to have implemented such a system. Yin [36] defines the case study research method "as an empirical inquiry that investigates a contemporary phenomenon within its real-life context; when the boundaries between phenomenon and context are not clearly evident; and in which multiple sources of evidence are used." The case study method enables a researcher to closely examine the data within a specific context and investigate contemporary real-life phenomena through detailed contextual analysis of a limited number of events or conditions, and their relationships.

Our research was carried out using a qualitative methodology including document analysis and interviews with managers to deepen our understanding of the impact of such changes on management behaviour. Document analysis implies the examination of some preliminary documents drafted by the Sardinian Region in order to understand what characteristics were required to develop the BO module. Moreover, twelve key informants working in different departments of the Sardinia Regional Government were interviewed over the period May–July 2014. These informants included:

- Two employees, components of the BO steering group, in charge of supervising the implementation and the development of the module;
- Two managers who played an active role in the planning and implementation phase of the BO module;
- Eight managers that worked in different departments of the Sardinia Regional Government and were selected according to their actual use of the BO module.

The interviews were audiotaped and transcribed; each lasted between 30 and 60 min. The content of the interviews was entered in a Hermeneutic Unit and analyzed using AtlasTi software [37] according to Grounded Theory methodology [38]. The main points of the content extracted from the text were marked with a series of codes (quotations) that were grouped into similar concepts to create families (code families) to foster the creation of new theories rather than beginning by testing a hypothesis (a bottom-up approach).

The aim of the research was to provide an understanding of which problems, positive aspects, and other dimensions underlined by the participants are more meaningful and relevant for describing the impact of the new module on individual working behaviour and can be used in the future implementation of the module.

5 Results

This section reports the results of the interviews which are divided into code families. A brief description of each code family is also provided.

5.1 Involvement in the Introduction/Implementation Process

Participants were asked to say whether or not they were involved in the new module introduction/implementation process and how. The majority of the participants were not involved. The interviews highlighted that a steering group was established and that it had limited consultation with other representatives from the real users of the BO module. It also emerged that limited attention was paid in this phase by the heads of the different organizational units (Assessorati and Direzioni) in participating actively in deciding what reports and, more generally, what kind of data managers would have needed to support their decision-making process.

5.2 BO Usage

All managers have a personal license for the new module but the interviews revealed that they make limited use of such access. In addition, some of the managers prefer to use the reports they receive every fortnight in a PDF format, instead of making specific queries to the BO module. No data on the effective use (such as frequency) of the licenses are available.

5.3 Training

Managers complain about the lack of training and communication about the new module. Some of them were involved once in a kick-off meeting but the majority were not involved at all. The interviewees highlighted the limited knowledge of the potential of the BO and they all agreed that more systematic training was necessary.

5.4 Strengths and Weaknesses

The interviewees were asked to point out the main strengths and weaknesses of the BO module. The strengths are as follows:

- Managers use the PDF reports they receive via e-mail, particularly at the end of the year (November and December) to check data related to the expenditure. They believe that having standard reports e-mailed or available on a website without querying the BO module is particularly useful; in particular, managers stated that BO is useful for managers that do not (or are not able to) use SIBAR because they can receive reports already collated;
- BO provides easy-to-read reports that are particularly effective and can be visualized in different ways (numerical or graphic) by choosing different methods of data representation (histograms, diagrams, pie charts, etc.).
- BO also provides reports for the elected councilors and for the National Court of Accounts, thereby increasing transparency and reducing the time needed to provide the National Court of Accounts with the required data.

The weaknesses are as follows:

- The database that supports SIBAR and BO is obsolete and overloaded; for this reason, queries are performed very slowly. BI is supposed to produce high-quality dashboards and reports using data from existing datawarehouses. However, the reports and dashboards generated by BO are static and not up-to-date. Managers often prefer to use SIBAR instead of BO to acquire reliable data and generate the reports that they need.
- BO data are superficial, generic and too aggregated, which is why managers prefer using SIBAR since they need more detailed data to make decisions.
- BO provides financial data only; there are no data available related to HR, the planning system or objectives that have to be achieved.

5.5 Support for the Decision-Making Process

BO was supposed to play a central role in producing information for operative and strategic decision-making processes. It should provide summarised information but leave users with the possibility to make more in-depth queries and allow personalized layouts. Currently, the module does not meet expectations and it is not used to make decisions, mainly because of the inefficiency in its use. Managers prefer to use SIBAR. Formally, BO should combine operational data with analytical tools to present information with the objective to improve the timeliness and quality of inputs to the decision process but currently it does not do so; it suffers from database inefficiency and a lack of data (only financial data are available).

6 Discussion and Conclusions

The interviews provided important insights that allow us to answer the research questions. Our analysis highlights that the introduction and the use of the new module have been innovative and useful for transparency (data available for politicians, National Court of Accounts, etc.) and important for the internal use for the standardization of the dashboards and reports it provides. Moreover, it provides the majority of managers (who are non-experts or who do not use the module) with timely and easy-to-use information.

The research also revealed a limited use of this module by managers and almost no use by councillors. The BO module was not tailored to the managers' specific needs because of a lack of communication between the steering group and the potential users.

Managers argued that their limited use was due to several reasons; the first is related to the limited information provided by the BI module (particularly if compared with what is already available with SIBAR). There is also limited knowledge about the BI module itself, and several managers even ignore its existence. Apparently, no systematic or organized training was delivered and just one kick-off meeting was organized. Other critical aspects reported by the interviewees refer to the inefficiency of the module, which may require considerable time to provide a specific report; as a consequence, managers often give up on the queries and eventually do not use the module.

In order to overcome this problem, additional investments in the underlying infrastructure have been planned and, in particular, a new data warehouse is going to substitute the existing one, with an estimated significant reduction in the response time. In addition, the available reports concern financial data only and no other kinds of data are available. Furthermore, the interviewees noted that the report they receive or that can be generated by the system are not always those they need. This fact is due, to a certain extent, to negligence in the design phase of the BO module, when all of the higher organizational units of the Regional Government (Direzioni Generali) were asked to recommend what reports they would need but did not give any indications. Moreover, it is possible to use the module differently, depending on one's level of expertise. Every fortnight, managers receive a selection of the reports they use in a PDF format but expert users complain about the reports being static, thus reducing their informative value. For these individuals, the present BO module is of little or no use at all. In fact, its inefficiency and the lack of the information provided make them believe that the ERP system (with the FI and CO modules) is more useful than the BI system. With regards to the positive aspects of the BO module, managers reported the possibility of having ready-to-use reports without have to be an expert in the use of the ERP system.

This study reports the case of the implementation of a BI system in an Italian region. Sardinia is an interesting case study because previously it was technologically out-of-date but has advanced significantly due to huge investments. Now, it has one of the most advanced ERP systems in Italy and is trying to make a BI module work to overcome the problems; in fact, BO is currently underused and is not exhibiting is full potential because of the following: (1) infrastructure problems, (2) lack of important data and (3) lack of training and communication. However, significant investments are already planned to overcome these problems.

Despite the limited number of interviews, this study highlights the problems and opportunities public organizations face when implementing an advanced BI system after large investments have been made to introduce an ERP system. Furthermore, BI systems are potentially very important, but they have to comply with some basic requirements. First of all, response times have to be quick in generating the required reports, and the BI module has to provide data and information other than those already available with the existing ERP system.

Concerning the database inefficiency, the main problem is related to the need for additional infrastructural investments. The literature on BI reports that the implementation of BI systems typically follows that of an ERP system. However, the physical infrastructure (mainly, the database) has to be gauged to support the BI module as well. In our case study, the decision to invest in BI overstimated the infrastructure, which was insufficient. In present conditions, the BI system is not ready to support managers in the decision-making process. In addition, there is a need to involve managers to help them understand the real advantages for them in using this advanced tool. In other words, a training plan is needed. In fact, as suggested by the literature, "although the potential of information technologies to support organizational transformation is acknowledged, evidence increasingly points to the importance of human agency in converting potential into practice" [39].

References

1. Markus, M.L., Axline, S., Petrie, D., Tanis, C.: Learning from adopters' experiences with ERP: problems encountered and success achieved. J. Inf. Technol. **15**(4), 245–265 (2000)
2. Umble, E.J., Haft, R.R., Umble, M.M.: Enterprise resource planning: implementation procedures and critical success factors. Eur. J. Op. Res. **146**, 241–257 (2003)
3. Harris, J.: Managing change in IT improvement initiatives. Gov. Financ. Rev. **22**(1), 36–40 (2006)
4. Sprecher, M.: The future of ERP in the public sector. Gov. Financ. Rev. **15**(4), 49–50 (1999)
5. Ward, M.A.: Information systems technologies: a public-private sector comparison. J. Comput. Inf. Syst. **46**(3), 50–56 (2006)
6. Rosaker, K.M., Olson, D.L.: An empirical assessment of IT project selection and evaluation methods in state government. Proj. Manag. J. **39**(1), 49–58 (2008)
7. Raymond, L., Uwizeyemungu, S., Bergeron, F.: ERP adoption for e-government: an analysis of motivations. In: *e*Government workshop'05, (*e*GOV05), Brunel University, UK, pp. 1–10 (13 Sept. 2005)
8. Parr, A., Shanks, G., Darke, P.: Identification of necessary factors for successful implementation of ERP systems. In: Ngwenyama, O., Introna, L.D., Myers, M.D., DeCross, J.I. (eds.) New Information Technologies in Organisational Processes, pp. 99–119. Kluwer Academic Publishers, Boston (1999)
9. Holland, C.P., Light B., Gibson, N.: A Critical success factors model for enterprise resource planning implementation. In: Pries-Heje, J., Ciborra, C., Kautz, K. Valor, J., Christiaanse, E., Avison, D., Heje, C. (eds.) Proceedings 7th European Conference on Information Systems, pp. 273–287, Copenhagen Business School, Copenhagen (1999)
10. Bancroft, N.: Implementing SAP/R3. Manning Publications, Greenwich (1996)
11. Botta-Genoulaz, V., Millet, P.A., Grabot, B.: A survey on the recent research literature on ERP systems. Comput. Ind. Elsevier **56**(6), 510–522 (2005)
12. Su, Y., Yang, C.: Why are enterprise resource planning systems indispensable to supply chain management? Eur. J. Op. Res. **203**(1), 81–94 (2010)
13. Hendricks, K.B., Singhal, V.R., Stratman, J.K.: The impact of enterprise systems on corporate performance: a study of ERP. SCM, CRM Syst. Implement. J. Op. Manag. **25**(1), 65–82 (2007)
14. Kemper, H.G., Rausch, P., Baars, H.: Business intelligence and performance management: introduction. In: Rausch, P., Sheta, A.F., Ayesh, A. (eds.) Business Intelligence and Performance Management: Theory, Systems, and Industrial Applications, pp. 3–12. Springer, U.K. (2013)
15. Hartley, K., Seymour L. F.: Towards a framework for the adoption of business intelligence in public sector organisations: the case of South Africa. In: Knowledge, Innovation and Leadership in a Diverse, Multidisciplinary Environment, Cape Town, South Africa (2011)
16. National Audit Office (NAO): Information and Communications Technology in Government. Landscape Review, London (2011)

17. Rouhani, S., Asgari, S., Mirhosseini, S.V.: Review study: business intelligence concepts and approaches. Am. J. Sci. Res. **50**, 62–75 (2012)
18. Pearce, F.T.: Business intelligence systems: the need. Dev. Integr. Idu. Mark. Manag. **5**(2–3), 115–138 (1976)
19. Nylund, A.L.: Tracing the BI family tree. Knowl. Manag. (1999)
20. Tyson, K.: Business Intelligence Putting it All Together. Leading Edge Publications, Illinois (1986)
21. Hannula, M., Pirttimaki, V.: Business intelligence empirical study on the top 50 finnish companies. J. Am. Acad. Bus. **2**(2), 593–599 (2003)
22. Negash, S.: Business intelligence. Commun. Assoc. Inf. Syst. **13**(15), 176–195 (2004). http://aisel.aisnet.org/cais/vol13/iss1/15
23. Thomsen, E.: BI's Promised land. Intell. Enterp. **6**(4), 21–25 (2003)
24. Herschel, R.T., Jones, N.E.: Knowledge management and business intelligence: the importance of integration. J. Knowl. Manag. **9**(4), 45–55 (2005)
25. Elbashir, M.Z., Collier, P.A., Davern, M.J.: Measuring the effects of business intelligence systems: The relationship between business process and organizational performance. Int. J. Acc. Inf. Syst. **9**(3), 135–153 (2008)
26. Azma, F., Mostafapour, M., A.: Business intelligence as a key strategy for development organizations. Procedia Technol. **1**, 102–106 (2012)
27. Koupaei, M.N., Movahedi, M.M.: An investigation on the effects of business intelligence and enterprise resources planning on TQM. Uncertain Supply Chain Manage. **2**(3), 191–198 (2004)
28. Boselli, R., Cesarini, M., Mezzanzanica, M.: public service intelligence: evaluating how the public sector can exploit decision support systems. In: RESER Conference on Productivity of Services NextGen—Beyond Output/Input. Fraunhofer Verlag, Stuttgart (2011)
29. Servers, E.N.: Public sector failing to benefit from business intelligence at a time when it could most use it, Enterprise Networks and Servers (Online) 1 (2007)
30. Nomisma: La Business Intelligence sul Territorio. Rome: Agra (2013)
31. Nomisma: La Business Intelligence in Italia. Rapporto Nomisma 2010. Rome: Agra (2010)
32. Nomisma: La Business Intelligence nella Pubblica Amministrazione. Rapporto 2011. Rome: Agra (2011)
33. Spano, A., Bellò, B.: The impact of using an ERP system on organizational processes and individual employees of an italian regional government organization. In: D'Atri, A., Ferrara, M., George, J.F., Spagnoletti, P. (eds.) Information Technology and Innovation Trends in Organizations, pp. 83–90. Springer, Berlin (2011)
34. Spano, A., Bellò, B.: Managerial and organizational impact of erp systems in public sector organizations. A case study. In: De Marco, M., Te'eni, D., Albano, V., Za, S. (eds.) Information Systems: Crossroads for Organization, Management, Accounting and Engineering, pp. 77–84. Springer, Berlin (2012)
35. Spano, A., Carta, D., Mascia, P.: The impact of introducing an ERP system on organisational processes and individual employees within an italian regional government organisation. Public Manag. Rev. **11**(6), 791–809 (2009)
36. Yin, R.K.: Case Study Research: Design and Methods. Sage Publications, Beverly Hills, Calif (1984)
37. Muhr, T.: ATLAS.ti a prototype for the suport of text interpretation. Qual. Social. **14**, 349–371 (1991)
38. Glaser, B.G., Strauss, A.I.: The Discovery of Grounded Theory: Strategies for Qualitative Research. Aldine, New York (1967)
39. Boudreau, M.C., Robey, D.: Enacting integrated information technology: a human agency perspective. Organ. Sci. **16**(1), 3–18 (2005)

Management Control Systems for the Water Concessionaires Governance: A Multiple Cases Study in the Italian Seaports

Assunta Di Vaio and Luisa Varriale

Abstract The purpose of this paper is to investigate the information and knowledge management regarding the carried out processes into the seaport relationships system in the Italian market. We focus on the relationships established between the water concessionaires and Port Authorities (PAs), in order to examine the main tools developed and adopted for facilitating their information and knowledge sharing, recognizing their role in the performing of tasks assigned to the PAs by the Law 84/1994. In the last decades, some reforms have significantly changed the port facilities management because of the need to reduce costs and guarantee high quality services. According to the main frameworks on the topic, we investigate how management control, information systems and reporting tools can facilitate the coordination and integration between water concessionaires and PAs in order to support the long-term decision in the seaport, following a systemic viewpoint. This qualitative work, adopting a multiple cases study methodology, compare four different ports in the Italian seaport system (Civitavecchia, Naples, Trieste, and Venice). Despite the crucial role played by the tools investigated in the information sharing and coordination process, we observe still the lack of an integrative information system—in terms of a shared digital platform—and, also, the presence of strong resistances by both the players to deeply communicate and effectively and efficiently interact to provide the water facility.

Keywords Port authority · Concessionaries · Water services · Outsourcing · External reporting · Management control · Information systems · Relationships system

A. Di Vaio (✉) · L. Varriale
Parthenope University, Naples, Italy
e-mail: susy.divaio@uniparthenope.it

L. Varriale
e-mail: luisa.varriale@uniparthenope.it

© Springer International Publishing Switzerland 2016
D. Mancini et al. (eds.), *Strengthening Information and Control Systems*,
Lecture Notes in Information Systems and Organisation 14,
DOI 10.1007/978-3-319-26488-2_11

145

1 Introduction

The public sector has been deeply changed since the 1980s by significant reforms assuming specific characteristics in the different countries. Thanks to these reforms the public institutions have defined new organizational and managerial models and processes in order to optimize the resources [1–3].

In the last decades the seaports system has been also affected by drastic changes dictated by several laws to improve the efficiency of the port infrastructures also through the participation of the private operators; as a consequence, the functions and responsibilities were significantly reorganized by this outsourcing process.

The port management reforms can be linked to the following pre-conditions: the application of labour practices very restrictive, the lack of appropriate solutions to manage the increasing demand, the low level of port services quality standards, and the absence of investments by many local governments in the capital port infrastructures [4, 5]. Hence, the reforms had to improve the attitude towards port clients/users and to decrease costs and prices, besides to advance port efficiency and service quality.

Thus, different organizational models were identified as an effect of the port reorder. Specifically, mixed public-private organizations characterize the Italian seaports, named as "landlord model", in which the infrastructures are provided by the Port Authority (PA), instead private companies outside invest in superstructure and port operations through the contracting out form [4]; while, the private sector has all the responsibility for the ownership and management of overall equipment and services [6].

In Italy the Law 84/1994 introduced these types of organizations, recognizing to PAs the tasks of orientation, planning, coordination, promotion and control of port operations and industrial and commercial activities (art. 6, c. 1, letter c). However, this rule interdicts PAs to directly manage port operations (art. 6, c. 6) and complementary services that have to be managed by the private companies in outsourcing.

Such Law (art. 6, c. 1, letter c) conceives also lighting, cleaning and waste collection, water, maintenance and repair, maritime stations, information technology, and other activities as services of "general interest", thus, mixed or private companies can manage them in outsourcing.

In this scenario, in which the laws require or stimulate outsourcing processes, we observe that PA increasingly needs to monitor and control the activities carried out by private operators avoiding to become their victims. With reference to the relationship between PA and concessionaire, we argue that critical factors are represented by the information selection and sharing about the performance measurement.

These criticisms have already been investigated in a previous study [7] focused on the analysis of water service outsourced in the Naples port experience, in which it was outlined that, although its reduced participation in the ownership of the water concessionaire, the use of management control and information system tools was limited. Drawing from this study, this paper aims to investigate other experiences in the larger Italian seaports, where the participation of PA in the ownership structures differs. In fact, we want to analyze if and how the role of the management control, information system, and reporting tools changes in the water service outsourced depending on the different ownership structure of the water concessionaire. We also clarify that the focus on the specific service on general interest, water supply, is justified from its relevance for all the seaport users, including the shipping companies or any other users, like shops or restaurants.

In Italy until nineties, local governments or concessionaires have managed the water services. The sector was completely reformed by the legislator because of the need to reduce public expenses and improve the quality of the service. Indeed, the water sector was completely reformed since 1994 by the Law n. 36, (named Galli Law). These reforms introduced some relevant elements about the water service: water services were integrated to realize economies of scope (water supply, wastewater and sewerage); water utilities were also merged to exploit economies of scale; water industries were industrialized to avoid the in-house solution; and finally, specific tariffs were defined to face current costs and investments.

In this direction, the water services have been interested by the outsourcing process to the new established private companies. In the Italian seaport system, the laws (Law 84/94 and the Ministerial Decree n. 36/94) have introduced a concession act through which the water infrastructures management was transferred from PAs to private operators. Nevertheless, after almost three decades in only 13 ports (Ancona, Bari, Brindisi, Cagliari, Catania, Civitavecchia, Livorno, Marina di Carrara, Naples, Palermo, Ravenna, Trieste, and Venice) the services have been outsourced to private companies.

Indeed, it is clear that, on one side, in the last decades in order to reduce costs it has been adopted the instrument of outsourcing; on the other side, the efficiency and increase of social effectiveness do not always occur. It is possible to identify several factors that can contribute to the failure of several privatization initiatives, such as the lack of cost reduction, low quality of the services provided, difficulties in monitoring and limitations in the social accountability.

In this direction, the control, monitoring and reporting of services outsourced become crucial for public managers especially to evaluate their respect of public administration objectives and strategies and safeguard the public interest.

This qualitative study, adopting a multiple cases study methodology, compare four different ports in the Italian seaport system (Civitavecchia, Naples, Trieste, and Venice). The findings evidence still the lack of an integrative information system (in terms of shared digital platform), and also the management control and reporting systems are not developed by the water concessionaires, otherwise strong resistances have been outlined by both the players to deeply communicate and effectively and efficiently interact to provide the water facility.

The paper is structured as follows: Sect. 2 is focused on the analysis of management control, information systems, and reporting in the relationships system between water concessionaries and PAs, also through a brief review of the literature on this complex issue. In Sect. 3 we compare the four cases study describing them and evidencing their similarities and differences. The Sect. 4 concerns the key performance indicators identified in order to better analyze the established relationships system for the water service. Section 5 outlines a brief discussion on the cases study and some final considerations.

2 Management Control, Information Systems, and Reporting in the Relationships System Between Water Concessionaires and PAs

In the seaports system the data and information collecting, processing and reporting are crucial for conducting all the activities, especially the supply of general services in outsourcing. Port managers have to guarantee the duty and accountability of disclosing information to all the stakeholders responding to the last laws and regulations. These obligations and needs, for the effective and efficient management of port infrastructures and the execution of operational activities and any services, imply the introduction of suitable tools able to fulfil the new informative requirements especially regarding external relations [8].

In the past the information system and any channels of communication were still undeveloped and irregularly issued over time, today we observe the adoption of a more complete system to manage data and information, though it is still fragmented and heterogeneous. Some authors recognize ICT (Information Communication Technology) as a critical success factor for achieving specific goals: to promote the connection of ports with their hinterlands [9], to improve high value added services, to increase logistic and transport system efficiency and competitiveness [10]. In addition, in the future years the European Union will pay more and more its attention and financial funds to ICT, in order to identify and implement new technologies able to increase efficiency, safety and competitiveness of current freight transport infrastructures [11]. From the technological and relational point of view ICT can be recognized as one of the most powerful enablers. ICT represents a strong networking and communication tool that allows data sharing and information flows, especially in B2B and supply chain management [12].

Otherwise, ICT applications have still a further and abundant potential to be explored in the port sector. ICT can significantly help to face some typical criticisms in the port system, such as the high level of competitiveness, the increase of stakeholders, the importance of high quality standards for the provided services, the outsourcing of some services, and so on. Scholars argue that ICT technology plays a strategic role because it allows the integration between different actors along the chain, supporting significantly all the information-sharing supply chain management and networking [13]. This recognized significant role of ICT is more important if we consider the outsourcing processes, because of the need to manage many players and PAs guaranteeing a continuous data and information integration. Otherwise, in the port system we observe the increasing need of controlling because of the relevant use of outsourcing processes, and this need can be satisfied thanks to the adoption and implementation of adequate ICT technologies. Qualitative and quantitative data are included in the information flows between the contracting and the contractor depending on the relationship between these players. PA needs appropriate and detailed information because of the great importance of the port services.

The concession contract allows to govern and regulate the relationship between PA and concessionaire. Otherwise, although a specific contract regulate the relationship between PA and concessionaire, there are still information asymmetries among these players for the management of their activities; however, it is possible to avoid information asymmetries only through the accuracy in these activities [14].

This study aims to investigate variables that are critical for the good functioning of this partnership: the management control, information systems and reporting used by the concessionaires to interface with PAs. Some critical factors, such as information, language codes, software, need to be managed for the successful development of the relationship [15].

In the literature on the topic, the control into inter-organizational relationships can stimulate the partners to act in a "performance oriented" way and to coordinate the input-output information process within the relationship [16]. Moreover, some authors on inter-organizational relationships argue that shared information, also coded in norms, contribute to activate a cooperation system among the partners, aligning their goals and behaviors and assuming a "performance orientation" [17, 18]. Thus, we analyze which instruments have been adopted to control and coordinate the players involved in the relationships system concerning the water service outsourcing. Specifically, we investigate the reporting tools (ex-post control mechanisms) [18, 19] introduced by the concessionaires to communicate data on the services provided to users. The electronic data processing represents a common tool used to collect and share information thanks to some spreadsheets, such as excel. During the recent years, we observe the implementation of Integrated Information Systems (IIS), like as an important source of competitive advantage [4].

In the seaport system, thanks to an IIS, the PAs can interact and be linked to the concessionaires and all the members of the port community, such as truckers, customs, ship agents and so on, sharing data and information and, consequently, providing high quality services. Otherwise, the implementation of an IIS implies high costs, so different factors can affect its introduction, like the strategic vision, the needs or competences, and the limited resources.

On the other side, the management control systems and its main tools (e.g. Balanced Scorecard) use information to evaluate the performance of the resources employed in the business processes. An efficient management control system might support and improve the decision system, above all when the strategic choices of one firm impacts on the other firms' behaviours, in order to obtain a competitive advantage for both. Indeed, according to Anthony [20] and Horngren et al. [21] the management control is defined not only as the process by which managers influence other members of the organization to implement the organization strategies, but also as an integrated technique concerning the coordination, resource allocation, and performance measurement.

Regarding the challenges faced in the implementation of IIS and, in general, the adoption of information management and control tools in the relationships system between the concessionaires and PAs for the supply of water services, in order to measure and control their performance, we consider one only study on the topic that exams the case of port in Naples (Italy). Drawing from this previous study [6], we deeply analyze other three cases (Civitavecchia, Trieste and Venice) to investigate the established relationships systems for the supply of water service. In Naples, the authors outline the establishment of the private concessionaire Idro Porto s.r.l. to manage the water service through a detailed contract, and because of the limited information collected and processed from the financial statements and formal documents, some key performance indicators have been developed to measure the performance the external provider and to monitor and control the execution of services and activities. It has been shown the activities provided by Idra Porto s.r.l. can be successfully monitored and controlled by the PA thanks to the IIS and any other information tools. Also, the Balanced Scorecard can allow the PA to build a clear vision of all the outsourced service provided by Idra Porto.

3   Multiple Cases Study

Adopting the case study methodology we have investigated three port experiences for the supply of water service: Civitavecchia, Trieste, and Venice. This is an explorative study conducted through semi-structured interviews to key actors in the investigated sector, more specifically we in-depth interviewed five key actors using different communication channels, that is Skype and face-to-face meetings. In details, we gathered information and data during our interviews to two administrative managers (one administrative manager for both Civitavecchia and Trieste), three individuals in Venice, one within port facilities area, one as administrative manager, and another one within the sales area.

In the final comparison among these cases we consider also the case of Naples, as shown in Table 1.

Regarding the customers and services provided, we observe that the water service supplied by all the water concessionaires investigated are: water supplied to the ships; water supplied to the other concessionaires, PA, maritime authorities, and other users (shops, restaurants, and so on); management and maintenance the water infrastructures in the seaport; lighting and electric distribution service. Moreover, in each case study regarding the relationships systems identified, the ship agent is the main player in the water supply to the ships.

Port Utilities S.p.A. (Port of Civitavecchia). The Port Utilities S.p.A. is the water concessionaire that operates in the Civitavecchia seaport (Port Authority of Civitavecchia, Fiumicino and Gaeta). It was established in 2002. The ownership

Table 1 Comparative analysis for the water supply in the Italian seaports system

Port	Year	Water concessionaire	Gorvernance PA	I.I.S.	Multi/mono utilities	Software
Civitavecchia	2002	Port utilities s.p.a.	18 %	No	Multi	Yes*
Naples**	2004	Idra porto s.r.l.	20 %	No	Mono	No
Trieste	2009	Trieste servizi s.p.a.	100 %	No	Multi	No
Venice	2010	Veritas s.p.a.	No	No	Multi	No

* The software is used only in the relationship between concessionaire and port users
**Data and information are collected by [6]

structure is composed by more shareholders, among them there is the PA of Civitavecchia that owns 18 % of the equity. It is a concessionaire that provides more "services of general interest" (multi-utilities provider), such as water, lighting, media communication and information technology services.

In Civitavecchia case, it is possible to identify the following relationships systems: (1) concessionaire and PA; (2) concessionaire and ship agents; (3) concessionaire and firms that manage tankers and small barges.

With reference to the first relationship system, at the beginning of the year and weekly revised, the PA shares data and information by email and fax regarding the activities planning and timing schedules about the ship arrivals without adopting an integrative information system through a shared software. Moreover, regarding the management control function on the carried out activities, PA analyses only budget and financial statements of the Port Utilities.

In the second and third relationships systems, regarding the water supply to the ships, data and information, that are usually shared by email, concern the quantity of water needed, the quays for mooring ships, and possible further services. Most water supply sub-services are automated, but the parts that are not able to be managed adopting advanced automatic systems are carried out to an external firm, which is responsible for the furnishing through the use of tankers and small barges. Starting from 2008, the Port Utilities has adopted a customized software, named SI. GE.FI., created by itself that is a shared platform between the administrative and technical departments; it allows the monitoring of processes mainly thanks to the use of a palmtop that can connect the electric box to the technical office transferring all the consumer data. This software plays a key role because performs the following functions: to communicate in real-time data to the administrative office (name of the ships and shipping companies, fees, consumption, and so on); to monitor and control automatically the consumption in order to avoid unethical and illegal behaviors; to print directly and automatically the commercial document ready for the signature; to draw up internal reports.

Idra Porto s.r.l. (Port of Naples). The water concessionaire Idra Port s.r.l. operates in the Naples seaport. It was established in 2004 and the PA owns the 20 % of the equity of the concessionaire. It is a mono-utility provider with only one service related to the water furniture.

In Naples case, we identify the following main relationships systems: (1) concessionaire and PA; (2) concessionaire and ship agents; (3) concessionaire and other concessionaires in the seaport. The main tool used for the management of the information in the relationship between Idra Porto and PA is the contract, that every year is checked and can be revoked if the water concessionaire does not deeply respect the rules. However, within all the relationships systems, data and information, regarding the activities planning and timing schedules, are shared mainly by email and fax. The previous study [7] shows that there is not a specific software able to integrate all the elements regarding the water supply and the role of the management control is very poor.

Trieste Servizi S.p.A. (Port of Trieste). The water concessionaire Trieste Servizi S.p. A. operates in the Trieste seaport. It was established in 2009 by the PA, which owns the 100 % of the equity. It is a multi-utilities provider with different "services of general interest", such as water, lighting, information technology services and the environment management (e.g. garbage, stretches of water, and so on).

In Trieste case, we identify the following main relationships systems: (1) concessionaire and PA; (2) concessionaire and ship agents; (3) concessionaire and other concessionaires in the seaport, such as the maritime station.

Within all the relationships systems, data and information, regarding the activities planning and timing schedules, are shared mainly by mail; hence, we observe the lack of a software to integrate these elements regarding the water supply. Indeed, a specific form is required in order to guarantee the data collecting and processing.

Veritas S.p.A. (Port of Venice). In Venice seaport, the water service management is carried out to a temporary joint between Veritas S.p.A. and Veritas Energia S.p.A., and it was established in 2010. More in detail, Veritas S.p.A. provides the water services, but also gas and electricity services. The Veritas S.p.A. is a public institution in which the ownership includes only local governments of the Veneto Region.

In Venice case, we identify the following main relationships systems: (1) concessionaire and PA; (2) concessionaire and ship agents; (3) concessionaire and other concessionaires in the seaport, such as the maritime station.

Within all the relationships systems, data and information, regarding the activities planning and timing schedules, are shared mainly by email and fax; although the technical staff adopts a palmtop for receiving the specific request for water furniture by fax, the water concessionaire does not adopt any softwares to share information and consequently monitor the processes.

The case studies evidence that the integrated information systems (IIS) are still missing in the data processes management among all the players involved in the water services in the seaports investigated (Table 1). First, the information about the water supplies is shared adopting the traditional tools, such as e-mail and fax and not software that will allow to the player data access data every time. This last is an important condition to support the decisions of the companies interested in the water supplier process. Second, neither the nature of the ownership structures of the water concessionaires nor the same business would seem to have a connection with the adoption of IIS. Finally, with regard to the instruments of management control the cases analyzed show that the financial statements of the water concessionaires are the main tool for performance assessment.

4 The Relationships System Between Concessionaires and PAs: Control, Reporting Systems and Key Performance Indicators

In our comparative study we can evidence that the contract is one of the most frequent tool adopted to manage the relationships system established among the players for the water supply, it is the formal act through which the public entity contracts out a service. In all the experiences investigated, like the previous case of Naples port, the act of concession contains all the rules needed to be respected by the water concessionaires, also their obligation for reporting periodically their activities to the PA in order to monitor the financial and economic aspects related to the service outsourced. These reports and data and information sharing mostly occur by hand, e-mail or fax, so we highlight the lack of a software to manage these activities (except to Civitavecchia experience) and also, any forms of IIS are not implemented.

Our study allows us to identify other useful key performance indicators to measure the performance concerning the water supply in the relationships system between the water concessionaires and PAs. These indicators can further develop the previous study on the same topic [6] (see Table 2), providing a more clear and complete vision of the phenomenon, considering the lack of effective tools from the technical point of view such as IIS or adequate software.

Following the key performance indicators in Table 2, developed on the basis of some perspectives from the Balanced Scorecard [22, 23], especially the adoption of specific management control systems [24], and considering the cases of Civitavecchia, Trieste and Venice in this study, it is possible to identify other key indicators allowing us to elaborate and apply measures of the internal processes, learning and growth, and IT.

More in detail:

(1) m^3 of water supplied in t_1/No. form received by the concessionaire in t_1
(2) Hrs for the training in a year/No. employee
(3) No. palmtops are not working in t_1

The indicator (1) helps to know the productive capacity of the water concessionaire in time t_1 and the indicator (2) measures the propensity of the water concessionaire to increase and improve the knowledge of the employee. In addition, starting from the recognized critical role played by the IIS mostly in the relationship between PA and concessionaire, and not in the concessionaires-customers relationship, we identify the key indicator (3). This last one evidences the efficiency of the technological tools in the relationships and processes identified.

Table 2 Key performance indicators for the water concessionaire to support the control of the PA

No. new services/total services provided	It measures the degree of attention to the development of new service that should integrate the already existing ones to improve the total quality and variety for clients
No. of complains/total users	It measures the degree of quality perceived by customers
No. information obtained in t1/no. information needed by PA on activities outsourced	They measure the efficiency of the IIS in the relationship between PAs and water concessionaires
Cost of IT training/IT cost	
% of process with feedback about time, cost and quality	

Source [6]

The decisions made by both partners might be supported by these key indicators also improving the relationship systems. Otherwise, our considerations allow us to overcome the limits of the previous study, developing even further a model that can effectively support the complex monitoring and reporting processes of services outsourced by PA.

5 Discussion and Final Considerations

This study can contribute to the existing literature by investigating the way needed to improve the PAs performance through effective tools to manage the quality and quantity of information about the services outsourced. Specifically, the paper investigates the external reporting, the management control and information system in the relationship between PA and water concessionaire and, finally, we suggest how the PA can improve its control activities using some useful key performance indicators and also tools like the Balanced Scorecard.

Our comparative analysis has evidenced some relevant criticisms in the relationship between PAs and the water concessionaires. In fact, the findings have outlined that the management control, information system and reporting differ in the port experiences depending on two main factors: the participation of PA in the ownership structure of the water concessionaire; the nature mono or multi-utilities of the concessionaire. We argue that these two variables significantly can affect the adoption of these tools and their effectiveness.

This study presents some limitations, related mainly to its qualitative content and the analysis of only four cases, but it can be considered as an interesting research starting point in order to find new and more intriguing aspects to investigate, which can explain the different role and use of the management control, information system and reporting tools in the seaports system.

Acknowledgements The authors are grateful for the contributions of the operators interviewed (the water concessionaires of Civitavecchia, Trieste and Venice) and for the support of the students of the University of Naples "Parthenope" involved in the research project, attending undergraduate and graduate courses. More in details, the authors thank Alessia Gracceva, Maria Anna Ludovico, and Arianna Petrosino. Any errors are entirely attributed to the authors.

References

1. Pollitt, C., Bouckaert, G.: Public Management Reform: A Comparative Analysis. Oxford University Press (2004)
2. Dunleavy, P., Hood, C.: From old Public administration to new public management. Public Money Manag. **14**(3), 9–16 (1994)
3. World Bank: Port Reform Tool Kit—Module 2—The Evolution of Ports in a Competitive World. (2008)
4. UNCTAD: Comparative Analysis of Deregulation, Commercialisation and Privatisation of Ports, UNCTAD/SDD/PORT/3, Geneva (1995)
5. Di Vaio, A., Medda, F.R., Trujillo, L.: An analysis of the efficiency of Italian Cruise terminals. Int. J. Transport Econ. **38**(1), 29–46 (2011)
6. Di Vaio, A., D'Amore, G.: Port authorities and water concessionaires: the role of reporting in management control and information systems. In: Accounting Information Systems for Decision Making, Vol. 3, Springer Series: LNISO, Springer Physica–Verlag, GmbH Publisher, pp. 315–323 (2013)
7. Parola, F., Satta, G., Penco, L., Profumo, G.: Emerging port authority communication strategies: assessing the determinants of disclosure in the annual report. Res. Transp. Bus. Manag. **8**, 134–147 (2013)
8. Almotairi, B., Flodén, J., Stefansson, G., Woxenius, J.: Information flows supporting Hinterland transportation by rail: applications in Sweden. Res. Trans. Econ. **33**, 15–24 (2011)
9. Ducruet, C., Van der Horst, M.: transport integration at european ports: measuring the role and position of intermediaries. Eur. J. Transp. Infrastruct. Res. **9**(2), 121–142 (2009)
10. Cepolina, S., Ghiara, H.: New trends in port strategies. emerging role for ICT infrastructures. Res. Trasp. Bus. Manag. **8**, 195–205 (2013)
11. Cepolina, S.: Fostering the garment industry competitiveness: the ICT contribution. Glob. J. Enterp. Inf. Syst. **3**(2), 5–14 (2011)
12. Kollberg, M., Dreyer, H.: Exploring the impact of ICT on integration in supply chain control: a research model. Norway: Department of Production and Quality Engineering, Norwegian University of Science and Technology (2006)
13. Marchi, L.: I sistemi Informativi Aziendali. Giuffré, Milano (1993)
14. Mancini, D.: Il Sistema Informativo e di Controllo Relazionale per il Governo della Rete di Relazioni Collaborative d'Azienda. Giuffrè, Milano (2010)
15. Dekker, H.C.: Control of inter-organizational relationships: evidence on appropriation concerns and coordination requirements. Account. Organ. Soc. **29**(1), 27–49 (2004)
16. Grandori, A., Soda, G.: Inter-firm Networks: Antecedents. Mech. Forms. Organ. Stud. **16**(2), 183–214 (1995)
17. Bensaou, M., Venkatraman, N.: Inter-organizational relationships and information technology: a conceptual synthesis and a research framework. INSEAD (1993)
18. Smith, K.G., Carroll, S.J., Ashford, S.J.: Intra-and interorganizational cooperation: toward a research agenda. Acad. Manag. J. **38**(1), 7–23 (1995)
19. Jensen, M., Meckling, W.: Theory of the firm: managerial behaviour, agency costs and ownership structure. J. Financ. Econ. **3**(4), 305–360 (1976)
20. Anthony, R., Govindarajan, V.: Management Control Systems. Mc-Graw-Hill IRWIN, Chicago (2007)

21. Horngren, C., Sundem, G., Stratton, W.: Introduction to Management Accounting. Pearson, New Jersey (2005)
22. Kaplan, R., Norton, D.: The balanced Scorecard—Measures that drive performance. Harv. Bus. Rev. (1992)
23. Olve, N.G., Roy, J., Wetter, M.: Performance Drivers: A Practical Guide to Using the Balanced Scorecard. Wiley (1999)
24. Otley, D.: Performance management: a framework for management control systems research. Manag. Account. Res. **10**(4), 363–382 (1999)

The Pros and Cons of XBRL Adoption in Italy: A Field Study

Francesco Avallone, Paola Ramassa and Elisa Roncagliolo

Abstract Our study responds to the call for more field-based research on XBRL focusing on the effects of its adoption with regard to: (i) knowledge and actual direct use of XBRL; (ii) existing limitations and future necessary improvements; and (iii) actual costs and benefits. In pursuit of these objectives, we have carried out a descriptive study based on interviews with different actors involved in the financial communication process in Italy, where the XBRL filing of financial statements has been mandatory for unlisted companies since 2009. Results suggest that five years of adoption have not led to a widespread awareness of XBRL features and potential benefits among professionals. Moreover, interviews highlight that so far the XBRL mandatory adoption has not achieved an overall substantial impact on real practice yet, if we exclude some financial statement users (e.g. financial analysts). Our findings have relevant implications for regulators, users, and companies as well.

Keywords XBRL · Information systems · Financial reporting · Field research

1 Introduction

In 1999 many of the world's leading accounting and financial reporting firms and major institutional organizations founded the XBRL consortium, aimed at building XBRL, promoting and supporting its adoption as an open standard language for the electronic communication of business information.

F. Avallone · P. Ramassa (✉) · E. Roncagliolo
Department of Economics and Business Studies, University of Genoa, Genoa, Italy
e-mail: ramassa@economia.unige.it

F. Avallone
e-mail: avallone@economia.unige.it

E. Roncagliolo
e-mail: roncagliolo@economia.unige.it

© Springer International Publishing Switzerland 2016   157
D. Mancini et al. (eds.), *Strengthening Information and Control Systems*,
Lecture Notes in Information Systems and Organisation 14,
DOI 10.1007/978-3-319-26488-2_12

After fifteen years from its foundation, XBRL International is now a not-for-profit consortium of more than 600 companies and government agencies and is comprised of 27 local jurisdictions focusing on the progress of XBRL in their area. This standard is currently put to practical use in more than 30 countries around the world (18 in Europe) on a voluntary or mandatory basis and its implementations keep growing in terms of uses and involved organizations.

Observing the diffusion of XBRL and its increasing pace, it seems to be less difficult now to resolve many doubts on the language adoption, while questions on its real costs and benefits for different kinds of entities are still unanswered, especially with reference to some forms of adoption and geographical contexts.

In such a perspective, any assessment of XBRL effectiveness should start from its expected benefits in the preparation, analysis and communication of business information. From a technical point of view, XBRL could offer considerable advantages to all players, from preparers to all classes of users interested in analysing accounting and financial data. However, it is reasonable to expect that these benefits can be obtained less or more easily by organizations depending on several factors, such as the form of adoption (mandatory vs. voluntary) and on the features of firms using XBRL in financial communication (e.g. listed vs. non-listed companies).

So far studies on XBRL adoption and its effects have been based mainly on quantitative research methods and have generally focused on voluntary adopters and listed companies, without a strict link with real XBRL practice. Our paper tries to fill this gap with a descriptive study exploring the effects of mandatory XBRL adoption by unlisted companies through an in-depth analysis based on interviews with a number of professionals involved in the financial communication process.

The main objective of our study is to assess the impact of XBRL adoption with regard to: (i) knowledge and actual direct use of XBRL; (ii) existing limitations in XBRL usage and future necessary improvements; and (iii) actual costs and benefits perceived by actors in XBRL financial communication.

Our study is focused on the Italian context where XBRL adoption is mandatory for unlisted companies from 2009 financial statements. This gives us an excellent research opportunity to explore the effects of this choice in terms of actual costs and benefits after five years from the first mandatory XBRL filing.

In particular, Italian unlisted companies preparing their financial statements according to the Italian Civil Code and national GAAP are subject to a mandatory filing of their annual financial statements in XBRL format to the Italian Business Register via the Chambers of Commerce. This requirement has been imposed from 2009 financial statements for the balance sheet and the income statement, while the XBRL filing of notes has been mandatory from 2015 after two experimental rounds of voluntary filings in 2013 and 2014. Contrary to other countries, the Italian regulator excluded all companies adopting IFRS (such as listed companies) from the XBRL presentation of financial statements and included XBRL in a list of possible formats to present financial statements (together with PDF and XML) without any mandatory filing in XBRL.

Assessing costs and benefits of mandatory XBRL adoption for unlisted companies is of particular interest for at least two reasons. Firstly, unlisted companies represent the backbone of the Italian (and European) economy and any positive effect on their financial communication can have a substantial impact on a number of actors involved in the communication process as preparers, intermediaries and users. Secondly, their features in terms of organizational structure (e.g. limited administrative staff) might affect the degree of pervasiveness of XBRL adoption and its related costs and benefits.

In order to explore the effects of XBRL introduction in this context, we have conducted a field study based on interviews with practitioners and professionals involved in XBRL adoption. This choice responds to the call for field research on XBRL, needed to assess issues and advantages of XBRL adoption not from a theoretical point of view or in very general terms with a large sample of respondents. Indeed, this approach is particularly suitable to explore more in depth the effects of XBRL on the practice through a direct dialogue with operators.

Our findings indicate that after five years of XBRL adoption the knowledge of this language is still limited among actors involved in the financial reporting process. Preparers and professional supporting companies in financial statement filings seem to limit their effort to the mandatory conversion of existing documents without trying to integrate this language in their practice in order to reap its potential benefits.

Evidence is mixed for financial statement users. Some actors seem to be not affected at all by XBRL in their activity or are experiencing some problems in the transition phase, still waiting for the first advantages, while other professionals (e.g. some financial analysts) have fully understood the XBRL potential and are already getting considerable savings and benefits. However, there is a consensus about the very limited costs for compliance, with increasing investments only for firms interested in more complete implementations that seem to be highly satisfactory in terms of cost-benefit ratio.

Our paper contributes to existing literature on XBRL by studying the effects of mandatory XBRL adoption by Italian unlisted companies after five years from transition. Findings increase our understanding of XBRL actual costs and benefits with particular reference to financial communication from preparers without a strong internal administrative structure. They have important implications for scholars, practitioners, and regulators as they contribute additional evidence on XBRL implementation and suggest relevant points to address for future XBRL evolution.

The rest of the paper is structured as follows. The next section reviews prior literature on XBRL with a particular focus on studies aimed at assessing the actual costs and benefits deriving from the standard adoption. Section 3 describes our research questions and the research design, then Sect. 4 discusses results emerging from our study. The final section provides conclusions.

2   Literature Review

As XBRL began to be adopted around the world, a considerable number of studies has explored various aspects of this standardized digital language.

Prior research on this topic mainly related to normative issues [1], particularly investigating XBRL implementation and its effects on the financial reporting process [1, 2], shifting afterwards to the development and quality of taxonomies and data [3], as well as costs and benefits of XBRL adoption [4, 5].

Examining potential benefits of XBRL adoption for all actors, prior research emphasised the role of XBRL in enhancing the financial reporting process [1, 2]. Particularly, XBRL could potentially enable preparers to save costs in producing and distributing financial information, removing manual data re-entry and reducing errors. It could additionally allow easier regulatory compliance and increase the efficiency in business decision-making and the use of information systems [6, 7].

However, potential benefits are mainly addressed to users of financial statements, providing more accessible financial reports and allowing more efficient investment decisions [6]. Actually, XBRL aims at improving comparability of financial statements [8] and simplifying their analysis, especially for banks and analysts.

Some potential benefits could arise for other categories of users as well. Particularly, auditors could gather financial information they need more easily and could be facilitated in the analysis of large data pools for anomalies and fraud [9]. However it would require auditors to extend audit procedures to include auditing the tags used [10].

Based on these discussions, other studies provide early empirical evidence on actual costs and benefits arising from XBRL implementation.

In the earliest stage of XBRL adoption, a survey among auditors and accountants in the US context indicates that respondents do not perceive the potential benefits of XBRL such as increased efficiency, effectiveness, usefulness, and various job-related performance enhancements [11].

Afterwards, Pinsker and Li [4] explore costs and benefits of XBRL adoption for early adopter companies, through four phone and e-mail interviews with business managers involved in the process in Canada, Germany, South Africa, and the US. Their results highlight larger benefits mainly in terms of cost savings related to a decrease in data redundancy as well as lower costs of bookkeeping. On the other hand, costs in XBRL initial implementation especially relate to uncertainty in an unproven technology and costs—time and money—needed for success.

Similarly, considering actual benefits for users of financial reports, especially non professionals ones, Hodge et al. [5] run an experiment in the US context and find out that XBRL enables acquisition and integration of financial information in order to make investment decisions. These findings are supported also considering the XBRL impact on analyst's forecast behavior. Particularly, as demonstrated for the US stock market, the mandatory adoption of XBRL is positively associated with the number of analyst followings as well as analyst forecast accuracy [12].

More broadly, the US capital market benefits from XBRL adoption because it has a positive effect on information efficiency [13], and mitigates information asymmetry [14], as demonstrated for the Korean stock market as well [15]. In spite of this, empirical evidence in the Chinese context suggests an increase in cost of capital and transaction costs after the initial mandatory XBRL adoption [16].

As regards research methods, prior literature mainly focused on single cases and gradually shifted towards advanced quantitative research techniques, even if some research questions might have been more effectively addressed using qualitative methods [17].

Additionally, academic research on XBRL needs to be more linked to the evolution of XBRL practice and to present a more comprehensive picture of the actual diffusion of this standardized digital language, as well as of costs and benefits related to its implementation for all the main actors involved in the process. In spite of this, previous studies focused mainly on quantitative methods and investigated special fields such as early adopters or listed companies.

Thus, our study aims at filling this gap providing a field-based research investigating actual knowledge of XBRL, as well as costs and benefits arising from its adoption, for a wide range of actors that so far have been examined by limited research.

Specifically, we refer to knowledge as the awareness of opportunities provided for these actors by XBRL, rather than the familiarity with technical issues.

Additionally, consistently with previous studies, we explore benefits in terms of potential advantages, such as cost and time savings, higher usability of data, and enhancement of financial communication. On the other hand, costs are investigated in terms of time and expenses required for XBRL implementation and its use.

Some recent European studies partially aim at reaching these objectives through questionnaire or online surveys. For example, Dunne et al. [18] undertake a survey in order to investigate the diffusion in the UK of XBRL and perceived potential benefits of this format for accountants, auditors, tax professionals, and users such as analysts and fund managers. These stakeholders consider greater data comparability, no need to re-key information, inter-operability, and improvements in data analysis as the most significant potential benefits of XBRL adoption.

Similarly, a general survey on professionals experience with ICT has been carried out in the Italian context, involving chartered accountants, lawyers, and labor consultants [19]. Professionals' opinions on XBRL have been partially investigated as well, and according to results chartered accountants know this language and think that their activity can benefit from its usage. Considering all the three categories of respondents, results provide evidence of perceived benefits from XBRL adoption. Although, most of respondents are lawyers (56 %) and these professionals are not actually involved in XBRL adoption.

3 Research Questions and Method

In the light of results from previous literature, this study aims at assessing the effects of XBRL adoption in the Italian context after five years from the first mandatory filing of financial statements in XBRL. In pursuit of this general objective, we have carried out a descriptive study addressing three broad research questions.

Firstly, we investigate the current level of knowledge on XBRL. In our view, the first substantial impact of XBRL adoption should consist in an increased knowledge of its key features and potential uses. Indeed, XBRL enables operators to streamline financial communication in many different ways, but its effective implementation definitively depends on choices made by informed actors (e.g. investing to integrate XBRL in their information systems) to exploit its potential.

In this perspective, our first research question can be expressed as follows:

RQ1: What are the current level of knowledge and the actual direct use of XBRL among the different actors involved in the financial communication process?

Professionals' perceptions of current limitations in XBRL use and their expectations about future improvements are another key point to have a better understanding of the current and future impact of XBRL.

It is important to recall that XBRL implementation is still recent and that a radical change in financial reporting practices cannot be expected as a sudden event. So, current perceptions of XBRL limitations and new ideas to address them are key points in shaping the future of XBRL diffusion and use. Additionally, the mandatory adoption for non listed companies in the Italian context might offer specific and interesting insights on the topic. Thus, our second research question is the following:

RQ2: What are the main present limitations and the future necessary improvements to exploit XBRL potential benefits?

Then, the complete assessment of the effects of XBRL adoption must be based essentially on the evaluation of actual costs and benefits perceived by preparers, financial reporting professionals, and financial statement users. This is a crucial question in the light of the number of potential benefits presented in XBRL literature. Therefore, our third research question can be stated as follows:

RQ3: What are the actual perceived costs and benefits of XBRL adoption for the different actors involved in the financial communication process?

To answer the above mentioned research questions, we opted for a qualitative research approach in order to gain a better understanding of experiences, perceptions, and feelings of professional operators involved in financial communication and to explore more in depth the effects of XBRL in the Italian context. So, we have carried out a field study in order to conduct a substantive investigation oriented towards providing bases for understanding the working of XBRL in action [17, 20].

To collect data, we conducted 16 semi-structured interviews with different classes of actors: eight chartered accountants, two employees in chartered professional accountant firms, a local partner of a big 4 auditing firm, an accounting service consultant in a big 4 auditing firm, a financial analyst, a bank manager, a country manager of a financial data provider, and a director of a local office of the Italian Revenue Agency (Table 1).

These interviewees, despite not representing exhaustively all classes of actors involved in XBRL financial reporting, are a considerable number compared to previous XBRL literature and are extremely relevant for our study. The reason is that they can share their own perceptions on XBRL adoption and additionally they also know many different experiences for being in touch with many other firms and individuals using XBRL. So, an interview with an auditor or with a chartered accountant can be interesting to increase our understanding of XBRL effects on both their professional activity and on their customers' practices.

The motivation for semi-structured interviews derives from the need to obtain information from interviewees leaving them free to express their opinion on the topic. This allows outlining a more comprehensive picture of XBRL effects, based more on real practical experiences and less on researchers' expectations [21].

Interviews regarded interviewees' knowledge about XBRL, their experiences in terms of direct use and their perceptions with reference to costs, current and future benefits of XBRL adoption. Questions were asked with a strict link to operating practices so to avoid interpretation problems that are common in indirect forms of data collection and in dialogues between individuals looking at the same phenomenon from different perspectives [22].

Interviews were conducted in June and July, 2014 and they had an average duration of one hour and fifteeen minutes. They were not audiotape recorded to favour the confidence of interviewees and to encourage them to be very frank in comments [23], but information have been collected in notes, integrated with as many details as possible immediately after interviews to avoid data losses.

Table 1 Number of interviewees for each class of actors

Class of actors	No. interviewees
Chartered accountant	8
Chartered accountant employee	2
Auditor	1
Auditor accounting service consultant	1
Financial analyst	1
Bank manager	1
Financial data provider	1
Director of a local office of the Italian Revenue Agency	1
Total	16

4 Results

Given the nature of our research questions, we got as close to the phenomena as possible by collecting information about the real pros and cons of XBRL after five years of implementation.

In order to collect enough data to adequately point out what users really think about XBRL, we went through an iterative process between "real" information (from interviews) and emerging paradigms (from the analysis of interviews).

The following analysis has been split into three subparagraphs that specifically examine results for each research question: (i) the knowledge of XBRL language and the real use of its taxonomy among users; (ii) existing limitations of XBRL and future required improvements, and (iii) costs and benefits related to XBRL.

4.1 Knowledge and Real Use of XBRL Among Users

Our first research question concerns the assessment of the actual knowledge and use of the XBRL language. XBRL is generally user-friendly, requiring no previous knowledge of IT background. Each entity can use XBRL to encode its financial statements, usually requiring explicit services to specialists (e.g. chartered professional accountants), and all users can use it to facilitate the analysis of financial data. In simple terms, XBRL is a tool that benefits all users of financial statements by providing increased functionality that comes from the standardization of business reporting terminology.

Focusing on the knowledge of XBRL among users, it is firstly useful to discriminate between the knowledge of the information technology background per se and the knowledge of the everyday use of the taxonomy.

Users unsurprisingly seem not interested in the IT background and features, but just limit their knowledge of the XBRL to the simple definition of the language. In other terms, people interviewed usually simply define XBRL as a mark-up language used to communicate financial and business data electronically.

It is interesting to point out that the higher the seniority of the interviewee, the lower is familiarity with XBRL. For instance, within the chartered professional accountant firms, employees that just produce and transmit financial statements have the more extensive and inside knowledge of the language, while senior chartered accountants seem not to be interested in XBRL. That situation can limit the use of XBRL to the simple respect of mandatory rules to transmit financial statements, instead of allowing users to explore its potential strengths. Thus, an appropriate XBRL knowledge by seniors could enhance the practical use of the language, permitting to take advantage of its increasing functionalities over traditional electronic formats and paper.

With reference to the auditors, it is interesting to point out that so far they seem to be not interested in taking advantages from XBRL potential benefits since the independent examination of records and financial accounts of a firm, in order to check their accuracy and compliance with established procedures, comes much before the release of financial statements that enclose that information.

Additionally, the interviewed bank manager and the director of the local Revenue Agency express the same view. Both states that the actual exploitation of the benefits of this language is still limited and provide additional evidence that XBRL simply represents a more sophisticated tool for mandatory filing of financial statements.

As regards financial analysts, on the contrary, some of them seem to use XBRL with considerable benefits. Firstly, the interviewed analyst takes advantage from XBRL through an in-house developed software that automatically reads and imports XBRL data, thus simplifying sorting and comparison of accounting information. Additionally, they are aware that this language can facilitate the massive upload of data to be used in the analysis (with substantial time savings). This is why they generally require companies to send them financial statements in XBRL format. In the light of these requests, the following case quote reveals that companies usually do not know what XBRL actually is:

Financial analyst

In my opinion it is important to empower the knowledge of XBRL among firms. If you ask a firm the financial statement in XBRL format, you can find it unprepared. Sometimes, firms with more than ten credit lines with banks do not know XBRL; this means that banks do not usually require financial statements in this format.

Finally, financial analysts believe that the transmission of financial statements through chartered accountants can drastically reduce the knowledge (and the use) of XBRL by the firms; each problem related with XBRL "is transferred" by the firms to chartered professional accountants. Chartered accountants are aware that software packages for professionals can solve the problem, without any significant increase in the software cost, and firms transferring the "problem" reduce their capability to benefit from potential uses of the language as well.

4.2 Existing Limitations and Future Necessary Improvements

From a theoretical point of view, XBRL presents different potential benefits, especially in order to improve the financial communication process. Particularly, it can provide more timely and efficient analysis of financial data both internally and across companies, and expand usability of externally reported financial information. Ideally, it can also improve cost accounting, performance measurement, and overall decision-making for firms, especially if a real and deep link with the general ledger exists.

That said, however, it is not a valid substitute for the financial accounting systems and the related procedures required to prepare Italian GAAP-compliant financial statements. XBRL, as a standardized language, just improves the usability and comparability of financial statement information, but it does not check the accuracy and completeness of financial statements for compliance with accounting standards. XBRL is useful in order to enhance the traditional financial reporting but it does not provide more data than standard financial statements do. It simply provides the same data in a format that enhances subsequent analysis and comparisons across companies. Even the taxonomy validation just allows preparers to validate the document for consistency and quality, but it does not check whether preparers have used the correct tag or assigned the right value to each tag.

At the same time, the mentioned extension of XBRL to notes could really boost the usefulness of the taxonomy. This is the opinion expressed by all the interviewees. The following quote reveals that tagging the notes could produce benefits to all actors:

Chartered professional accountant

Tagging the notes could really boost the use of XBRL. Firstly, filling in a mandatory form should reduce the present practice to talk a lot on a mandatory item but saying nothing, or simply eluding the mandatory requirements. If a specific tag on a mandatory data exists, you can't avoid filling in the data or the existence of missing information should rise.

Secondly, if an authentic link should exist between XBRL tags and general ledger, software could check whether preparers have used the correct values to generate the financial statement, thus improving the real use of XBRL even in the audit procedures.

It is necessarily to point out that the mandatory extension of XBRL to the notes (in Italy from 2015) could really change the usability of financial data and improving the comparability across companies.

The experimental version of XBRL notes in Italy uses tags on specific items of both tables and narratives identifying quantitative data and text blocks. For instance, there should be a significant improvement in information on details of cost of administrators, leasing, changes in intangibles and tangible assets, and details of credits with a split for geographical area as well. All these data could help to better compare firms, improving the efficiency of financial analyses.

That said, the real benefit for users could arise, however, if a clear link between tags in financial statements (and notes) and general ledger exists, enabling to check for accuracy of financial information with a clear understanding of the origin of data and improving a real comparison between the same items and values of different companies.

Even if some improvements seem to be possible, at the moment some limitations exist. Firstly, a local office of Revenue Agency exposes the existence of problems in displaying XBRL documents, thus increasing the amount of time required for each analysis. A real use of XBRL potentialities by the Revenue Agency is postponed over the medium or long term. Secondly, the scarce knowledge on XBRL strengths among firms reduces the practical use of the taxonomy in cost accounting, performance measurement, and overall decision-making procedures. Lastly, the exclusion of notes significantly reduces the power of XBRL, only facilitating the uploading of financial data in more usable ways.

The extension of XBRL to notes could improve the comparability across firms, enabling better knowledge of financial data and enhancing the transparency of financial statements.

4.3 Who Benefits from XBRL?

As confirmed by our interviewees, the main cost of XBRL is just the initial (*una tantum*) time required by the implementation phase. Even if there are no costs for users, at present the benefits seem to be modest as well.

Actually, excluding the clear improvement in the uploading of financial data, the real comparability of data across firms is subject to the correct typing of the right value to each tag, and any other potential improvement is subject to both XBRL extension to notes and the existence of a clear link between general ledger and tags.

Specifically, the following quote highlights that the lack of such a connection prevents the existence of internal benefits for firms. So far, the only current benefits of XBRL seem to be for external users of financial information.

Auditor

There will not be an internal benefit for firms from XBRL language until there is a real (and clear) connection between general ledger and tags. If it is not a case, the only benefits of XBRL are for external users of financial data. Specifically, I think that the main benefits of this taxonomy are currently limited to a simpler comparability across firms, and especially to the easier massive upload of financial data for data aggregators firms.

With reference to comparability, I think that a significant improvement could come from the use of a standard chart of accounts (as the so called "plan comptable général" in France) that only discriminates some industries, strictly linked with both tags and general ledger. In this case, XBRL could become useful for auditors as well.

Thus, financial analysts and data aggregators (Bureau Van Dijk, Thomson Reuters, etc.) seem to be the ones obtaining the main benefits from XBRL implementation. The former could reduce time employed in the upload of financial data. The latter could both significantly reduce costs previously required to replicate companies' financial statements into the database (or acquiring information at a lower price from external data aggregators), and reduce the time needed to update data, thus improving the timeliness of data. The existence of a specific tag for each item enable massive and immediate upload of financial data without any manual typing, thus significantly reducing initial costs for data aggregator firms.

Actually, other users of financial information (e.g. banks, chartered accountants, auditors) do not benefit from XBRL but at the same time they do not have any cost from it. The real challenge for the usefulness of the taxonomy is in its extension to the financial statement notes. Even if the taxonomy is not a disclosure checklist, the implementation of the right tags on the notes could enhance the quality and transparency of financial data, thus improving the practical use of taxonomy by all users, especially in comparisons across firms, but also for auditing procedures and for internal use of data in cost accounting, performance measurement, and overall decision-making for firms. The following quote from an interview to a bank manager highlights the current lack of direct benefits for some categories of users.

Bank manager

> So far, we do not have direct benefits from the XBRL mandatory adoption for non listed firms. XBRL has not brought any change in our procedures: we still collect data on companies requiring loans from a data provider and then supplement their analyses looking at financial statements in paper format.
>
> Talking about future, we might expect an increase in notes disclosure due to the new taxonomy, that might be seen by firms as a sort of guidance. This is the only indirect benefit which I can foresee at the moment.

The emerging absence of costs related to XBRL implementation is an interesting aspect to emphasise as well. In order to avoid a no-cost no-benefit paradigm, it is useful to further promote XBRL enhancement (e.g. through a better tagging of notes) in order to create the conditions for an extensive diffusion of benefits among all users, avoiding the current appropriation of benefits from a few users (such as analysts and data aggregator firms).

5   Conclusions

Our study aims at investigating the effects of XBRL adoption for a wide range of actors involved in this process, focusing on the professionals' XBRL awareness as well as actual costs and its present and future benefits.

Based on previous research and in pursuit of our objectives, we have carried out a descriptive research on the Italian context using a qualitative approach. Indeed, Italy represents an interesting context for this field study because of the mandatory filing of financial statements in XBRL for unlisted companies since 2009. This gives us the opportunity to shed light on the impact of XBRL after some years from its adoption by companies that generally have a limited administrative structure and that so far have been rather neglected by academic research.

We collected data with semi-structured interviews to different categories of actors involved in XBRL reporting, such as chartered accountants, auditors, bank managers, analysts and a director of a local office of the Revenue Agency.

Our results suggest that five years of mandatory adoption have not led to a widespread awareness of XBRL features and considerable benefits among professionals yet. This is in line with a very limited use by preparers that generally rely on practitioners to simply convert financial statements. Overall, it seems that so far XBRL has very scarce practical applications in the majority of actors' activities providing little benefits with extremely modest costs as well. Only some users (e.g. some financial analysts) have already integrated XBRL in their practice and are getting considerable savings and benefits from its adoption.

In summary, our findings highlight that so far the XBRL mandatory adoption in Italy has not achieved an overall substantial impact on real practice yet.

This study has important implications from several points of view.

Firstly, it has public policy implications by delivering insight into present limitations and effects of XBRL, thus supporting regulators and government agencies in their decisions to enhance an effective and more pervasive XBRL implementation. Additionally, results from the current study draw attention to the need to foster awareness of XBRL potential benefits.

In such a perspective, public agencies, together with the local jurisdiction, and professional associations can play a key role in promoting XBRL. An increased XBRL awareness also needs the effort of the academic community through additional research and education initiatives directed to both practitioners and future accounting professionals.

Finally, our findings have practical implications by showing the existing gap between XBRL potential benefits and real practice. It highlights the opportunity for professionals to integrate XBRL in their activities in order to achieve a competitive advantage over competitors and, more generally, to enhance the financial reporting process and to improve effectiveness in resource allocation.

However, the study's findings should be considered in light of certain limitations. Particularly, it could be interesting to involve more categories of actors in order to obtain a more comprehensive picture of real XBRL impact. Additionally, it is to note that XBRL mandatory adoption in Italy was limited to balance sheet and income statement, with XBRL transmission of notes required only from 2015.

Future research can contribute additional evidence to further identify and explain the real impact of XBRL adoption involving a wider range of actors and exploring contexts with different requirements on XBRL adoption.

References

1. Debreceny, R., Gray, G.L.: The production and use of semantically rich accounting reports on the internet: XML and XBRL. Int. J. Account. Inf. Syst. **2**, 47–74 (2001)
2. Bonsón, E.: The role of XBRL in Europe. Int. J. Digit. Account. Res. **1**, 101–110 (2001)
3. Bonsón, E., Cortijo, V., Escobar, T.: Towards the global adoption of XBRL using international financial reporting standards (IFRS). Int. J. Account. Inf. Syst. **10**, 46–60 (2009)
4. Pinsker, R., Li, S.: Costs and benefits of XBRL adoption: early evidence. Commun. ACM **51**, 47–50 (2008)
5. Hodge, F.D., Kennedy, J.J., Maines, L.A.: Does search-facilitating technology improve the transparency of financial reporting? Acc. Rev. **79**, 687–703 (2004)
6. Baldwin, A.A., Trinkle, B.S.: The impact of XBRL: a delphi investigation. Int. J. Digital Account. Res. **11**, 1–24 (2011)
7. Doni, F., Inghirami, I.E.: Strategy Management Systems e XBRL: mutui rapporti e interconnessioni. In: Zambon, S. (ed.) XBRL e informativa aziendale. Traiettorie, innovazioni e sfide, Part III, pp. 286–311. Franco Angeli, Milano (2010)
8. Piechocki, M., Felden, C., Gräning, A., Debreceny, R.: Design and standardisation of XBRL solutions for governance and transparency. Int. J. Discl. Gov. **6**, 224–240 (2009)

9. Ward, G.: How XBRL can enhance the credibility of audited financial statements. IFAC, New York (2004)

10. Boritz, E.J., No, W.G.: Security in XML-based financial reporting services on the internet. J. Account. Public Policy **24**, 11–35 (2005)

11. Pinsker, R.: XBRL awareness in auditing: a sleeping giant? Manag. Auditing J. **18**, 732–736 (2003)

12. Liu, C., Wang, T., Yao, L.J.: XBRL's impact on analyst forecast behavior: an empirical study. J. Account. Public Policy **33**, 69–82 (2014)

13. Efendi, J., Park, J.D., Smith, L.M.: Do XBRL filings enhance informational efficiency? Early evidence from post-earnings announcement drift. J. Bus. Res. **67**, 1099–1105 (2014)

14. Yoon, H., Zo, H., Ciganek, A.P.: Does XBRL adoption reduce information asymmetry? J. Bus. Res. **64**, 157–163 (2011)

15. Kim, J.W., Lim, J.-H., No, W.G.: The effect of first wave mandatory XBRL reporting across the financial information environment. J. Inf. Syst. **26**, 127–153 (2012)

16. Liu, C., Luo, X.R., Sia, C.L., O'Farrell, G., Teo, H.H.: The impact of XBRL adoption in PR China. Decis. Support Syst. **59**, 242–249 (2014)

17. Alles, M., Debreceny, R.: The evolution and future of XBRL research. Int. J. Account. Inf. Syst. **13**, 83–90 (2012)

18. Dunne, T., Helliar, C., Lymer, A., Mousa, R.: Stakeholder engagement in internet financial reporting: The diffusion of XBRL in the UK. Br. Account. Rev. **45**, 167–182 (2013)

19. Ossevatorio ICT&Professionisti: Se parliamo di Professionisti, in realtà, parliamo di imprese! Politecnico di Milano (2014)

20. Hopwood, A.G.: On trying to study accounting in the contexts in which it operates. Acc. Organ. Soc. **8**, 287–305 (1983)

21. Rubin, H.J., Rubin, I.S.: Qualitative interviewing: the art of hearing data. Sage Publications, Thousand Oaks (1995)

22. McCracken, G.: The long interview. Sage University Paper Series on Qualitative Research Methods. Beverly Hills, Sage (1988)

23. Stoner, G., Holland, J.: Using case studies in finance research. In Humphrey, C., Lee, B. (eds.) The Real Life Guide to Accounting Research: A Behind-the-Scenes View of Using Qualitative Research Methods, Section One, pp. 37–56. Elsevier, Oxford (2004)

Benefits and Barriers of Social/Collaborative ERP Systems: A State of the Art and Research Agenda

Davide Aloini, Riccardo Dulmin, Valeria Mininno
and Alessandro Spagnesi

Abstract Despite a growing interest on the topic of a "social or collaborative" evolution of ERP systems, studies analyzing the suitability and more in general managerial implications of this process are lack in the literature. This research aims to explore key benefits and obstacles of such software integration providing a systematic in-depth investigation of the academic literature in the field. Fourteen main benefits and eight barriers were identified and analyzed while a first interpretive framework is drawn in order to provide valuable direction for further research.

Keywords Enterprise resource planning (ERP) · Social, business process management · Benefits · Barriers · Literature review

1 Introduction

The topic of a "social or collaborative" evolution of ERP systems (also ERP 2.0, intended as the inclusion of Web 2.0 tools e.g. social networks, wikis, mashups and tags into the traditional ERP system's backbone), has recently attracted the attention of practitioners and academicians [1]. On one hand because of the orientation of Web 2.0 tools toward collaboration, flexible communication and knowledge sharing which seems to be able to address, at least partially, some of the recognized ERP problems leading to sub-utilization (e.g. high complexity, centralized control, administrative orientation, poor adaptability of the system to local needs, imposing best practices, over-standardization of communication and loss of social interaction among users). On the other, because the new functionalities provided by Web 2.0 and Social software are promising innovation for typical back-end activities such as in R&D, Purchasing, Sales and Marketing, innovating the way of working and

D. Aloini (✉) · R. Dulmin · V. Mininno · A. Spagnesi
University of Pisa, Pisa, Italy
e-mail: davide.aloini@dsea.unipi.it

© Springer International Publishing Switzerland 2016
D. Mancini et al. (eds.), *Strengthening Information and Control Systems*,
Lecture Notes in Information Systems and Organisation 14,
DOI 10.1007/978-3-319-26488-2_13

definitely getting a new life for their processes in an Enterprise 2.0 perspective. The growing interest for the Enterprise 2.0 concept and related IS support is confirmed from in academic [2] and in the practitioners literature [3].

Evidence shows that a new class of company is emerging, the one that uses collaborative Web 2.0 technologies intensively to connect the internal efforts of employees and to extend the organization's reach to customers, partners, and suppliers [4]. As a consequence, the changing needs of "knowledge workers" interacting with the Enterprise Information System, particularly their call for a higher flexibility in the workflow management and support in managing social work connection, is another incentive for such an integration [5].

In this context, ERP and Web 2.0 seem complementary in their features: the ability of ERPs to provide support and control of company's business processes by pursuing centralization and standardization of the control flow, and the flexibility in addressing communication, collaboration, social interaction and knowledge sharing typical of a user-centric web 2.0 approach. This evidence clearly leads to a broadly perception of the potential value of ERP 2.0 solutions. However, new risks and managerial challenges also arise: fundamental problems may be related for example to safety and data protection for some business conversations, or to inconsistency or low reliability of some data flows which are intolerable for core ERP modules (e.g. HR, Accounting, Production Planning, etc.).

The debate on the topic is still embryonic and there is a need to shed further light by a more systematic and in-depth investigation. Particularly, this paper would be a first step in order to identify and analyze potential benefits and barriers of such innovation in order to allow a technical and managerial analysis of related implications.

2 Research Background

2.1 ERP 2.0: Embedding Web 2.0 into ERP Systems

Enterprise Resource Planning (ERP) systems are integrated software solutions used to manage organization's resources. Over time, ERP systems evolution has contributed to extend their coverage in terms of modules and functionalities so offering much more than the literal meanings. Actually, they integrate all departments and functions of a company into a single computer system that can serve different departments' needs [6, 7] and potentially extend functionalities also to external partners and process participants. In this process, Vendors, Consultants and also Academicians have been frequently called to evaluate the potential and applicability of adapting or embedding new functionalities to ERP systems, basically in order to improve support for company business processes taking advantage by emerging tools and technologies.

In recent years, companies increased the use of Enterprise Social Networks (ESN), thus trying to enter in the business world the ease of communication linked to the functionality of Web 2.0, such as social collaboration platform; instant messaging (chat); tagging people and document; creation of interest groups; share internal content; share external content; use new symbols for create information hashtagging# and mentions @; use of unstructured information (videos, images, conversations); internal search engine to search for people, documents and information; posts creation; tips on users with common points.

First examples of social software integration are available in the companies practice: for example in the HR area where social software can enhance social onboarding/social recruitment activities, Learning processes and Talent Management; or in Sales where social software may contribute to streamline processes as collaborative opportunity management, CRM, Sales on Demand; in Marketing to manage collaborative campaign; and even in Service and Post-sales to perform a collaborative service request resolution, for example building an ad hoc team (people from Sale, R&D, other functions) to solve customers' complaints, responding more effectively and efficiently to their needs. Moreover many financial processes are cross functional as it happens for collaborative budgeting, policies, procedures. In this context we cannot neglect to consider the potential support of Semantic Web Technologies for information management and process control (Semantic analysis of contents). Enterprise 2.0 tools, in fact, do not provide formal models for the creation and the management of such complex systems with large amounts of data [8].

With Enterprise 2.0, the collaborative philosophy of Web 2.0 is adopted in the company to support business processes and social software finds its way also in traditional systems such as ERPs. Main benefits might embrace typical structured back-end activities (standardized business processes) and especially ad hoc informal processes (highly variable) which are supported by agile and adaptive user centric software (e.g. project planning or customer relationship management).

The use of the collaboration tools might lead to capabilities applicable to a number of traditional company processes in order to streamline activities and fully support an agile and interactive management of intra and extra company workflow: working in groups with distant people directly from the office; using also informal communication for business activities; enabling users to track and extrapolate the information flowing within the company, both formal (reports, economic data, budget, delivery notes ...) and informal (chat, post images, video, ...); making conversations leaner without having to use long sessions of e-mail; working with conversations in real-time; simplifying contacts with partners, the management of warehouses, orders and production schedule; facilitating relationship with the customer before and after sales.

They might also contribute positively to the system adoption improving system usability. ERP systems are complex and rigid systems so that many modules are often under-used, skipped or neglected, while the ESN platforms tend to be abandoned if they are not strictly related to the core business. According to this perspective, the integration between ERP systems and ESN might help the usability of ERP technology and also aid ESN systems to be closer to company core processes.

2.2 Literature Review

Literature is polarized around two different positions: Academics and Practitioners. Their initiatives are going on with different speeds and following complementary directions. If Web 2.0 irruption in the ERP world is already a reality for some Vendors (particularly in CRM, SALES and HR modules), the existing market solutions are not mature but still in an experimental phase and there is a lack of research in the field. Nevertheless, a more systematic approach is needed in Academic research. The state of academic literature, in fact, is still embryonic and the amount of production decreases vertiginously if we leave the classical concept of ERP adding keywords of "social/collaborative integration".

With the exception of Grabor et al. [1] which suggest a step-by-step method supporting the identification of ERP business processes which could be of interest for the integration of Web 2.0 functionalities, the most of academic contributions focus more in general on the Enterprise 2.0 topic and on the use Social Software from a strategic perspective. Papers are spread among different research communities and countless publications from Computer–Human Interaction to System Sciences [9] dealing particularly with the fields of innovation [10–14] and knowledge management [15, 16]. Most of the works are theoretical or conceptual, while empirical works are about experimental/ stand-alone solutions which are scarcely integrated with company processes and information systems.

Just recently research on the use of social technologies moved in operation management areas. Preliminary studies started to be assessed in social Customer Relationship Management (CRM) [17] promising direct market access, interactive contact, better demand understanding [18–21]. Introductory discussions have taken place on topics related to social Business Process Management (BPM) [22–24] and social software-driven SCM innovation.

In this context, the practitioners' world (Companies, Vendors and Consultants) played as first mover. First pioneering experiences of social software adoption can be dated at the beginning of 2000s when some big corporate (e.g. UK, British Telecom) and consulting firms activated experimental implementations. Grabot et al. [1] assess a wide review on these cases investigating both software, and implemented functionalities, and also offering a detailed classification of the industrial applications. Nevertheless, major consulting groups (among the others IBM and McKinsey) [25–27] launched studies on the social phenomena in order to identify and classify potential and perceived business benefits [28]. Finally, most active ICT players (e.g. SAP, Oracle, IBM, Infor) started intensive investigations and experimental developments of social information platform/systems embedding social functionalities into the most promising ERP modules. See, for example, SAP (Jam), Oracle (WebCenter), IBM (Social Connections), Infor (Ming.le).

Whether these evidences are neither exhaustive nor conclusive, they show:

- a growing interest of the companies for the 2.0 tools in different key business areas
- a low integration of the 2.0 functionalities to the existent processes and systems
- a call for integration with the main IS of companies in order to making operational the Enterprise 2.0 paradigm.

3 Research Objectives

This research aims to explore key benefits and barriers (obstacles) of including Web 2.0 functionalities into the ERP systems. It would be a first step in order to assess a systematic and in-depth investigation of such innovation. At our best knowledge, in fact, studies analyzing the applicability of such software integration are lack, if not completely absent in the literature. Thus, research directions are twofold: on one hand, investigating the business value of social software integration into ERP, on the other hand to analyze the technical and managerial concerns which could affect such a process.

Here following the main research objectives:

- Investigate the applicability of integrating Web 2.0 functionalities into the ERP systems
- Identify potential benefits and perceived risk and barriers
- Draw a first interpretive framework to analyze their relations, differences and impact on the business processes
- Identify research areas needing further attention and deployment.

4 Research Methodology

In order to achieve the previous objectives and due to the exploratory nature of the research, a systematic review on the topic was assessed in order to analyze the state of the art of the academic literature. It goes through three main stage: data/article collection and screening, data analysis including benefits and barriers identification and article classification, and finally synthesis and evaluation.

Stage 1—Data collection. The examined papers consist of articles published by the most important world-wide specialists: Emerald, IEEE-Xplore, Science Direct, Springer and, due to the novelty of the topic and the very latest development, also most recent IS conferences. Initially we collected approximately 500 articles using web facilities (Fig. 1). After a preliminary screening (we decided to keep just peer-reviewed documents from journals, books, conferences with more than 2 pages, also skipping those addressing simply the use of social and web 2.0 tools outside from specific business processes), we fell to 121 papers. After that, a second

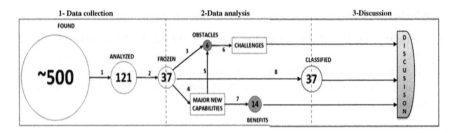

Fig. 1 Literature review: data collection and analysis process. **Description**: *1* reading the abstracts and extraction of potentially interesting documents; *2* document analysis performed by Publish or Perish and Nvivo10; *3* content and citation analysis by Nvivo10 and document analysis to find out obstacles; *4* analysis and re-reading of documents to find the most important new enabled capabilities; *5* analysis of additional potential obstacles deriving from the new capabilities; *6* obstacles put the company in front of new challenges; *7* the achievement of new capabilities lead to the expected benefits of integration; *8* classification of the article accordingly to the dimensions of the analysis

and more in-depth document analysis was performed by Publish or Perish and Nvivo10 tools to obtain information and documents definitively consistent with the research. Finally, the sample of interest was made of 37 papers.

Stage 2—Data analysis. Once selected, papers were analyzed:

In a first step, benefits and risks were identified and a first classification of articles was achieved in order to homogenize the different definitions and meanings of words used (see Fig. 1). Through the use of research software as "Nvivo10" a content analysis was performed in order to extract the most interesting concepts from various papers. A second step was finalized to design a framework in order to provide a picture of the state of the art of academic research. We have explored the literature following two dimensions:

1. *Research scope and focus*, that is the core objective of the paper in terms of process applicability and the investigation focus. In this perspective here the main dimensions for papers' coding and classification:

   - Scope: distinguishing between research addressing specifically the core ERP processes, general BPM interactions, B2B collaboration in a SCM perspective or Marketing/CRM related processes (ERP, BPM, SCM, CRM),
   - Focus: Technology (collaborative technology and functionalities), People (support to employee interactions), Documents (support to documental workflow).

2. *Research type and methodology*, we distinguished among conceptual (descriptive vs normative) and empirical (qualitative vs quantitative) contributions.

   Stage 3—Discussion. Contributions were analysed in order to catch how web 2.0/social software functionalities and technologies can benefits company business processes. Preliminary findings allow to define the state of the art in the field and to draw possible interesting directions for further research.

5 Findings and Discussion

5.1 Benefits and Barriers

The study reviewed the current state of academic research about the integration of social collaboration tools and management software. The benefits founded are listed and explained in Table 1. They are mostly related to improved internal-external

Table 1 Business process benefits

ID	Benefit	References
B.1	Control and storage of data	Erol et al. (2010), Koskinen (2006), Wu and Chao (2008)
B.2	Customer experience	Malthouse et al. (2013), Woodcock and Green (2010)
B.3	System usability for employees	Brambilla et al. (2012), Hawryszkiewycz (2010), Kemsley (2010), Nitsche et al. (2009), Ozkan and Abidin (2010), Schmidt and Nurcan (2009), Tapscott (2008)
B.4	Enterprise agility and innovation capability	Brambilla et al. (2012), Grabot et al. (2014), Schmidt and Nurcan (2009), Wang et al. (2011)
B.5	External collaboration	Adebanjo and Michaelides (2010), Hawryszkiewycz (2010), Koskinen (2006), Wu and Chao (2009), Brambilla et al. (2012), Reinhold and Alt (2011)
B.6	External communication	Adebanjo and Michaelides (2010), Bruno et al. (2010), Jussila et al. (2014), Koskinen (2006), Lee et al. (2011), Malthouse et al. (2013), Schmidt and Nurcan (2009), Wu and Chao (2009)
B.7	Internal collaboration	Brambilla et al. (2012), Erol et al. (2010), Hawryszkiewycz (2010), Kemsley (2010), Koskinen (2006), Wang et al. (2011)
B.8	Internal communication	Jussila et al. (2014), Koskinen (2006), Wang et al. (2011)
B.9	Knowledge and information capture	Adebanjo and Michaelides (2010), Hawryszkiewycz (2010), Koskinen (2006), Lee et al. (2011), Reinhold and Alt (2011), Schmidt and Nurcan (2009), Shafiei and Sundaram (2004),Wu and Chao (2009)
B.10	Productivity of employees	Kemsley (2010), Lee et al. (2011), Ozkan and Abidin (2010), Nitsche et al. (2009)
B.11	Understanding of the market	Adebanjo and Michaelides (2010), Deng et al. (2009), Jussila et al. (2014), Reinhold and Alt (2011)
B.12	Time savings in marketing	Jussila et al. (2014), Mohan et al. (2008)
B.13	Operational costs	Adebanjo and Michaelides (2010), Elragal and Haddara (2012), Erol et al. (2010), Jussila et al. (2014), Kemsley (2010), Ozkan and Abidin (2010), Woodcock and Green (2010)
B.14	Customer related costs	Jussila et al. (2014), Mohan et al. (2008), Ozkan and Abidin (2010), Woodcock and Green (2010)

Table 2 Obstacles

ID	Obstacle	References
O.1	Data security	Bruno et al. (2010), Jussila et al. (2014), Kemsley (2010), Koskinen (2006)
O.2	Architecture and language integration	Wang et al. (2011), Wu and Chao (2009), Bogel et al. (2013), Reinhold and Alt (2011)
O.3	Overestimation of financial benefits	Bruno et al. (2010), Jussila et al. (2014)
O.4	Privacy respect	Malthouse et al. (2013), Ozkan and Abidin (2010)
O.5	Data quality versus quantity	Erol et al. (2010)
O.6	Resistance to internal change	Adebanjo and Michaelides (2010), Jussila et al. (2014), Koskinen (2006), Li et al. (2012), Woodcock and Green (2010)

communication, coordination and collaboration capabilities typical of social tools' agility and flexibility, but also to the improvement of process operations and monitoring, typical of ERP (data storage and management, transactional processing and operational planning and control).

Possible obstacles are listed in Table 2. They mostly deal with the themes of integration between the different architectures of software systems and the ability to allow an exchange of information in order to be more agile and flexible without compromising safety of data exchange.

5.2 State of the Art

Figure 2 reports paper distribution analysed according to the investigated dimension of the analysis.

Evidence shows that academic research in the field is mainly focused on general topics and widely refers to ERP and BPM support more than to single processes. More specific contributions concern with CRM/SCM processes. Proposals analyze the issue from a technological perspective emphasizing the support to internal-external employee's interaction.

As concerning research type and methodology, we can assert that the topic is discussed both conceptually by theoretical model or proposal analysing issues on integrating web 2.0 functionalities into ERP systems/processes and empirically

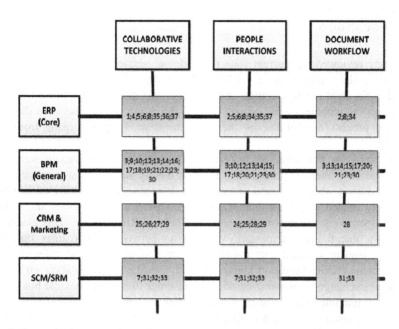

Fig. 2 Research aim: dimensions. *Numeration of reported papers is coherent with Appendix A

mostly by qualitative analysing of case study or ideas of experimental application of such software and systems. Real and complete implementation project of the proposed models are however very lack. Quantitative studies are rarely present in the literature (Table 3).

Table 3 Research scope versus type and methodology

		Research type and methodology			
		Conceptual		Empirical	
		Descriptive	Normative	Qualitative	Quantitative
Research scope	ERP	1; 2; 9; 37	6; 36	4; 5; 7; 8; 11; 34	35
	BPM	10; 13; 14; 16; 17; 21	3; 18; 19	12; 15; 20; 22; 23	30
	CRM	27	–	24; 25; 26; 29	28
	SCM	32	–	31	33

6 Conclusions

The study reviewed the current state of academic research about the integration of social collaboration tools and ERP software. Benefits and obstacles are discussed at the light of the literature and then analysed in order to define a research agenda on the emergent topic on one hand highlighting the link between the first and new process capabilities, on the other the new challenges rising from the seconds.

Findings show that academic research on the subject is at an initial/developing stage. The ERP/Web 2.0 integration topic is mostly discussed at a conceptual/theoretical level while empirical research is lack or absent. The identified benefits are mainly related to the communication area, typical of social tools, and to the process operations and monitoring area, typical of ERP software. This evidence confirms a potential complementarity and synergy between the two areas. Possible obstacles, instead, concern with the challenge of integrating radical different software systems architectures and languages, and with the ability to allow an easier and faster exchange of information and data in order to be more flexible but at the same time guarantee safety for the company data.

Thus, the research offer interesting insights at different levels. Firstly, at a theoretical level, providing an interpretative framework explaining the value and the potential risks of embedding social software functionalities into ERP systems. While the benefits, risks and feasibility of ERP social evolution are still mostly hidden, the subsequent impacts could be potentially huge in life of companies because of the numerous and deep interactions with the way people work, human-process-system interactions, information flows (integration) within and outside the company, management practices, systems of incentives and rewards, decision making/management, human resource management, intellectual capital sharing. The present work covers just some aspects of the topic but can hopefully open many directions for further research, as for example in Management theory, IT Management, and also IT-Project Management.

As for managerial implications, the research would set a first step to understand how to apply social media into Enterprise software in order to support different business processes and enhance reengineering and optimization opportunities. Approaching a first empirical evaluation of the benefits and risks of such integration, we also hope to contribute to the evolution of future EIS/ERP 2.0 systems.

Appendix A

See Table A.4.

Table A.4 Coding table of analyzed papers

ID	Article
1.	Elragal, A. and Haddara, M. (2012). The future of ERP systems: Look backward before moving forward. 4th Conference of ENTERprise Information Systems—aligning technology, organizations and people (CENTERIS 2012)
2.	Shafiei, F. and Sundaram, D. (2004). Multi – Enterprise collaborative enterprise resource planning and Decision support systems. Proceedings of the 37th Hawaii International Conference on System Sciences—2004
3.	Hawryszkiewycz, L.T. (2010). A framework for synchronizing collaborative technology with changing enterprise environment. 2010 International Symposium on Collaborative Technologies and Systems (CTS)
4.	Heden, R. and Sedera, F. et al. (2012). Archival analysis of enterprise resource planning systems: The current state and future direction. Thirty Third International Conference on Information Systems, Orlando 2012
5.	Wang, Y. and Reaseley, A. et al. (2011). Combining ERP systems with enterprise 2.0. ENTERprise Information Systems Communications in Computer and Information Science Volume 219, 2011, pp 198–207
6.	Grabot, B. and Houè, R. et al. (2012). Introducing "2.0" functionalities in an ERP. Advances in Production Management Systems. Competitive Manufacturing for Innovative Products and Services IFIP Advances in Information and Communication Technology Volume 398, 2013, pp 104–111
7.	Li, M. and Chen, G. et al. (2012). A social collaboration platform for enterprise social networking. Proceedings of the 2012 IEEE 16th International Conference on Computer Supported Cooperative Work in Design. Wuhan China
8.	Wu, H. and Chao, L. (2009). Community Collaboration for ERP Implementation. Journal software IEEE. Volume 26. Issue 6
9.	Andriole, S.J. (2012). Seven Indisputable Technology Trends That Will Define 2015. Communications of the Association for Information Systems: Vol. 30, Article 4
10.	Appleford, S., Bottum, J.R., and Thatcher, J.B. (2014), Understanding the social web: towards defining an interdisciplinary research agenda for information systems, ACM SIGMIS Database archive Volume 45 Issue 1, Pages 29–37
11.	Ebrahimi, S. (2012). Knowledge Management For Enterprise Systems: A Review Of The Literature. PACIS 2012 Proceedings. Paper 72
12.	Bogel, S. and Stieglitz, S. et al. (2013). Bringing together BPM and social software. Proceedings of the Nineteenth Americas Conference on Information Systems, Chicago, Illinois, August 15–17, 2013
13.	Erol, S and, Granitzer, M. et al. (2010). Combining BPM and social software: contradiction or chance?. Journal of Software Maintenance and Evolution: Research and Practice. Volume 22, Issue 6–7, pages 449–476, October–November 2010
14.	Kemsley, S. (2010). Enterprise 2.0 meets business process management. International Handbooks on Information Systems 2010, pp 565–574. Springer
15.	Bider, I. and Johanneson, P. Et al. (2010). In search of the Holy Grail: Integrating social software with BPM experience report. BPMDS 2010 and EMMSAD 2010, LNBIP 50, pp. 1–13, 2010. Springer-Verlag Berlin Heidelberg 2010
16.	Schmidt, R. and Nurcan, S. (2009). BPM and social software. Business Process Management Workshops. Lecture Notes in Business Information Processing Volume 17, 2009, pp 649–658. Springer

(continued)

Table A.4 (continued)

ID	Article
17.	Lee, J. and Jang, J.Y. et al. (2011). Processcodi: A case study on social BPM through integration of SNS, mind map, and BPMS. Future Generation Information Technology Lecture Notes in Computer Science Volume 7105, 2011, pp 378–383. Springer
18.	Brambilla, M. and Fraternali, P. et al. (2012). BPMN and design patterns for engineering social BPM solutions. Business Process Management Workshops. Lecture Notes in Business Information Processing Volume 99, 2012, pp 219–230. Springer
19.	Molhanec, M. (2012). Enterprise systems meet social BPM. Advanced Information Systems Engineering Workshops. Lecture Notes in Business Information Processing Volume 112, 2012, pp 413–424. Springer
20.	Kurz, M. and Scherer, M. et al. (2013). Applying BPM 2.0 in BPM implementation project. OTM 2013 Workshops, LNCS 8186, pp. 42–46, 2013. Springer-Verlag Berlin Heidelberg 2013
21.	Bruno, G. and Dengler, F. et al. (2011). Key challenges for enabling agile BPM with social software. Journal of Software Maintenance and Evolution: Research and Practice. Volume 23, Issue 4, pages 297–326, June 2011. John Wiley & Sons, Ltd
22.	Fraternali, P. Brambilla, M. et al. (2011). A model-driven approach to social BPM applications. Social BPM Handbook, BPM and Workflow Handbook series, Future Strategies. Pages 95–112, USA, June 2011
23.	Niehaves, B. and Plattfaut, R. (2010). Collaborative Business Process Management: Exploring Themes, Achievements, and Perspectives. ECIS 2010 Proceedings. Paper 30
24.	Malthouse, E.C. and Haenlein, M. et al. (2013). Managing Customer Relationships in the Social Media Era: Introducing the Social CRM House. Journal of Interactive Marketing. Volume 27, Issue 4, November 2013, Pages 270–280
25.	Deng, X.L. and Zhang, L. et al. (2009). Implementation and research of social CRM tool in mobile boss based on complex network. The 1st International Conference on Information Science and Engineering (ICISE2009)
26.	Reinhold, O. and Alt, R. (2011). Analytical Social CRM: Concept and Tool Support. 24th Bled eConference eFuture: Creating Solutions for the Individual, Organisations and Society. June 12–15, 2011; Bled, Slovenia
27.	Mohan, S. Choi, E. et al. (2008). Conceptual modelling of enterprise application system using social networking and web 2.0 "social CRM system". International conference on Convergence & Hybrid Information Technology 2008, Daejeon, Korea. Published IEEE Computer Society
28.	Woodcock, N. and Green, A. (2011). Social CRM as a business strategy. Journal of Database Marketing & Customer Strategy Management (2011) 18. Pages 50–64
29.	Petrovic, O. (2010). A digital platform for marketing communications in the mobile and social media space. Software Services for e-World. IFIP Advances in Information and Communication Technology Volume 341, 2010, pp 182–192. Springer
30.	Andriole, S.J. (2010). Business impact of Web 2.0 technologies. Commun. ACM 53, 12, 67–79. DOI=10.1145/1859204.1859225http://doi.acm.org/10.1145/1859204.1859225
31.	Adebanjo, D. and Michaelides, R. (2010), Analysis of Web 2.0 enabled e-clusters: A case study, Technovation, Volume 30, Issue 4, Pages 238–248, ISSN 0166-4972, http://dx.doi.org/10.1016/j.technovation.2009.09.001
32.	Koskinen, T., (2006). Social Software for Industrial Integration, Proceeding OZCHI'06 Proceedings of the 18th Australia conference on Computer-Human Interaction: Design: Activities, Artefacts and Environments Pages 381–384

(continued)

Table A.4 (continued)

ID	Article
33.	Jussila et al. (2014), Social Media Utilization in business-tobusiness relationships of technology industry firms. 30, Computers in Human Behaviour pp. 606–613
34.	Ozkan, N. and Abidin, W.Z. (2010). Suggestion of web 2.0 mashups for human resource management. International Conference on Education and Management Technology (ICEMT), 2010, Cairo, Egypt
35.	Babaian, T. Lucas, W. et al. (2012). Evaluating the collaborative critique method. CHI 2012, May 5–10, 2012, Austin, Texas, USA
36.	Hofmann, P. (2008). "ERP is Dead, Long Live ERP", IEEE Internet Computing, vol.12, no. 4, pp. 84–88, July/August 2008, doi:10.1109/MIC.2008.78
37.	Nitsche, M. and Kindsmuller, M.C. et al. (2009). Social adaption of ERP software: Tagging UI elements. Online Communities and Social Computing. Lecture Notes in Computer Science Volume 5621, 2009, pp 391–400. Springer

References

1. Grabot, B., Mayere, A., Lauroua, F., Houe, R.: ERP 2.0, what for and how? Comput. Ind. **65**, 976–1000 (2014)
2. McAfee, A.P.: Enterprise 2.0: the dawn of emergent collaboration. MIT Sloan Manage. Rev. **47**, 20–28 (2006)
3. Kiron, D., Palmer D., Phillips, A.N., Kruschwitz, N.: Social business: what are companies really doing? MIT Sloan Manage. Rev. 1–28 (2012)
4. Bughin, J., Chui, M.: The rise of the networked enterprise: Web 2.0 finds its payday. McKinsey on Bus. Technol. **22**, 1–9 (2011)
5. Hawryszkiewycz, L.T.: A framework for synchronizing collaborative technology with changing enterprise environment. In: 2010 International Symposium on Collaborative Technologies and Systems (CTS) (2010)
6. Botta-Genoulaz, V., Millet, P.A.: A classification for better use of ERP systems. Comput. Ind. **56**, 573–587 (2005)
7. Klaus, H., Rosemann, M., Gable, G.G.: What is ERP? Inf. Syst. Frontiers **2**, 141–162 (2000)
8. Fensel, D., Bussler, C., Ding, Y., Omelayenko, B.: The web service modeling framework WSMF. Electron. Commer. Res. Appl. **1** (2002)
9. Giuffrida, R., Dittrich, Y.: Empirical studies on the use of social software in global software development: a systematic mapping study. Inf. Softw. Technol. **55**, 1143–1164 (2013)
10. Burger-Helmchen, T., Cohendet, P.: User communities and social software in the video game industry. Long Range Plann. **44**, 317–343 (2011)
11. Carbone, F., Contreras, J., Hernandez, J.Z., Gomez-Perez, J.M.: Open innovation in enterprise 3.0 framework: three case studies. Expert Syst. Appl. **39**, 929–939 (2012)
12. Hienerth, C., Keinz, P., Lettl, C.: Exploring the nature and implementation process of user-centric business models. Long Range Plann. **44**, 344–374 (2011)
13. Parmentier, G., Mangematin, V.: Orchestrating innovation with user communities in the creative industries. Technol. Forecast. Soc. Change **83**, 40–53 (2014)
14. Martínez-Torres, M.R.: Application of evolutionary computation techniques for the identification of innovators in open innovation communities. Expert Syst. Appl. **40**, 2503–2510 (2013)
15. Richard, D.: A social software/web 2.0 approach to collaborative knowledge engineering. Inf. Sci. **179**, 2515–2523 (2009)
16. von Krogh, G.: How does social software change knowledge management? Toward a strategic research agenda. J. Strateg. Inf. Syst. **21**, 154–164 (2012)

17. Faase, R., Helms, R., Spruit, M.: Web 2.0 in the CRM domain: defining social CRM. Int. J. Electron. Customer Relat. Manage. **5**, 1–22 (2011)
18. Ang, L.: Is SCRM really a good social media strategy? J Database Market. Customer Strategy Manage. **18**, 149–153 (2011)
19. Baird, C.H., Parasnis, G.: From social media to social customer relationship management. Strategy Leadersh. **39**, 30–37 (2011)
20. Alt, R., Reinhold, O.: Social customer relationship management. Bus. Inf. Syst. Eng. **5**, 287–291 (2012)
21. Woodcock, N., Broomfield, N., Downer, G., Starkey, M.: The evolving data architecture of social customer relationship management. J Direct Data Digital Market. Pract. **12**, 249–266 (2011)
22. Neil, S.: The rise of "social" business process management. Manag. Autom. **25**, 38–41 (2010)
23. Erol, S., Granitzer, M., Happ, S., Jantunen, S., Jennings, B., Johannesson, P., Koschmider, A., Nurcan, S., Rossi, D., Schmidt, R.: Combining BPM and social software: contradiction or chance? J. Softw. Maintenance Evol. Res. Pract. **22**, 449–476 (2010)
24. Bruno, G., Dengler, F., Jennings, B., Khalaf, R., Nurcan, S., Prilla, M., Sarini, M., Schmid, R., Silva, R.: Key challenges for enabling agile BPM with social software. J. Softw. Maintenance Evol. Res. Pract. **23**, 297–326 (2011)
25. McKinsey: Building the Web 2.0 enterprise. McKinsey Global Survery Results. The McKinsey Quarterly, June (2008)
26. McKinsey: How companies are benefiting from Web 2.0. The McKinsey Quarterly, June (2009)
27. McKinsey: Evolution of the networked enterprise. The McKinsey Quarterly, March (2013)
28. Andersson, D.: Selecting ERP for enterprise 2.0 and social media functionality. IFS White Papers, IFS Labs, available at www.ifsworld.com (2011)

Implementing Accrual Accounting in Italian Universities: Critical Aspects of an Information System

Lucia Giovanelli, Federico Rotondo and Sonia Caffù

Abstract This paper presents the experience of research, analysis and implementation of a new information system, and especially its accounting side, with the purpose of supporting management and improving performance of a centuries-old academic institution. The underway process of change, started in 2010 and based on the action research approach, is analyzed all along its different steps, from the identification of the best accounting information system in relation to the complexity and specificity of universities to the investigation of its impact on governance and operational routines. In particular, the experimentation of U-GOV, the IT system chosen to support the accounting change, highlights that the main criticalities deal with not only technical, but also cultural and organizational aspects.

Keywords Universities · Information system · Accrual accounting · Governance

1 Introduction

In the early Nineties, while the public sector was generally undergoing a profound reform inspired by New Public Management (NPM), public universities delayed the introduction of managerial practices and tools making this sector appear underdeveloped in comparison with other public sectors [1].

L. Giovanelli (✉)
Department of Economics and Management, University of Sassari, Sassari, Italy
e-mail: giovanel@uniss.it

F. Rotondo
Department of Humanities and Social Sciences, University of Sassari, Sassari, Italy
e-mail: frotondo@uniss.it

S. Caffù
Accounting Office, University of Sassari, Sassari, Italy
e-mail: scaffu@uniss.it

© Springer International Publishing Switzerland 2016   185
D. Mancini et al. (eds.), *Strengthening Information and Control Systems*,
Lecture Notes in Information Systems and Organisation 14,
DOI 10.1007/978-3-319-26488-2_14

Actually, however, in the preceding period, the university sector had been affected by changes which had modified its organization, management and accounting practices. While the main actors of public university governance (deans, principals, department heads) benefitted from a political legitimation, they basically learned "hands on" how to manage organizations [2], showing a cultural gap as the reason for the delay in implementing managerial logic, tools and practices. Additionally, the dramatic financial situation generally and the public finance problems of Italy determined budget cutting policies, particularly for universities.

In this scenario, in 2010, the management of the University of Sassari realized that in order to achieve long-term improvements in performance within a context of decreasing resources, it was essential to introduce planning, control and evaluation practices and a new information system, especially an accounting one so as to support decision-making and promote enduring effectiveness and efficiency. A process of change began, based on the introduction of new information tools such as the passage from cash accounting (used with different methodologies by the individual University sub-structures) to accrual accounting with a single budget and financial statement.

This paper presents the experience of research, analysis and implementation of the new information system of the University of Sassari, with particular attention paid to the accounting side, in order to highlight results as well as criticalities and unanswered questions the ongoing experimentation should be able to address.

This paper is organized as follows. Section 2 outlines the research objectives and methodology; Sect. 3 discusses the process of change in accounting information systems of Italian universities and provides a literature review about this topic; Sect. 4 shows characteristics of U-GOV, an information system for the governance of universities; Sects. 5 and 6 illustrate results, final discussion and suggestions for the future.

2   Objectives and Methodology

This paper aims at identifying an information system able to adequately support management in improving university performance, which is evaluated under the multiple dimensions which define universities' missions: didactics, research, health and socio-economic outcomes. The first step of research focuses on the accounting information system used to plan, monitor and report the results of operations, assets and financial position of the organization. Subsequently, the structure of such an information system is investigated with special attention to the elements enhancing the effectiveness of a performance indicator system, made up of financial and non-financial measures, in a university.

From a methodological perspective, the action research approach is used due to the fact that the action researcher is not an external observer but, as was in the current case, part of a specific process of change which becomes the object of research [3, 4].

This paper reports the experience of the University of Sassari (Italy), where, beginning in 2010, a process of change of the information system, and in particular of the accounting one, was undertaken, utilizing a methodological approach of repeated steps of development, test and adjustment. The final purpose of the change process was to better support management and so improve decision-making quality. Previously, the accounting information system of the organization was based on cash accounting and could be defined as "fragmented" as there were a large number of units (faculties and departments) each one with its own accounting but no common guidelines used to harmonize budgeting and reporting practices and documents. This made the identification of the global financial situation, economic results and assets of the university very difficult. Thus the need to harmonize the accounting of the different units of the organization and to adopt a unique master budget articulated into the single budgets of each structure in order to effectively guide budgeting, reporting and enhance accountability of the entire organization; after the first period, when the existing accounting information system based on cash accounting was used, it was decided to adopt, in line with the change required by Law no. 240 of 2010 which in the meantime reformed the Italian public university sector, accrual accounting.

The action research approach was believed to be the most appropriate one to cope with the change of the accounting information system especially when considering the importance of research, a pillar of universities' mission, in such an organization. Although the authors were aware of the existence of other affordable methodologies for achieving the research objective, an empirical and iterative approach based on planning, acting, observing and reflecting was preferred [5]. After a pre-step activity aimed at understanding the context and focusing the purpose, the following steps of data gathering, feedback and analysis relied on a social process involving both researchers and practitioners; this process was also followed in the consequent steps of action planning and implementation. Action research was particularly suitable to understand changing practices, which are constituted in social interaction between people [6], and contributed both to academic theory and to practical action by promoting a continuous learning process within the organization. A key element was the evaluation step which permitted the modification of rationales and tools in relation to context features [7].

The top-management of the University supported the research purpose and work groups, including practitioners of the organization in addition to the authors, were constituted. The authors, in particular, held important positions in the organization, both political (Vice-Chancellor and member of the Accounting Committee) and technical (head of the Accounting Office), and were actively involved in the work groups. Groups' activity was constantly oriented to experiment accounting innovations, analyze their outcomes on the organizational structure and the decision-making, reflect on the criticalities and propose adjustments to continually improve the information system support for management.

3   The Accounting Change in Italian Universities

As mentioned above, in the first years of Nineties, while Italian public sector underwent reform in the wave of NPM theories, universities remained quite completely outside the process of change. This circumstance is even more curious when considering that the universities were the first public organizations to be affected by managerial innovations introduced, for instance, by the Law no. 168 of 1989 affirming the principle of autonomy (confirmed for local governments with the Law no. 142 of 1990). Autonomy in statute and regulation (art. 6) set by the Constitution (art. 33) for public universities potentially paved the way to organizational, managerial and administrative innovations. Universities had, however, suffered from huge changes during the Eighties, initially from an organizational and managerial reform (DPR 382/1980 enacting the delegated Law no. 28/1980) and successively from an accounting reform (DPR 371/1982), which conditioned the acceptance of the new regulation. Public universities, in fact, remained anchored to the models introduced by Eighties reform.

In 1993, with the Law no. 537, new financing and human resource management mechanisms replaced the centralized approach to financial management of universities, which had undermined for a long period their autonomy [8]. The new approach fostered university organizational and financial autonomy by introducing an Ordinary Financial Fund (FFO) to be allocated partly on the basis of historical expenses and partly (an equilibrating share) on criteria determined by decree of the Ministry of University and Research related to *"standard production costs for each student and for objectives of research quality, considering dimensions, structural and environmental conditions of universities"* (article 5, l. no. 537/93). The introduction of a performance-based principle in resource allocation, an absolute novelty for the time in the public sector, was followed by the institution of the "internal evaluation offices". The Observatory for the evaluation of the university sector was replaced, in April 2000, by the National Committee for the evaluation of the university sector, operating until the institution of the National Agency for the evaluation of universities and research (ANVUR) with the Law no. 286/2006.

The innovations inspired by NPM, although potentially feasible in light of the mechanism of resource allocation increasingly based on results, were barely implemented by Italian universities. The principle of autonomy was not accompanied by an adequate assumption of responsibility and the context was characterized by a very poor managerial culture, leading to organizational choices (open-ended contracts, career advancement) and managerial choices (property investments, degree courses not related to the job market and so on) driven by a short-term perspective. These choices quickly revealed negative effects for universities performance and sustainability.

The change process for universities, except for a few cases, was stalled and only regained momentum when the university system's resources were cut. With the approval of Law no. 240 of 2010 and the following enabling decrees, in fact, a season of deep changes in governance, organization, management and accounting of universities begins. The key words of change are rationalizing, value, evaluation, responsibility and accountability. In reference to the accounting matter, legislative decree no. 18/2012 and inter-ministerial decree no. 19 of 14 January 2014 revolutionize accounting practices and the display of assets and financial situations.

When the new regulation was issued the Italian university sector was characterized by various accounting models. Accounting autonomy (article 7, comma 7, Law no. 168/1989) had emphasized diversity among public universities and, within each of them, among central bodies and peripheral bodies which constituted responsibility centers (faculties and departments). Actually, it must be said that DPR 371/1982 established a cash accounting with some accruals elements for central bodies while maintaining a pure cash accounting for peripheral bodies.

Such a situation made it difficult for universities to draw up single consolidated financial statements and the Ministry could not compare the financial situations of different universities [9], even though the criteria for preparing statements of universities in a homogeneous way had already been set, as well as the rules to build the Information System for Public Sector Operations (SIOPE) to address European reporting requirements. Furthermore, public finance constraints provoked a significant reduction of resources for universities, increasing budgeting constraints for many organizations, in particular those with higher personnel cost and debts.

Cash accounting shows all its limits in such a scenario, as it is basically a short-term model oriented to the concept of authorization rather than to that of accountability. It neither makes organizations accountable in the long-term for financial and asset equilibrium (essential conditions of longevity for centuries-old institutions), nor for technical-operational results related to university activities (research, didactics, services for students, transfer of technology to the local territory).

Specific steering actions, at the system level, become important to guarantee transparency and homogeneity of accounting models among universities, in order to improve the reporting of public resource use and to compare different economic, financial and assets situation [10], as occurred in other European countries [11].

The accounting situation identified by legislators for universities seems to address a central point of the long-standing debate about the best accounting model in the public higher education system [9, 12–17], as it establishes the passage, on or before January 1st, 2015 (originally January 1st, 2014), to accrual accounting and cost accounting. Cash accounting, at least officially, remains, as legislators require universities to draw up the single budget, without authorization power, and the single financial statement for the entire university following cash accounting (art. 1, comma 3, decree no. 18/2012). This proviso, which creates some technical problems as it requires the reclassification of financial data (cash inflows and outflows) following the rules of European reporting (SIOPE) and international comparisons (missions and programs and COFOG classification), aims at enhancing the consolidation and monitoring of public sector accounts in order to fulfill the requirements of State reporting for European purposes.

This is the context where the University of Sassari projected the process of change of its information system, particularly of the accounting part of it.

4   U-GOV: An Information System for the Governance
of Universities

U-GOV is an information technology (IT) system designed to play a key role in the success of the change process. An accounting information system, based on accrual accounting and cost accounting techniques, designed to support management of the university, must also respect the information duties required by central administrations for the purpose of public finance control.

The IT system must guarantee the coherence of the new accounting model with accrual principles, ensuring that the accounting records actually embrace the information needed for management control and could be used to monitor the soundness of public sector's accounts. In addition, it should promote the effectiveness of strategy formulation and implementation, as well as resource planning and control in relation to objectives and guidelines set by the Ministry.

This process implies both an overall view on the main strategic areas and the necessity to monitor all the single specificities of the University. For this reason U-GOV was viewed as the best solution. It is, in fact, an integrated IT system developed for the governance of universities by Cineca (a non-profit consortium, made up of 54 Italian universities, two national research centres, and the Ministry of Universities and Research) by mixing the competencies and innovations held by Italian universities. The system integrates processes and information about human resource management, research, accounting and services to students. Authors, in line with the research purpose, focused the analysis on the structure of the IT system related to accounting, being aware that the system, potentially, makes it possible to design different levels of integration between complex and cross processes.

As illustrated in Sect. 3, the minimum requirements for an IT system include recording the following information: double-entry accounting events, accrual accounting, cost accounting, synthetic statements of cash accounting, life cycle of research projects and didactics. In addition to the external information obligations, further requirements for an IT system are related to the effectiveness of planning and controlling the financial, economic and assets performance of the university, as whole and for each single activity. The system should permit recording student fees and other contributions, following accrual principles and shared in cost centers (degree courses), as well as human resources (in terms of working time related to didactics, research and other institutional tasks).

Within the context which characterizes every university's daily activity, the IT system should permit the coexistence of accrual, cash and cost accountings through an integrated reading of the accounting information previously cleansed from duplications of data and activities. Administrative processes, carried out by means of a coordinated cycle management, enable a prompt reporting for internal and external purposes.

The necessity to gather a complete information highlights the high level of complexity, from an administrative and accounting point of view, that the University faced under this new framework. The IT system architecture covers all the aspects required by the legal framework, both mandatory and for authorization purposes. The overall view, in fact, is important to outline the accounting situation in a neat, controlled and computerized way. This facilitates the respect of the mandatory accrual accounting principles and also the drawing up of the budget plan, which has an authorization purpose for the single responsibility centers. Finally, it allows the constant monitoring of budget determinations and the ex-post performance evaluation through cost accounting.

The analysis of the IT system architecture showed the following strengths:

- fair and complete records all along the management cycle in order to gather thorough information for accounting and management control;
- strong attention to the authorization function, with the possibility to secure budget shares to costs related to obligations not yet accrued;
- automation in the project management following the cost-to-cost method;
- possibility of reclassifying the chart of accounts on the basis of the reference models of the Ministry and the IV EU-Directive;
- possibility of distinguishing, at every moment, between the commercial and institutional sides, both for the profit and loss account and the balance sheet;
- possibility of showing accounting statements for each responsibility center;
- possibility of gathering all data, without any other further elaboration, needed to control public finance objectives.

Nevertheless, in a continuous improvement perspective, some weaknesses must be addressed:

- necessity to develop reports more compliant with the internal information needs of the University. Reports are currently used but the process and the content must be refined;
- necessity to improve some aspects of cycle management in order to facilitate practitioners during their ordinary routines;
- strengthen the flexibility of the IT system architecture so as to make it more suitable to every university's peculiarities.

In light of the analysis, U-GOV IT system, currently used in 37 Italian universities, revealed itself to be an adequate architecture to support accounting change in universities. It also appears to be useful to promote informed decision making of University management by integrating and sharing information between accounting and planning, both before and at the end of the accounting period.

5   Evidence from the Implementation

With the aim to clarify the meaning of the project it is important to reconstruct, at least broadly, the organizational context where it was developed. All the planning and implementation phases of the project, in fact, occurred in what can be defined as a constantly changing context.

The turning point was the 2010, when the top-management of the University realized that transforming management attitude, and the tools to manage, was the key to obtain notable changes. In brief, the University clearly defined long-term objectives and strategies, that were approved by the management bodies (Board of Directors and Academic Senate), and then communicated to all personnel.

From a strategic point of view, some ongoing projects were confirmed (and speeded up), other new projects were identified to support and promote the achievement of the new objectives. These new projects included moving towards the unified budget and financial statement of the University and the accrual accounting [10]. In this phase, also relying on other similar experiences of change management in the public sector [18], the importance of intervening on the administrative and technical side of the organization, at various levels, clearly emerged:

- by designing supporting units, roles and positions;
- by developing competencies and motivations of the involved actors;
- by defining new tools for management and information exchange.

Additionally, from the outset it was decided to invest in monitoring and evaluating the project, both in itinere and ex-post, the same amount of resources devoted to the activities of planning and designing it.

In 2012, the work group took the following important actions:

- mapping, monitoring and analyzing the administrative and accounting processes: checkup on the accounting system structure and the internal auditing;
- listening to the principal actors involved in the administrative-accounting processes;
- identifying the macro-model to be used as a reference point and consequent mapping of data needed for its implementation;
- defining the model and choosing the software;
- defining common processes and methodologies and then formalizing them, testing and eventually going back over them;
- implementing and starting the software.

The debate with the actors concretely involved in the process permitted the identification of the conditions for success which qualified, time after time, each single step and the consequent capitalization and sharing of best practices [19]. In the meantime, internal legislation related to managerial, administrative and accounting practices was thoroughly reviewed.

The next phase—still in progress—is focused on the circulation of information as the basic assumption is that for the proper functioning of the system actors must be in the best position to exchange information with each other without any hierarchical order. The rationale behind such an internal communication is related to the concept of "network" where real-time conversations permit "nodes" to give and gather essential information, at every moment, on their relative activities [20]. The main challenges of the ongoing process are basically two, a technical one and a cultural one, and the development of the new accounting system is not sufficient to meet the challenges. In this regard, the constant maintenance of technical and cultural aspects is required for success.

The checkup of the accounting system structure and the internal auditing revealed the need to completely change the administrative-accounting processes in light of the introduction of the single budget and financial statement and especially to gather accurate data on assets of the organization so as to draw up the first balance sheet under accrual accounting. In particular, an external company was designated to carry out a detailed survey of movable assets, indispensable for a 450-year-old University, while the State Land Administration was charged with the task of determining the market value of the property assets. As a result, an updated configuration of property assets of the organization was obtained, although the accounting standards for public universities did not allow the use of the new data to draw up the first balance sheet.[1]

Through the checkup of the existing structures and the systematic confrontation with the actors, all data required by the following phases for the review of processes and the strategic actions to be taken to start the new accounting system were mapped. Particularly, the following activities occurred:

- detailed analysis of unexpended balances and residual liabilities, in order to correctly classify them in credits/debits;
- introduction of common methodologies and languages to manage research/didactics projects.

The identification of the macro-model of reference focused on the technical-accounting structure and the responsibility of each actor involved in the process. From a "static" point of view, every event deserving to be recorded is recorded just one time, is considered by the related accounting systems (accrual accounting and cost accounting) and is anchored to specific entities. The accounting system reflects the organizational structure of the University by defining the units responsible for performance: management centers, cost centers and projects.

Management centers are formally defined as organizational units which have resources made available to them and which are so accountable for the correct use of them and the achieving of specific objectives (Centers with Managerial and Administrative Autonomy and Management Offices) [21]. In particular, in order to make management as flexible as possible, it was decided to charge Centers with the highest responsibility as they can autonomously manage the account payables of the accounting cycle. In this regard, cash management was also carefully changed. Finally, considering the introduction of a single budget and financial statement, and so of a single bank account, it was decided to manage cash at a central level.

Cost centers were identified, during the starting phase of the process, in the offices/laboratories/libraries of the organizational structure. The evolution of the model of control anticipates defining the cost centers for each degree course/PhD/postgraduate school. Generally speaking, the system enables cost

---

[1]Art. 5, comma 1, letter a, Inter-ministerial Decree of January the 14th, 2014, no. 19.

addressing in relation to responsibility and other objects of control defined in the model.

Within the accounting system, forecasting cost accounting represents the means by which financial balance is monitored and expenditures are pre-emptively authorized. When defining the model two criticalities emerged. The first one is related to the rigidity of pre-emptive control; the second to the possibility of uni-vocally relating cash information to accrual and analytic information. In relation to the first problem, a budget control at center level was developed, so as to avoid periodical changes in resource supply. The second problem was resolved by developing an integrated chart of accounts in order to logically connect cash, accrual and cost accounting point of views. This was seen as an effective way to facilitate practitioners in daily routines related to each single elemental transaction.

As regards the process, the system is oriented to integrate planning, management and reporting activities. The third phase was devoted to the formal building of the above mentioned processes, with special regard to the "cycle of control" shared in 4 steps: middle-term planning, short-term planning (budgeting), management and evaluation. Particularly, the development, monitoring and approval of budget is a complex process which crosses the vertical structure of the organization to involve all areas and departments and formalizes phases and actors.

The change process had a strong impact on management and operations and, since the beginning, revealed some criticalities not yet completely resolved.

First of all, a sort of "resistance to change" in the organization appeared, in relation to both the accounting aspects and the new point of view about resource management [22]. Actually, all the personnel involved in the process underwent professional training. Special attention was paid to improve competencies of those personnel involved in accounting issues in reason of the passage from cash accounting to accrual accounting. Many central services supporting practitioners during the change were reinforced and theoretical training was accompanied by intense practical training in the use of the new IT system [23].

During the project, some technical problems related to the IT system had a strong impact on both the administrative-accounting processes and the daily activity of practitioners. In particular:

- the decision (need) to manage single elementary transactions as a whole high-lighted the incomplete incorporation of the new accounting principles: practi-tioners sometimes underestimated the importance of essential information to correctly record accounting data, causing consequent analyses and reviews at the end of the accounting period;
- changing some processes, during the development of the system, provoked continuous "refinements" generating uncertainties about the correctness of procedure and need for stronger support;
- the IT system required significant adjustments during the first year.

People involved in the change process had to cope with a strong organizational stress. They had to devote a considerable part of their time to extraordinary activities causing delays in ordinary activity [24]. Finally, adopting the new accounting system entailed the review of the reporting system, both at operational and management levels, through the inclusion of reports and communications in ways never used before inside the organization.

A year after starting the new model the system is not yet at full speed and its cultural and managerial impact has not been completely absorbed. In the immediate future actions to carefully monitor the fine-tuning of the system under a broad perspective (including technical, organizational and cultural aspects) and to start special on-the-job training programs are planned.

6 Concluding Remarks

This paper illustrates a project, methodologically based on the action research approach, to define and implement an information system capable of supporting management and so to improve performance of the University of Sassari. In 2010, this organization started a process oriented to introduce principles and tools for planning, controlling and reporting as well as changing the information system, particularly the accounting one.

The need to maintain an overall view on the strategic areas while monitoring the single areas of the organization, led to the selection of the U-GOV IT system, developed by Cineca. The system is based on the integration and sharing of information between accounting, planning and control systems, both before and at the end of the accounting period.

Beginning with the assumption that in order to achieve the change goals, a transformation of management attitude and tools was required, the University clearly defined the strategic actions and objectives and, once approved by the management bodies, communicated them to all personnel.

In line with the project purpose and methodological approach, work groups, composed by the authors and key practitioners, were constituted. Authors, each one holding political or technical roles in the organization, were responsible for steering, coordinating and supporting groups.

The technical-administrative structure was perceived, since the beginning of the process, as one of the key variable influencing the evolution of the system and thus determining its success or failure. For this reason adequate resources were devoted to monitoring and evaluating, in itinere and ex-post, the process. Exchanging information and debating with practitioners involved in the day to day processes were also important elements to identify success conditions and capitalize best practices.

In the meantime, a thorough reform of the internal regulations, related to managerial, administrative and accounting aspects, was carried out. The concept which inspired the new communication system inside the organization, still to be completely developed, was that of the "network".

A decisive moment was the checkup of the accounting organization and the internal audit system, which revealed some crucial points for the effective development of the new system of single budget and financial statement. These are the total review of the administrative-accounting processes and the acquisition of accurate information on assets. Simultaneously, in order to make operational procedures as simple as possible, centers with managerial and administrative autonomy were given even more responsibility and power.

When defining the model some criticalities emerged, such as the rigidity of pre-emptive control and the link between cash information and accrual and analytic information. From a dynamic point of view, the project, since the beginning, intended to integrate processes related to planning, management and reporting, as it was viewed as another crucial point. In this regard, special attention was paid to the formal structure of control, which was articulated along a 4-step cycle able to bridge the vertical structure of the organization and involve all areas and departments of the University.

Furthermore, the experience permitted the identification of general problems which can affect similar processes of change in universities or other public organizations, and so should be considered. Among those, the "resistance to change" coming from the actors, both related to the technical-accounting innovations and the new point of view in resource management. Doubts were regularly raised, within the organization, on the meaning of such a deep and painful change, at least in relation to the short-term effects on organizational and operational practices. The impact was even harsher considering the centuries-old traditions of the institution (the University of Sassari was founded in 1562), which had fed the belief about a sort of immortality of the organization, quite apart from the development of management techniques.

The cultural and operational impact of such major changes in the information systems, in such contexts, certainly represents a crucial point to be considered in advance in order to take proper actions to attenuate negative effects. The experience carried out by the University of Sassari, in this regard, highlighted the importance of some specific interventions to effectively implement the system, such as:

- the development of practical training programs for all the involved actors;
- the reinforcement of central services to support practitioners at all organizational levels;
- sharing technical solutions;
- the review of the reporting system, both at operational and management levels, following the principles of horizontal and integrated communication.

The experimentation showed the complexity of a change process dealing with not only technical, but also cultural and organizational aspects. It revealed the information potentialities of the new accounting model for both the internal purpose, related to management, and the external one, related to accountability. The single budget and financial statement system enhances transparency of essential dimensions to evaluate the whole University efficiency (production cost of services in relation to revenues in turn connected to performances), as well as the conditions of long-term sustainability through the clear display of assets. Monitoring cash flows and cost accounting complete the information system and promote the formulation of strategies capable of improving operational performance and in the meantime respecting the essential cash, financial, economic and assets equilibriums of the organization.

In the near future, the project intends to overcome the criticalities revealed by the accounting experimentation and in the meantime to refine the information system with the inclusion of the elements needed to support the system of indicators, both financial and non financial, used to monitor performances and enhance the achievement of the University mission.

References

1. Busetti, S., Dente, B.: Focus on the finger, overlook the moon: the introduction of performance management in the administration of Italian Universities. J. High. Educ. Policy Manag. **36**, 225–237 (2014)
2. Dente, B.: Tre Nodi dell'Università Italiana. Astrid-rassegna, n. 92, Roma (2009)
3. Lewin, K.: Action research and minority problems. J. Soc. Issue **2**, 34–46 (1946)
4. Jönsson, S.: Action Research in Management Accounting Studies. In: Gothenburg Research Institute Report, Gothenburg (1999)
5. Coughlan, P., Coghlan, D.: Action research for operations management. Int. J. Oper. Prod. Manag. **22**, 220–240 (2002)
6. Kemmis, S., McTaggart, R.: Partecipatory action research. In: Denzin, N.K., Lincoln, Y.S. (eds.) The Sage Handbook of Qualitative Research, pp. 559–603. Sage, Thousand Oak, CA (2005)
7. Checkland, P.: Framework through experience to learning: the essential nature of action research. In: Nissen, H.E. (ed.) Information System Research: Contemporary Approaches and Emergent Traditions. Elsevier, Amsterdam (1991)
8. Giovanelli, L.: Le Amministrazione Pubbliche tra Autonomia e Vincoli di Sistema. Azienda Pubblica **3**, 293–304 (2013)
9. Catalano, G.: La Contabilità Economico-Patrimoniale nelle Università. Aspetti Metodologici e Principi Contabili. Il Mulino, Bologna (2009)
10. Agasisti, T., Catalano, G.: Debate: innovation in the Italian public higher education system: introducing accrual accounting. Pub. Money Manag. **33**, 92–94 (2013)
11. Christiaens, J., De Wielemaker, E.: Financial accounting reform in flemish universities: an empirical study of the implementation. Financ. Account. Manag. **19**, 185–204 (2003)
12. Palumbo, R.: L'Università nella sua Dimensione Economico-Aziendale. Giappichelli, Torino (1999)
13. Miolo Vitali, P.: I Sistemi di Misurazione Economico Finanziaria nelle Università Italiane: Problemi e Prospettive. Cedam, Padova (2001)
14. Cinquini, L.: Il Bilancio Consuntivo delle Università. Verso una Nuova Informativa Economico-Finanziaria. Giappichelli, Torino (2002)
15. Capodaglio, G.: L'Introduzione della Contabilità Economico-Patrimoniale nelle Università Italiane. Metodologie e Soluzioni Operative. Rirea, Roma (2004)
16. Paletta, A.: Il Governo dell'Università. Tra Competizione e Accountability. Il Mulino, Bologna (2004)
17. Cugini, A.: La Misurazione delle Performance negli Atenei. Logiche, Metodi, Esperienze. Franco Angeli, Milano (2007)
18. Giovanelli, L., Marinò, L., Rotondo, F., Fadda, N., Ezza, A., Amadori, M.: Developing a performance evaluation system for the italian public healthcare sector. Pub. Money Manag. **35**, 297–302 (2015)

19. Brown, K., Waterhouse, J., Flynn, C.: Change management practices—is a hybrid model a better alternative for public sector agencies? Int. J. Public Sector Manag. **16**, 230–241 (2003)
20. Klijn, E.H., Koppenjan, J.F.M.: Public management and policy networks. Public Manag. **2**, 135–158 (2000)
21. Romzek, B.S., Dubnick, M.J.: Accountability in the public sector: lessons from the challenger tragedy. Public Adm. Rev. **47**, 227–238 (1987)
22. By, R.T., Macleod, C.: Managing Organizational Change in Public Services: International Issues, Challenges and Cases. Routledge, London and New York (2009)
23. Wise, L.R.: Public management reform: competing drivers of change. Public Adm. Rev. **62**, 555–567 (2000)
24. Kelman, S.: Unleashing change: a study of organizational renewal in government. Brookings Institution Press, Washington DC (2009)

Innovations in Accounting Information System in the Public Sector. Evidences from Italian Public Universities

Elisa Bonollo, Simone Lazzini and Mara Zuccardi Merli

Abstract The paper analyzes how the accounting information system supports the transition from the traditional public accounting to the accrual accounting and the new budgeting and reporting system in public universities, with a specific reference to the bookkeeping of research projects. The accounting treatment of the research projects is particularly interesting because of the relevance of this item in the university budget, the options indicated by the lawmaker for its valuation criteria and the effects the valuation criteria have on the economic and investment budget of the university. Therefore the configuration of the accounting information system is not a mere technical problem, but involves the whole management. The research is based on the case study method applied to the University of Genoa. The research method is based on in-depth description of the role of the accounting information system in supporting the various phases of the research project accounting.

Keywords Accounting information system in public organizations · University · Research project

1 Introduction

Since the 1990s, in Italy as in other countries, public organizations have been involved in a modernization process to overcome the traditional bureaucratic model typical of a formal legal administration system [1–3]. During this modernization

E. Bonollo (✉) · M. Zuccardi Merli
Department of Economics and Business Studies, University of Genoa, Genoa, Italy
e-mail: bonollo@economia.unige.it

M. Zuccardi Merli
e-mail: zuccardi@economia.unige.it

S. Lazzini
Department of Economics and Management, University of Pisa, Pisa, Italy
e-mail: simone.lazzini@unipi.it

© Springer International Publishing Switzerland 2016
D. Mancini et al. (eds.), *Strengthening Information and Control Systems*,
Lecture Notes in Information Systems and Organisation 14,
DOI 10.1007/978-3-319-26488-2_15

process, characterized by being legislation-driven, great importance was attached to financial management reforms, so much so that some scholars coined the term "New Public Financial Management" [4–6]. This set of reforms led to the adoption of accounting information systems derived from the business world (i.e. accrual accounting, cost accounting, etc.), as this was considered to be more appropriate than traditional systems to fulfil the information needs of internal and external stakeholders, support the achievement of a higher level of efficiency and empower the staff to use public resources.

In recent years, these changes have also involved public universities, initially with academic studies focused on the criticalities of the traditional public accounting system and subsequently with empirical research describing the state of the art throughout the country or focusing on the experiences of a few innovative pioneering universities; finally, with legislative initiatives addressed to all public universities [7–13].

More specifically, Law no. 240 of 2010, Legislative Decree no. 18 of 2012 and Ministerial Decree no. 19 of 2014 renewed the accounting information system of public universities, which passed from the traditional cash- and commitment-based accounting system to accrual accounting with an annual economic and investment "authorizing" budget. The main innovation introduced was that universities are now required to approve a single economic and investment budget rather than having separated and independent budgets (with revenues and expenditure) prepared by the central administration and by each individual department. As a consequence, there will be only one economic and investment budget of the university, including all the revenues, costs and investments of the different university activities (teaching, research and administration), so the accounting information system has to be completely re-designed.

In this context, the paper aims to investigate how the information system supports the use of the accrual accounting and the new budgeting and reporting system in the university, with specific reference to the management of research project accounting.

The accounting treatment of research projects is particularly interesting because of the relevance of this item in the university budget (in terms of revenues, costs and investments), the options indicated by the lawmaker for its valuation criteria and the impact of valuation criteria on the economic and investment budget. Therefore, the configuration of the accounting information system [14, 15] is not a mere technical problem, but involves the whole management of the university [16].

The method of analysis used consists of a case study [17] that has provided a picture of the main elements that characterize the configuration of the accounting information system of the universities, with particular reference to the accounting and IT procedures prepared for the reporting of research projects. The use of this qualitative method of investigation is consistent with the objective of the paper, as it is based on an in-depth description of all the elements of the issue studied and interactions between these elements. More specifically, our research analyses how the information system supports the management of research project accounting in the University of Genoa. The choice of this case stems from the fact that the University of Genoa has introduced the accrual accounting system since the beginning of 2013 and has already highlighted some criticalities in connection with this change. The sources of data used for the case study were internal documents and interviews with the personnel of the accounting unit of the central administration.

The paper is structured as follows: it starts with a brief literature review on the accrual accounting in the public sector and an in-depth analysis of the renewal of public university accounting information systems within the framework of the New Public Financial Management; secondly, the paper presents the peculiarities of the management of research projects accounting, and finally the case of the University of Genoa is described and discussed.

2 Accrual Accounting in the Public Sector: A Brief Literature Review

The Italian university system has recently been going through a process of deep change that has ended up by also involving its accounting information system [18, 19]. In fact, the need to adequately respond to the information requirements of internal and external stakeholders (for management and control purposes) and the need to make executives accountable for an efficient use of resources have required that lawmaker introduces changes in the accounting systems to be mandatorily adopted by universities. These changes should be seen within the wider framework of a deep reform process that also concerns other public organizations and that, with different timing, is set to introduce accrual and cost accounting systems to be implemented with or in replacement of traditional public accounting [12, 20].

To tell the truth, the cash- and commitment-based accounting system had already been criticised in the fifties [21, 22], but it has been at the beginning of the nineties, with the new public management, that many authors suggested again that lawmaker should innovate the accounting information system of public organizations. According to these authors, the traditional public accounting system was inappropriate to provide the necessary information for an effective management of policies, resources and for the control of results [1, 23–25]. That is when the adoption of accrual accounting was proposed [6, 26, 27].

In addition to that, the adoption of cost accounting is also proposed to meet the information requirements connected with the development of the "cost awareness" in services and political programs. This can improve the decision-making process and establish the responsibilities of executives not only on contractual and procedural issues, but also on the use of the available resources [12, 28]. In fact, some authors pointed out that the benefits connected with the accrual accounting would be, inter alia, associated with the use of the cost accounting system particularly in those public organizations that are characterised by a high number of heterogeneous activities and services delivered [1, 28–30], because it would provide more accurate information on the economic dimension of management. Other authors also associated the introduction of accrual accounting with a greater focus on the management of assets, the availability of complete information on liabilities and the improvement of transparency and accountability towards external stakeholders [25, 31, 32].

The accounting system change does not just impact on technical aspects, but reveals its effects on the whole management, also and above all on the organization. In fact the accounting system as part of the information system is not a mere technical tool, but it is at the same time the result of a progressive accumulation and stratification of experiences, procedures, processes, and information needs and the factor that affects the future development of the organization [32–34].

Innovations of accounting information systems are often considered as essential in the processes of organizational change and have been of interest to many scholars in recent decades. Some authors, as part of the so-called critical approach, are focused on the mutual influence between power relations and information systems. Based on the belief that accounting information systems reflect the configuration of the interests of the ruling class in different historical periods, they propose to change the existing accounting information system in order to change the *status quo* [35, 36]. Other studies as part of the so-called new-institutional approach, are focused on the role of the accounting information systems in supporting the change in existing power structures and organizational culture and in legitimizing the organization itself [37, 38]. According to this approach, the adoption of a particular accounting information system, in this case the accrual accounting, is influenced by the will more to conform to rules, norms and values (often imposed from outside) than to consider its efficiency and effectiveness on management [39, 40].

Finally, we should also point out that some studies have highlighted the criticalities associated with the replacement of the traditional public accounting system with accrual accounting [32, 41], just think of: the challenge of valuating the starting capital and the operating capital, particularly in connection with some asset items, such as assets with a cultural or historical value, art and museums [42–45], the risk of a poor control of expenditure [12], the difficulty of interpreting the result for the year [46, 47], the need to define uniform accounting principles to ensure comparability in space and time, and the reliability of annual report items [48, 49].

3 The New Accounting Information System of Universities

In order to adapt the accounting information system of universities to the requirements of the context, lawmaker issued, within the university reform, Law no. 240 of 2010, Legislative Decree no. 18 of 2012 and Ministerial Decree no. 19 of

2014. These legislative provisions require the introduction of an accrual and cost accounting system "in order to ensure consistency with the three-year planning of the universities, more transparency and consistency, and allow for the identification of the exact financial and equity situation of the university, as well as its global management trends" (Law 240/2010, art. 5), and the preparation, based on the accounting principles and reporting forms defined by the Ministry, of the documents specified in Table 1.

The main innovations introduced compared to the past can be summarised in the following points:

- Universities are required to adopt accrual accounting, unlike in the past, when they were independent as to accounting system (and could adopt the accounting information system they preferred). The accounting reform does not provide the coexistence with the traditional public accounting. The non-coexistence between cash- and commitment-based accounting and accrual accounting has been established to prevent the risk, highlighted by several authors, of generating confusion in executives who could receive inconsistent information from the joint presence of the two accounting systems and end up by basing their decisions on the traditional public accounting system [23, 28, 46].
- "Cost accounting systems and procedures for management control" must be mandatorily used in order to provide information on costs (and revenues) for the decision-making process and to make executives accountable in terms of use of resources, investments, and so on [19]. In this regard, no further regulation detail has been issued, but one may assume that cost accounting should not only be integrated with the accrual accounting system, but also connected to the reclassification of expenses for missions and programs to prepare the "chart of

Table 1 University documents in budget and final phases

Budget reporting (within 31/12/n − 1)	Final reporting (within 30/04/n + 1)

Consolidated three-year budget
  • Economic budget
  • Investment budget
Consolidated annual budget
  • Economic budget
  • Investment budget
"Chart of expenses classified by missions and programs"
Consolidated traditional public accounting budget
	Consolidated annual report
	  • Statement of assets and liabilities
	  • Income statement
	  • Accompanying notes
	  • Cash flow statement
	  • Report on operations
	  • SIOPE[a] statements
	  • "Chart of expenses classified by missions and programs"
	  • Board of Auditors' report
	Consolidated traditional public accounting report
	Consolidated financial statements
	  • Statement of assets and liabilities
	  • Income statement
	  • Accompanying notes

[a]SIOPE = *Sistema informativo sulle operazioni degli enti pubblici* (Information System on Public Organizations' Operations)

expenses classified by missions and programs" and increase the degree of accountability towards stakeholders as to the allocation of resources.

- The consolidated three-year budget (called "economic-financial plan" in Law no. 240 of 2010) must be prepared to ensure the economic and financial sustainability of all the activities of the university in the medium term. This, compared to the past, will reinforce medium/long-term planning, which, according to the lawmaker, must require the consistency of the contents of all its related formal documents (consolidated three-year budget, three-year programming and personnel recruitment plan, three-year planning, performance plan, etc.).
- The consolidated annual budget, consisting of the economic budget and the investment budget, becomes an authorization document, thus avoiding the reduction of the degree of control on available resources.
- The annual budget for the year (as well as the annual report) is a single "consolidated" document, which means that it is referred to the university as a whole, including both the central administration and any decentralized (or peripheral) units, thus avoiding the fragmentary production of different accounting budgets that characterised the pre-existing accounting system and favouring the coherence of management by objectives [50, 51].
- The consolidated traditional public accounting budget and report must in any case be prepared and accompanied by a reclassification of expenses for missions and programs (connected with COFOG codes), in order to allow for the consolidation and monitoring of public organizations' accounts. However this budget has lost its authorisation function to become a simple annex produced to meet ministerial information requirements.
- The consolidated financial statements must be prepared in compliance with the accounting consolidation principles set forth by the Ministry, in order to ensure a higher level of external accountability concerning the consolidated economic, financial and equity situations of the university, any university foundations, subsidiaries and other organizations where the university has the majority of votes in the shareholders' meeting or the power to appoint the majority of the members of the boards of directors.
- All the initial and final accounting documents (budgets and year-end statements) must be submitted to the Ministry (inter-institutional accountability) and published in the institutional website of the university as required by the so-called "Brunetta Reform" (Law no. 15 of 2009, Leg. Dec. no. 150 of 2009) to ensure the utmost transparency vis-à-vis stakeholders (external accountability).
- General accounting principles (or postulates), the Statement of Assets and Liabilities, the Income Statement and Cash-Flow Statement, valuation criteria for annual report items and criteria for the preparation of the first Statement of Assets and Liabilities have been introduced by Ministerial Decree to ensure the comparability and reliability of the accounting documents prepared by the universities (because they ensure a better consistency between the times and methods used to report administrative events) and to regulate some peculiar items that are typical of universities.

Clearly, the lawmaker, considering past experiences, wished to adjust the need to ensure the required attention for the economic aspect of management (accrual accounting), the control of the resources used compared to those planned (consolidated annual budget with authorization purpose), the consolidation of accounts (reclassification of expenses for missions and programs), accountability and transparency vis-à-vis stakeholders (obligation to publish accounting documents online, obligation to prepare the consolidated financial statements) and comparability over time and space (accounting principles and annual report forms imposed by Ministerial Decree).

Although several studies have been published on the accounting system of Italian universities since the approval of Law no. 240 of 2010, most of them have focused on an analysis of the implementation stage of the new accounting information system [13] and on existing best practices [18]. There is a lack of studies investigating specific annual report item valuation problems in terms how the choice of different valuation criteria, as suggested by regulatory provisions, impacts the actual operations of organizations and the determination of the year's result. The next sections of our work will analyse in depth one of these cases, connected to the accounting management of research projects.

4 The Management of Research Project Accounts

The introduction of accrual accounting in universities, already a significant innovation in itself, has been only a part of a thorough reconfiguration of the relationships between the central administration and peripheral units (Departments and service facilities of the university), and has become one of the most complex situations universities had to face over the last few years.

In the current configuration, departments are no longer independent as to accounting. The former budgeting and financial reporting documents are no longer required; now all these documents have been unified at university level.

So, the accounting information systems of the universities had to be configured for two main requirements: apart from the essential requirement of passing from traditional public accounting to accrual accounting, the need to support the new competencies of peripheral units within the framework of the accounting system.

The main point is to define which economic and financial flows each structure can record autonomously and how they are interconnected at central level. To this purpose, it is essential for the accounting information system to reflect the delegation system, where powers are conferred upon structures, and the reconciliation processes. The choice of a more or less extended delegation between the central administration and peripheral structures affects many aspects of the management of universities: payment of suppliers, treasury control, contract management, utility cost allocation, and particularly the management of research projects.

Under this perspective, the management of research projects takes on a crucial role both for the importance of research within the university framework and for the complexity of their accounting. The management of research projects is not only a peculiarity of universities, but also entails the need to allocate tasks between the department that carries out the research activity and the central administration that has to report said activity in the consolidated financial statements, and therefore determine its accrual in each financial year.

The accounting structure of universities is mainly dealt with in Ministerial Decree 19/2014, which sets forth the principles for the preparation of the consolidated annual report.

The legislation identifies specific accounting principles for universities and refers, for any specific item not dealt with in the Ministerial Decree, to civil law provisions and the accounting practices defined by the *Organismo Italiano di Contabilità* (OIC), the Italian commission for accounting. We can, therefore, acknowledge how the lawmaker elected to intervene selectively on the preparation of the annual report by specifying only the criteria concerning those items that, being peculiar of universities, could not have been easily dealt with in the civil law or in the accounting principles established by the OIC.

Article 4 of the Decree indicates annual report item valuation criteria to be adopted by distinguishing provisions into those referred to the Statement of Assets and Liabilities, and those referred to the Income Statement. Valuation criteria and the principles for the reporting of research projects are contemplated in letter "g" of the above-mentioned article dedicated to the item of accruals and deferrals. More specifically, the lawmaker highlighted how the valuation of accrued income or deferred income in the university context takes on a peculiar significance in connection with the accrual of income derived from ongoing projects and research funded or co-funded by third parties.

Research projects are booked to the Income Statement among positive income items summarised in the macro-class "A—Operating income", and particularly in the sub-class "Income from typical activities". The lawmaker identifies two types of research projects: "competitive" research projects and "commissioned" research or research deriving from "technological transfer". The first class of projects is usually accessed by taking part in competitive selection procedures that are generally proposed by national or international public institutions (Ministry of University and Research, European Union, etc.) or by private or public foundations that have an interest for specific fields of research. The second type of projects consists of research activities commissioned to one or more departments by external entities, called "outsourced research projects".

After highlighting the different nature of the projects, the legislation regulates their assessment and distinguishes between projects of different duration. Projects or research may last for multiple years or be annual, depending on the agreements made with the funder and on the type of activity to be carried out.

Projects that start and finish within the same financial year are assessed on the basis of the cost criterion, where annual report items are valued based on cost. Pursuant to art. 2, cost "should be intended as the whole expense born to procure a given good or service, including those that can be directly or indirectly allocated for the reasonably allocable portion".

As regards multi-year research projects, the legislation leaves each individual university free to choose a valuation based on the cost criterion or as a function of the progress of works. We also point out that, once made, this choice will be univocal, which means that it will concern all the research projects of that university, subject to the condition that the Accompanying Notes will specify all the necessary information on the method used and criteria adopted.

For annual researches, valuation is extremely easy because all the costs incurred for the implementation of the project accrue during that year and are allocated to it based on the pertinence between the cost and the revenue [20].

Instead, the valuation and accounting of projects seems to be much more complex when the projects are due to last for several years. This situation requires the identification of the portion of costs and revenues to be allocated to the year considered as distinguished from the portion that must be transferred to future years.

Abstractly speaking, the applicable methodologies can substantially be reduced to the following two types:

1. The first consists in the determination of the portion to be allocated to the year considered by assuming that the revenue to be allocated corresponds to the costs incurred during the year and, consequently, proceeding to a write-off operation by booking a deferred or integration income by recording an accrued income.
2. In the second the accounting of research projects is considered similar to work in progress [49], so the portion of costs incurred during the year is determined and, correspondingly, the capitalization is made by booking a positive income components that sterilizes the income effect in the Income Statement, as a counter-entry to the evidence in the Statement of Assets and Liabilities of the annual report component in the current assets section.

Article 4 continues by specifying that the income derived from the projects is recorded as revenue and not as advance payment. In the case that costs exceed income in the year considered, the year's income will be recorded as accrued income in the Statement of Assets and Liabilities, while in the opposite case, if the income recorded exceeds the costs allocated to the project, the corresponding revenue will be written off and that portion will be transferred to the subsequent years with the accounting tool of deferred income.

Between these two options, the lawmaker seems to prefer the former solution, which requires research projects to be accounted for by identifying the portion accruing to the year in connection with the revenue amount allocated to the year. If this is lower than the cost incurred for the implementation of the project, an accrued income will be booked, vice versa a deferred income is recorded.

The accounting method identified has two important consequences: the first is that this approach implies the income neutrality of the research projects during their implementation period. The revenues allocated during the various years always corresponds with the cost of those years, so no impact is expected on the formation of the year's result. In fact, any margin will emerge only during the closing year, and usually in outsourced research. The second consequence consists in the fact that the accrued income or deferred income has originated from the progression of costs (*cost to cost*) between the different years rather than in connection with the time relevance of the economic component to the year, as traditionally happens.

The positive or negative difference between the amount of allocated revenues and costs incurred during the year depends on the time when the revenue is booked in the accounts. Since the lawmaker does not contemplate the option of booking advance payments on research projects (art. 4), the following options remain: the first consists in booking the revenue derived from the research project when the administration is formally obliged to a third party, with whom it has agreed to finance a given project: for example, the ministerial decree that designates the winners of public funds for research or the signature of a contract for outsourced research. In this case, the revenue is entirely allocated to the first year, therefore costs progressively incurred will be lower or equal to revenues. Therefore, based on the cost to cost criterion, a deferred income is booked to write off the portion of revenue to be transferred to subsequent years, whose amount corresponds to the difference between the allocated cost and the previous revenue.

The second option consists in booking the revenue when it is financially realized. In this case, there is a real possibility for revenues to be lower than costs, so they must be integrated by booking accrued income for the same amount of the cost allocated to the year, so as to neutralize the incidence of the economic result.

Consequently, the accounting of research projects first of all requires the definition of specific competencies between the peripheral structures where the activities are carried out and the central administration that takes care to reflect them in the consolidated annual report. Then the configuration of the information accounting system must ensure the allocation of the individual cost items to the different projects, their subdivision by peripheral structures, and finally, the determination of the portion of revenues to be allocated to the year considered and the closing of account at the end of the year [19].

In the next sections of this paper we will describe, by using a case study, the main characteristics of the accounting information system configured in the University of Genoa.

5   The Case Study of the University of Genoa

The University of Genoa has adopted accrual and cost accounting since January 2013, two years in advance with respect to the legislative requirement.

In particular, on 28 March 2012, its Board of Directors passed a resolution for the purchase of Cineca's U-GOV application platform for the introduction of an integrated accrual and cost accounting system. In this regard, we should point out that the charts of accounts for accrual accounting and cost accounting are distinct, but, obviously, interconnected. More specifically, the chart of accounts for cost accounting is the tool used to enter the provisions of the consolidated annual authorization budget in the U-GOV system. Subsequently these provisions, when the management operations are carried out, will be checked for budget availability in order to proceed with cost accounting (the latter being kept by using the single-entry book-keeping method) and/or accrual accounting bookings.

The U-GOV system has been designed, inter alia, for the management of research project accounting. More specifically, it allows to:

- Manage research project master data with a taxonomy that has been previously defined at central level;
- Connect the research project with the responsible organizational units, human resources and funders involved;
- Book and report on the acquisition and use of the financial resources connected with the costs and revenues of the projects.

In order to describe the management of research project accounting, the following steps will be summarised:

- Configuration of the project form;
- Management of research projects during the year;
- Closing of the year.

The *configuration of the project form* has been managed centrally (that is the accounting unit of the central administration) during the start-up of the U-GOV system and required the specification (through successive screen pages) of:

- Taxonomy of projects, developed at three levels (classes, macro-typologies, typologies);
- Cost/revenue statement forms (with lists of the possible cost/revenue items to be booked and reported) and activity statement forms (that list the possible typologies of activities to be reported);
- Typology of funders and related master data;
- Financing schemes on the basis of the different types of reporting requested.

Therefore, potential connections between projects, cost and revenue items for accrual and cost accounting, activities to be carried out, funders and reporting criteria are already created during the initial stage. Always during the configuration stage (within the more general framework of "Accounting configurations"), the Genoa University decided to assess research projects by reporting their value with the *cost to cost method.*

The *management of research projects during the year* involves decentralized structures (Departments, Centres of excellence, etc.) which can enter the data of the research project proposals and label them as "draft". Then when there is a signature of an agreement, convention, resolution, ministerial decree, etc. the decentralized structures confirm the data and label them as "final". The data to be entered allow for the creation of the actual connections between the individual research project and:

- The organizational structure, by entering the organizational units involved in the project;

- The human resources, by entering the names of the university employees involved, their role and commitment in terms of time;
- External funders, by entering their names and respective cash contribution in absolute and relative terms;
- The accrual and cost accounting system, through the project codes, the amount of financial resources available, the project start and end dates, the project typology, the financial scheme, and finally the cost/revenue statement form adopted.

The transition to accrual accounting has led to a redesign of responsibility between the central administration and decentralized structures.

The Fig. 1 shows the procedures between the old and the current situation.

From the point of view of bookkeeping, when the research project has reached the "final" stage, upon issuing the so-called "Pro-forma Invoice", the revenue is determined as specified below:

- A so-called "advance accrual accounting bookkeeping entry" (Invoices to be issued@Revenues from research projects), called "advanced" because it precedes the reception of the actual invoice;
- A so-called "regular cost accounting bookkeeping entry", which books a revenue according to the cost accounting chart of accounts.

If, conversely, the invoice receivable is immediately issued based on the research agreement in force or if there is another similar document (for example a ministerial decree), the revenue is determined as follows:

- A so-called "regular accrual accounting bookkeeping entry" (Receivables@Revenues from research projects);
- A so-called "regular cost accounting bookkeeping entry", which books the revenue according to the cost accounting chart of accounts.

In both cases, the U-GOV system requires that the period of accrual of the revenue be defined; it is a particularly significant piece of information because, at year-end, in adjusting entries, the IT procedure will automatically connect the non-accrued revenue portion to the following period. Then the central administration checks the validity of documents and authorizes the decentralized structure to use the financial resources.

In the case of a purchase of goods or services, the order for the supplier will cause the creation of an "advance cost accounting bookkeeping entry", so called because it precedes the time when the actual cost arises, that is to say the time when the good is delivered or service is provided. When the order is accounted for with the "advance cost accounting bookkeeping entry", the budget availability for the research project is checked (as the project is connected to the booking of the issuing of the order through its code) and then, if the outcome is positive, the relative amount is reduced. In the U-GOV system, the availability of the budget can be checked by choosing between two control modes: an analytical control (on the

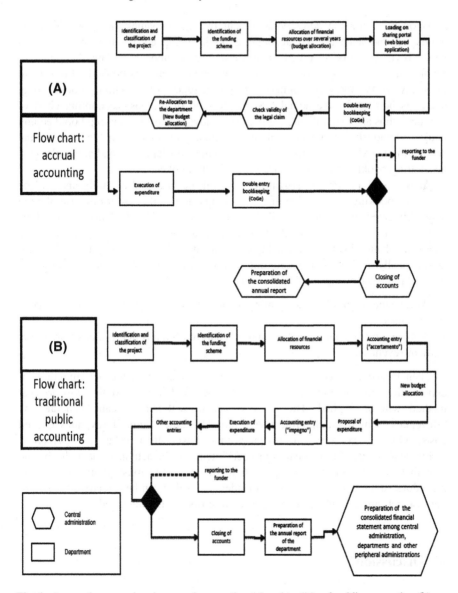

Fig. 1 Accounting procedure in accrual accounting (**a**) and traditional public accounting (**b**)

budget availability of the individual cost item used for the booking) or a synthetic control (on the resources globally available during the year for the research project). For reasons connected with the necessary management flexibility in conducting research projects, the University of Genoa uses this availability check not on the individual cost accounting item, but synthetically on the global budget availability of the project.

Upon receiving the delivery document that accompanies the entrance of the goods, an "advance accrual accounting bookkeeping entry" must be booked—Cost@Invoices to be received—and subsequently, upon receiving the purchase invoice, a "regular accrual accounting bookkeeping entry" is booked—Invoices to be received@Payables to suppliers. Then a "regular cost accounting bookkeeping entry" is booked for the actual cost in the item of the cost accounting chart of accounts, thus also neutralizing the previous "advance cost accounting bookkeeping entry". Obviously, in the case of an accompanying invoice, a "regular accrual accounting bookkeeping entry"—Cost@Payables to suppliers—and a "regular cost accounting bookkeeping entry" are immediately booked.

At *year-end*, the *cost to cost* procedure will be managed centrally and will be started by booking depreciation in cost accounts, so that the cost for the use of fixed assets allocated to the project will be considered in said calculation. Only afterwards will the *cost to cost* method be applied on each typology of project, in the submenu of the closing records. In particular, it is the U-GOV system itself that automatically in the cost accounting adjusts revenues to the year's costs, by recording the following as a single entry:

- A revenue item (cost accounting chart of accounts item), if costs exceed revenues;
- A lower revenue item (cost accounting chart of accounts item), if costs are lower than revenues.

Then in accrual accounting the procedure is made up of the determination of depreciation, the determination of the "project balances" and the *cost to cost* method will be applied. The U-GOV system will automatically generate the "Revenues from research projects@Deferred income" item, if revenues exceed costs. On the contrary, if revenues are lower than costs, an "Accrued income@Revenues from research projects" item will be activated manually by the user that allocates the accrued portion to the year. We must point out that the procedure summarised above only considers costs that can be directly allocated to the research project, while general structure costs are not allocated.

6 Discussion

The paper aims to investigate how the information system supports the implementation of the accrual accounting and the new budgeting and reporting system in the university, with a specific reference to the accounting treatment of research projects. Focusing on this particular aspect stems from the relevance this item takes on in the university, from the complexity of the accounting of research projects, as well as for their emblematic significance in bookkeeping processes.

The outcome of research activities shows how accounting for research projects, and more generally the transition from traditional public accounting to accrual accounting, is not only a technical accounting problem exclusively limited to the administrative sphere, but definitely becomes a managerial issue as it impacts planning and programming processes, organizational layouts, accountability processes and governance processes.

The management of research project accounting needs a precise definition of the organizational layout that clearly conveys the differences between competencies and responsibilities in the peripheral structures where the project activities are conducted and the central administration that has the task of reporting those activities in the accounts and also of reflecting their incidence in the annual report.

For all these reasons, the accounting information system is important both as a tool closely connected with the operation of processes of the entity and for its prescriptive value, as it affects the definition of accounting procedures, responsibilities and organizational tasks. In fact, the analysis conducted shows how the role of the accounting information system in support of research projects is not a neutral item, i.e. perfectly adaptable to the peculiarities of the administration, but has restrictions and boundaries that affect and, or better condition, the same formation of accounting procedures and the operation of the organization. For example, in some cases the IT application facilitated accounting choices, but in other cases it conditioned the steps and the characteristics of other procedures; in other situations, finally, it even implied total reorganizations.

From the organizational point of view universities have gone from a situation in which the peripheral units had its own budget and its annual report to a situation in which the management forecasting and reporting are under the responsibility of the central administration. In addition to the problems of learning the new accounting system by the operators the University of Genoa had to reconfigure all the accounting procedures that currently operate simultaneously at the central and peripheral level. The approach adopted by the Genoa University for the configuration of its IT application is essentially oriented to an integrated management of research projects. This integration spans over three different but interconnected planes:

- A first plane concerning technical-accounting integration, which takes form in the single chart of accounts that links cost accounting entries to accrual accounting entries;
- A second plane regards integration at the level of attributions between peripheral structures and the central administration. The accounting information system allows to break down the research project booking process into sub-processes that are attributed to different entities. For example, we point out how peripheral structures prevalently operate on cost accounting items, while the central administration has taken upon itself the task of booking the main entries in accrual accounting, particularly those connected with the closing of accounts and reporting of research projects in the consolidated annual report;
- The third integration plane concerns the decision-making process. Here the accounting information system operates as a carrier of regulations for the decision-making process. The management of research projects implies integration between the different fields of independence in making decisions that

link peripheral structures to the central administration. The accounting treatment of research projects is fed by a decision-making process that is developed in the individual departments that can develop their own decision-making process within the scope of the delegations assigned to them and this process, in its turn, will trigger the system of decisions made by the central administration.

As regards technical-accounting issues, our investigation showed how, for certain aspects, including the most significant, the information system requires manual actions from the operator. The definition of accrued income, for instance, requires the operator to identify the portion of revenues accrued during the year, to be booked with the integration entry. Although the cases where booking accrued income is required are much less than those where deferred income must be booked, if we consider the number of ongoing projects in a university, which is much more than 10,000, the circumstance of having activities to be done manually involves a quite large amount of work and exposes to the risk of errors and inaccuracies.

Further research perspectives may concern an extension of the cases examined in order to understand, by means of comparisons, whether other universities using the same application or those that chose other software application, made different choices in terms of accounting procedures, and which challenges and weaknesses they found.

References

1. Borgonovi, E.: Principi e sistemi aziendali per le pubbliche amministrazioni. Egea, Milano (2002)
2. Anselmi, L.: Percorsi aziendali per le pubbliche amministrazioni. Giappichelli, Torino (2003)
3. Mussari, R.: Public sector financial reform in Italy. In: Guthrie, J., Humphrey, C., Jones, L.R., Olson, O. (eds.) International Public Financial Management Reform: Progress, Contradictions and Challenges. Information Age Press, Greenwich (2005)
4. Guthrie, J., Olson, O., Humphrey, C.: Debating developments in new public financial management: the limits of global theorizing and some new ways forward. Financ. Account. Manag. **15**, 209–228 (1999)
5. Lapsley, I.: Accounting and the new public management: instruments of substantive efficiency or a rationalising modernity? Financ. Account. Manag. **15**, 201–207 (1999)
6. Olson, O., Guthrie, J., Humphrey, C.: International experiences with 'new' public financial management (NPFM) reforms: new word? small word? better word?". In: Olson, O., Guthrie, J., Humphrey, C. (eds.) Global Warning: Debating International Developments in New Public Financial Management. Capelen Akademisk Forlag As, Oslo (1998)
7. Agasisti, T., Arnaboldi, M., Catalano, G.: Reforming financial accounts in the public sector: the case of Universities. Ir. Account. Rev. **15**, 1–29 (2008)
8. Arcari, A.: Il controllo di gestione negli Atenei. Egea, Milano (2003)
9. Campedelli, B.: Il sistema di rilevazione delle informazioni e la contabilità analitica. In: Azzone, G., Campedelli, B., Varasio, E. (eds.) Il sistema di programmazione e controllo negli atenei. Il Mulino, Bologna (2011)
10. Cantele, S., Martini, M., Campedelli, B.: Factors affecting the development of management control systems in Universities. Economia aziendale Online **4**, 167–183 (2013)

11. Catalano, G., Tomasi, M. (eds.): Esperienze di contabilità economico-patrimoniale nelle università. Il Mulino, Bologna (2010)
12. Catturi, G., Grossi, G., Riccaboni, A.: Evoluzione storica e prospettive della contabilità negli Atenei italiani. Annali di storia delle Università italiane **8**, 1–14 (2004)
13. Paolini, A., Soverchia, M.: Le università statali italiane verso la contabilità economico-patrimoniale ed il controllo di gestione. Manag. Control **3**, 77–98 (2013)
14. Marchi, L.: I sistemi informativi aziendali. Giuffrè, Milano (2003)
15. Marchi, L., Mancini, D. (eds.): Gestione informatica dei dati aziendali. Franco Angeli, Milano (2009)
16. Mancini, D., Vaassen, E.H.J., Dameri, P.R.: Trends in Accounting Information Systems. In: Mancini, D., Vaassen, E.H.J., Dameri, P.R. (eds.) Accounting Information System for Decision Making. Springer, London (2013)
17. Yin, R.K.: Case Study Research: Design and Method. Sage Publishing, Beverly CA (1984)
18. Azzone, G., Campedelli, B., Varasio, E. (eds.): Il sistema di programmazione e controllo negli atenei. Il Mulino, Bologna (2011)
19. Azzone, G., Campedelli, B., Cantele, S.: La progettazione del sistema di programmazione e controllo negli Atenei. In: Azzone, G., Campedelli, B., Varasio, E. (eds.) Il sistema di programmazione e controllo negli Atenei. Il Mulino, Bologna (2011)
20. Sostero, U.: Il postulato della competenza economica nel bilancio d'esercizio. Giuffrè, Milano (1998)
21. Zappa, G., Marcantonio, A.: Ragioneria applicata alle aziende pubbliche. Giuffrè, Milano (1954)
22. Cassandro, E.: Le gestioni erogatrici pubbliche. Utet, Torino (1979)
23. Anessi Pessina, E., Steccolini, I.: I sistemi contabili degli Enti locali: stato dell'arte e prospettive di riforma. Egea, Milano (2007)
24. Anessi Pessina, E.: La contabilità delle aziende pubbliche. Egea, Milano (2000)
25. Pezzani, F.: L'evoluzione dei sistemi di contabilità pubblica. Azienda pubblica **4**, 561–565 (2005)
26. Hood, C.: A public management for all seasons. Public Adm. **69**, 3–19 (1991)
27. Hood, C.: The new public management in the 1980s: variations on a theme. Acc. Organ. Soc. **20**, 93–109 (1995)
28. Anthony, R.N.: The fatal defect in the federal accounting system. Pub. Budg. Financ. **20**, 1–10 (2000)
29. Paulsson, G.: Accrual accounting in the public sector: experiences from the central government in Sweden. Financ. Account. Manag. **22**, 47–62 (2006)
30. Sicilia, M., Steccolini, I.: Vent'anni di riforme dei sistemi contabili degli enti locali: principali evidenze empiriche. In: Anessi Pessina, E., Sicilia, M., Steccolini, I. (eds.) Bilanci pubblici tra riforme e prassi: quali sfide per il futuro? Egea, Milano (2011)
31. Buccoliero, L., De Nardi, F., Nasi, G., Steccolini, I.: L'implementazione della contabilità economico-patrimoniale negli enti locali italiani: i risultati di un'indagine empirica. Azienda pubblica **4**, 591–614 (2005)
32. Steccolini, I.: Accountability e sistemi informativi negli enti locali. Giappichelli, Torino (2004)
33. Hopwood, A.G.: The archaeology of accounting systems. Acc. Organ. Soc. **12**, 201–234 (1987)
34. Hopwood, A.G.: Accounting and the domain of the public-some observations on current developments. In: Guthrie, J., Parker, L., Shand, D. (eds.) The Public Sector—Contemporary Readings in Accounting and Auditing. Harcourt Brace Jovanovich, Marrickville (1990)
35. Laughlin, R.: Accounting systems in organizational context: a case for critical theory. Acc. Organ. Soc. **12**, 479–502 (1987)
36. Broadbent, J., Jacobs, K., Laughlin, R.: Organizational resistance strategies to unwanted accounting and finance changes. Account. Auditing Account. J. **14**, 565–586 (2001)
37. Covaleski, M.A., Dirsmith, N.W.: An institutional perspective on the rise, social transformation and fall of a university budget category. Adm. Sci. Q. **33**, 562–587 (1988)

38. Covaleski, M.A., Dirsmith, N.W., Samuel, S.: Changes in the institutional environment and the institutions of governance: extending the contributions of transaction cost economics within the management control literature. Account. Org. Soc. **28**, 417–441 (2003)
39. Steccolini, I.: Cambiamento e innovazione nei sistemi contabili pubblici. Egea, Milano (2009)
40. Meyer, J., Rowan, B.: Institutionalized organizations: formal structure as myth and ceremony. Am. J. Sociol. **83**, 340–363 (1977)
41. Hyndman, N., Connolly, C.: Accruals accounting in the public sector: A road not always taken. Manag. Account. Res. **22**, 36–45 (2011)
42. Christiaens, J., De Wielemaker, E.: Financial accounting reform in Flemish universities: an empirical study of the implementation. Financ. Account. Manag. **19**, 185–204 (2003)
43. Carnegie, G., Wolnizer, P.: Unravelling the rhetoric about the financial reporting of public collection as assets: a response to Micallef and Peirson. Australian Account. Rev. **9**, 16–21 (1999)
44. Micallef, F., Peirson, G.: Financial reporting of cultural, heritage, scientific and community collections. Australian Account. Rev. **7**, 31–37 (2008)
45. Barton, A.D.: Accounting for public heritage facilities—Assets or liabilities of the governments? Account. Auditing Account. J. **13**, 219–235 (2000)
46. Guthrie, J.: Application of accrual accounting in the Australian public sector: rhetoric or reality? Financ. Account. Manag. **14**, 3–19 (1998)
47. Garlatti, A., Pezzani, F.: I sistemi di programmazione e controllo negli enti locali. Etas, Milano (2000)
48. Borgonovi, E.: Principi contabili: anche nell'amministrazione pubblica? Azienda pubblica **2**, 173–178 (2004)
49. Agasisti, T., Catalano, G.: Una proposta di principi contabili per il settore universitario. In: Catalano, G. (ed.) La contabilità economico-patrimoniale nelle università-aspetti metodologici e principi contabili. Il Mulino, Bologna (2009)
50. Coran, G., Sostero, U.: I sistemi contabili universitari come strumenti per il monitoraggio dell'economicità: un'evoluzione possibile? In: Cugini, A. (ed.) La misurazione della performance negli Atenei. Franco Angeli, Milano (2007)
51. Salvatore, C.: Il cambiamento della governance delle Università italiane come strumento di corretto governo, Quaderni monografici 9. Rirea, Roma (2012)

The Role of the CIOs on the IT Management and Firms' Performance: Evidence in the Italian Context

Katia Corsi and Sara Trucco

Abstract This research aims to analyze the ways in which skills and personal features of the Chief Information Officers (CIOs) could affect the ERP (Enterprise Resource Planning) implementation and management in the Italian context. Furthermore, we attempt to analyze how the different ways of ERP implementation and management could contribute to improve the firms' performance. Prior studies demonstrated the link between the adoption of an IT (Information Technology) and the financial and non-financial performance ratios of a firm. Even if scholars found controversial results about it, they all seem to agree that deeper and more positive improvements related to an ERP adoption could be introduced only after a certain lag of years. Recent literature about this topic also highlights that the CIOs' role with his/her features, such as background, managerial competencies, technical skills are essential factors in obtaining positive economic returns for IT investment and in improving the overall firms' performance. Despite these considerations, it has not still been paid enough attention to the recent and evolving role of the CIOs' personal features and how the different ways of ERP implementation and management could contribute to improve the firms' performance. In order to reach our main aim, we carry out 10 in-depth pilot interviews to Italian CIOs to elicit early qualitative feedback and we send the survey questions to the CIOs who are willing to have collaboration with our research project. The survey has the main aim to test research items identified from the pilot interviews, in an exploratory and subjective viewpoint. Results contribute to the theoretical and practical definition of the relevant profiles attributable to CIOs and the impacts of each profile to firms' performance.

Keywords CIO's role · Information technology · ERP · Italian firms · Firms' performance

K. Corsi
Economic and Management Sciences Department, University of Sassari, Sassari, Italy
e-mail: kcorsi@uniss.it

S. Trucco (✉)
Faculty of Economics, Rome University of International Studies, Rome, Italy
e-mail: sara.trucco@unint.eu

© Springer International Publishing Switzerland 2016   217
D. Mancini et al. (eds.), *Strengthening Information and Control Systems*,
Lecture Notes in Information Systems and Organisation 14,
DOI 10.1007/978-3-319-26488-2_16

1 Introduction

Recent literature highlights the pivotal role of the CIOs on the IT management and on the overall firms' performance [1–3]. The role of this managerial function was introduced in the 1970s, even if its responsibilities and its tasks have increased in the recent decades. Specifically, according to the literature and professional associations, the CIO is the person responsible for investments in technology and able to demonstrate how this technology can properly drive to create value within the firm [4, 5]. In pursuing its functions, the CIO needs to be coordinated with the other top managers, such as the Chief Executive Officer (CEO), the IT auditor and the Chief Financial Officer (CFO) [6]. In the Italian setting, the topic of CIOs role is quite new. In this framework, a fundamental role is played by the IT governance that should be oriented toward developing processes, organizational structures and relational mechanisms for the IT decision making process, in accordance with the mission of the firm [7, 8].

Aim of this paper is to analyze the ways in which skills and personal features of the CIOs could affect the ERP implementation and management in the Italian context and how they could contribute to improve the firms' performance.

Paper is organized as follows. Section 2 provides the literature review about this topic; Sects. 3 and 4 define research design, sample and data collection; Sects. 5, 6, and 7 propose preliminary findings, final discussion and suggestions for future researches.

2 Literature Review

A literature stream about IT systems focuses on the potential corporate performance benefits due to an ERP implementation [9–15]. Even if most of academics agree that it is important to have an holistic view of ERP implementation effects [10, 16, 17], they highlight mixed results about the possible impacts that an ERP adoption could have on the financial and non-financial performance of a firm. Moreover, scholars agree that the ERP adoptions produce the full effects after a certain time-lag [18, 19].

On the basis of this perspective, recent literature investigates the CIO's role in the ERP management, the CIOs' features and the overall IT governance and their impacts on business performance.

The concept of the IT governance is relatively new and it becomes relevant from the late 1990s with the definition of an information system framework [20], to describe relationships among managers in order to achieve strategic alignment between business and IT [21]. Subsequently, other scholars highlight the needs to transform the simple IT system management into an IT governance [22]. The IT governance should be developed within each firm that deals with IT [23]. Recently, the concept of IT governance has evolved and concerns the needs to integrate the business and the IT plans, to allocate IT responsibilities and to define the priority of IT investments within a firm [23, 24]. The IIA's International Professional Practices Framework defines IT governance as "the leadership, organizational structures, and processes that ensure that the enterprise's information technology supports the organization's strategies and objectives." According to recent literature, the most common framework to evaluate IT governance is the Control Objectives for Information and related Technology, COBIT [25, 26]. COBIT, largely used into the organizations, helps top managers to control their information systems, processes, investments and risks in order to achieve a better IT governance [23, 27]. Prior studies highlighted that the IT governance structure should be complementary to the organizational IT architecture to achieve the IT alignment [28]. The IT alignment could be defined as the level to which the IT function supports the main goals of an organization's line functions [29]. Within this framework, a literature stream deals with IT governance contingency influences [30]. Specifically it focuses on which option could be the best one for an organization, thereby analyzing factors that could affect the IT governance success. The evolving IT governance framework, which is closer to new strategic and organizational needs, also affects the managerial structure, responsibilities, activities and abilities of CIOs.

The evolvement of the CIO's role in recent years has led to proliferation of studies about the different aspects of the IT governance, such as studies regarding the different structures of the IT function [31]; the activities performed by the IT staff and by CIOs [32, 33]; the relationships between CIOs and business functions [34], and between CIOs and top management team [35] and finally the impacts of CIOs' role on organizational performance [1, 36]. This proliferation in the literature shows the richness and versatility of CIOs' features and a high fragmentation of these studies.

In order to overcome this fragmentation, we consider useful contributions that propose several profiles of CIOs, characterized by specific skills, activities and relationship. Guillemette and Paré propose five profiles of CIO, although they could be overlapped [37]: architecture builder, partner, project coordinator, systems provider and technological leader. Authors provide skills, mission, activities, relationships and governance for each profile of CIO. Furthermore, scholars propose different features of CIOs, namely "CIO role Performance": business visionary, business system thinker, value configure, entrepreneur, IT architect planner, organizational designer, relationship builder and informed buyer [38]. The several attempts to configure the CIOs role, all agree on the growing influence acquired by this position in recent years, because ERP increasingly play a pivotal role in business processes. In this way, CIOs often sit at the table of top management team and assume a huge influence role, even out the IT function. According to the "upper echelon theory" [39, 40], the CIO, as a member of the firm's C-level executive team, assumes a strategic role and can affect organizational performance, adding value to the firm by enhancing an effectively use of the IT, an achievement of organization's objectives and an overall improvement of performance [36, 41]. This can be demonstrated by some researches which show that market reacts positively to the creation of the new CIO position and to the appointment of the CIO as a firm's leader [42, 43]. The increasing pivotal role of the CIO in business processes open up new research interests on this topic, especially with regard to two main issues: (1) the relationships between CIO and top management team and (2) the skills and abilities of the CIO. About the former, some contributions point out the relationships between CIO and other CXOs (other C-level Officers), as social capital. A recent study analyzes the social capital in three dimensions (structural, cognitive and relational), investigating how each dimension of social capital can support exchange of knowledge and alignment between the organization's IT strategy and business strategy. Scholars demonstrate that these facts finally affects the firm's financial performance [35]. Other studies focus on the relationship between CIO and some specific members of top management team, especially CEO and CFO. Therefore, the CIO should report to CEO or CFO; this choice should depend on firm's strategic position and strategic IT role. It is likely to have a CIO who reports to a CEO, if the firm pursues IT initiatives that help the differentiation strategy; on the other hand, a CIO should report to a CFO in order to lead IT initiatives in facilitating cost leadership strategy [6, 44].

Several contributions regarding the latter topic, point out how skills and background of CIOs affect the IT orientation and how this position contributes to the firm's performance improvement. CIO should have a technical background, as basic training, even if this know-how could support just an utilitarian orientation of his/her role, emphasizing rigid support of operations [1]. Innovative approaches of IT in supporting long-terms goals (strategic orientation) and in improving the overall firm's performance should require managerial and leadership skills [45].

According to the literature, there are a lot of taxonomies which describe the CIO's skills. Chen and Wu [38] identify IT and managerial skills which affect the IT management effectiveness and the CIO's role performance. In addition to these considerations, Khallaf and Majdalawieh [46] argue that the CIO's competencies can have several sources, such as experience and education. These sources can be both present into three dimensions identified as: "Know-what", Know-how" and "Know-how to be" [47]. Although the education is important to affect the overall know-what, the experience aids to obtain the Know-what contextualized to a specific sector or firm, allowing the development of skills, relating to leadership, strategic thinking, diplomacy, visionary, reading the market, delivering, relationship building, etc. [48, 49]. The previous knowledge allows to generate the "know-how to be", which regards procedures useful to formal know-how.

3   Research Design

This research focuses on the wide concept of the "organizational role". The concept of role, in fact, has an organizational and social meaning: firstly, it refers to a specific organizational position (formal role) and, secondly it regards to skills, relationships and expectations obtained in covering the role (substantial role). The "substantial role" represents the set of actions performed by a person in relation to

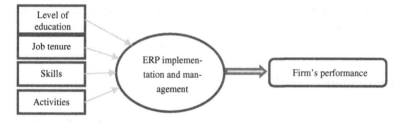

Fig. 1 Research framework

his/her expectations, the results achieved and the interactions with other organizational positions. On the basis of this concept, we build the conceptual framework (Fig. 1). Therefore, we attempt to fill the literature gap, using a subjective analysis based on the CIOs' viewpoint to answer the following two research questions:

RQ1: *In which way skills and personal features of the CIO could affect the ERP implementation and management?*
RQ2: *How the different ways of ERP implementation and management could contribute to improve the firm's performance?*

4 Sample Selection and Data Collection

In order to answer our research questions, we conduct our study on a sample of CIOs in large and small/medium Italian companies. Firstly, we personally contact CIOs taking numbers of telephone directly from the website of each firm. Due to a low response rate (just two CIOs agree to participate in the interviews and in the consequent survey), we use the LinkedIn social network, as some scholars highlight that social media applications are largely used among people [50] and LinkedIn is becoming essential for business professionals [51]. From LinkedIn we select all the Italian CIOs and we obtain 135 contacts. Secondly, according to the literature [52], we carry out 10 in-depth pilot interviews in order to elicit early qualitative feedback and to better refine our research design and the subsequent survey. We select 10 interviewees from our LinkedIn contacts on the basis of their willingness to cooperate in university research projects [53, 54]. In the interviews, we use an open semi-structured questionnaire for a total of a maximum of 30 min per subject. In these interviews, we ask subject to define his/her role, the responsibilities, the type of relationships with other managers, the way in which an ERP can be implemented and how this fact affects the firms' performance. After this preliminary phase, we send the survey questions to the CIOs. The survey has the main aim to test research items identified from the pilot interviews, in an exploratory viewpoint [55]. The survey is split into 5 sections as follows: 1—personal data of the interviewee; 2—

training; 3—professional background; 4—the definition of the role of the CIO; and 5—final section.

5 Preliminary Findings

This paragraph is split into two sections: in the first one we propose the processing and interpretation of pilot interviews and in the second one we propose preliminary findings about the survey.

5.1 First Section: Pilot Interviews

In-depth pilot interviews elicit early qualitative feedback and help us to better refine our research design. Specifically, interviews allow us to define CIOs' role in the ERP adoption and management. The interviewees come from different contexts, from both small and large firms (from a minimum of 50 employees to a maximum of 70.000 ones), from both private and state-owned companies and from different industrial sectors. The interviews are recorded, transcribed in a file and encoded in a synthetic grid in order to compare CIOs' answers. The interviews are carried out through a semi-structured questionnaire which requires to categorize answers into five pivotal items: (1) CIOs' responsibility and activities; (2) relationships between CIO and the other managers; (3) CIOs' role in the ERP investment decision; (4) CIOs' role in the ERP adoption and management and (5) recent changes in the CIOs' role.

1. *Responsibilities and activities*

The CIO's role is wide and multitasking, as the CIO is simultaneously responsible for several projects which correlate him/her with various stakeholders and he/she simultaneously performs traditional functions regarding maintenance, implementations and management of the IS. All the interviewees argue that they carry out activities which support the business growth. These activities may lead the CIO to have relationships with various functions, thereby highlighting problems of communication. The CIO needs to develop relational skills and to use an administrative language in order to assume a pivotal role in the decision process. This leads to a partial overcoming of the traditional functional barriers.

> Over the years, I have deliberately lost the pulse on the situation about technological aspects, since these aspects can be directly handled by my employees: today I mainly deal with the organizational aspects, which regard processes and inter-functional projects.

2. *Relationships with other managers*

The CIOs traditionally deal with external stakeholders, as suppliers. Moreover they need to have a lot of contacts, especially with the operational managers. They should not provide products, but solutions of problems. For this aim, it is important that CIO develops listening skills in order to perceive all requests from operational functions. The relationship between CIOs and managers should be collaborative, even if this is often hindered by the following elements: the procedures, a different mind-set among managers, an interference of the property that "*does not give enough space to the CIO*", the difficulty of overcoming traditional conflicts between functional effectiveness and efficiency. The relationship especially depends on the capability to be an appealing function that provides services and creates value.

> One thing is to establish relationship with the operational managers offering them an updated version of a software and another thing is to sit in the same table and say: -look! I can reduce your time of orders management for ten days-.

3. *Role of the CIO in ERP investment decisions*

In general, the CIO is the promoter of the investment, even if the sponsor is often the top managers. This sponsorship supports the CIO in overcoming barriers and reluctance that are typical of the implementation step and it legitimates him/her to solve the conflicting relationships and the changes often generated in the following investment management phase. Sometimes, the CIO may be the sponsor of a project, but he/she needs to acquire it through two main actions: understanding which projects can create value in the company and sharing them with the managers who should benefit from these projects. They are, in fact, functional managers who should realize the real changes to make productive the investments and the projects.

> It is important, just from the beginning, to take on board the internal customer.
> In the face of an IT investment, there are often relevant resistances and a strong mandate helps to smooth the way.

4. *The way in which an ERP can be implemented and its impacts on firm's performance*

The implementation of an ERP could generate a shift in the paradigm, as this project has both a technical and an organizational complexity. With an ERP, the IT function may not have a product-based approach, but an approach based on the composition of products, procedures, processes and results. "*If this new approach is not accepted, it is likely to propose something that it will never be applied by firms*".

The ERP cannot be implemented in an adaptive way, such as a pre-packaged product, since results can even worsen, producing unused information or information not properly used. The purely technical approach runs the risk of never being applied. The best approach should be the proactive one, conveying the wills of all people to solve the problems that arise from the ERP implementation and to avoid the politics of "passing the buck". This approach allows the optimization of the processes, creating value for the company.

We must be careful to not fall into the logic "redo everything, reassess the entire company," because this is the way to activate projects for which you know from where you start, but you do not know where you end. When project ends, we are all unhappy, since the project has been expanded so much, that finally we are not able to reach the expected objective.

5. *Recent changes in the CIO's role.*

In recent years, the CIO has moved from an operational connotation to a managerial one: he/she is becoming a consultant in the management of processes and projects. In fact, he/she is often the best problem solver, as he/she is able to perceive the needs of the company, to propose technical solutions and especially to manage them. He/she is a qualified interface, as a sort of translator between the computer technician and the users who work in various operational functions. *"The CIO is pulled by the hair to participate in the definition of processes"*; this aspect not always shows its management and strategic impacts, because the benefits of this CIO's involvement regard the formal procedures and internal control systems or because sometimes it prevails the concept of the IT function, as a mere cost-centre. The changes are due both internal factors, such as increasing complexity, and external factors, such as the recent innovation of the cloud. Technical innovation bring about the barriers down that confine the CIO respect to the business, so that nowadays the CIO may be considered an innovation officer or an integration officer.

If the CIO does not understand the necessity to change himself/herself and if he/she is not able to act as a collector of opportunities for organizational improvements, he/she will be intended to be confined as a mere manager of low-level services.

6. *Conclusive considerations from preliminary interview-step*

This first preliminary phase allow us to define different approaches that CIOs could use in the ERP implementation and management, which we codify into four main profiles, in relation to the prevalence of a different professional and background focus:

(1) the informatics one, which is based on technical and informatics aspects, such as the choice of a new ERP, the solution of technical problems in the ERP implementation and the maintenance of the software in order to provide the basic IT services at a minimum cost; (2) engineering/process related one, which focuses on the process management through business procedures analysis and process mapping, in order to optimize the processes and to provide a competitive advantage; (3) organizational/managerial one, which is based on the operational and functional problems that could be solved through the IT solutions, and strong relationships between CIOs and other functional managers and other C-level managers in order to emphasize the capabilities of IT in supporting new business strategy; and (4) marketing/relational one, which focuses on the CIO's skills to propose himself/herself either to external subjects (especially suppliers) and internal managers in order to operate as an organizational collector.

5.2 Second Section: Survey Results

From this phase, we obtain 50 answer forms from CIOs (rate of answer: 37 %). Respondents are all men (with the exception of a woman) with an average age of 46 years (minimum age: 32; maximum age: 61). The greatest number of CIOs (9 out of 50) are located in Milan and, in general, in the North of Italy. Regarding the second section of the survey (training of the CIO), we find that 50 % of our sample attended a high school and 50 % attended a technical institute. As university education, results underline that most of the CIOs have an engineering degree (20 out of 50) and 30 % of CIOs do not have a degree. Finally, as postgraduate education, we find that most of the CIOs do not have any postgraduate qualifications (82 %), even if many CIOs declare that they also attended several informatics courses and courses for project management. Most of the CIOs highlight the relevance of a deep field experience and the possibility to have a professional growth thanks to free courses organized by the firms in which they worked. The third section of the survey (professional background) highlights a high turnover of this professional figure, as CIOs tend to have a long experience in this field, even if a short work experience in the current firm (as shown in Fig. 2).

Survey results underline that CIOs mainly report to the Chief Executive Officer (CEO) (31 out of 50). The remaining CIOs report to the Chief Financial Officer (CFO) (7 out of 50) and to the Board of Directors (8 out of 50). They have a team work of around 33 people (with a maximum in our sample of 300 people in big firms and a minimum of 2 workers in small/medium firms). CIOs' survey is consistent with the previous in depth-interviews, confirming the presence of four main professional orientations of respondents (Table 1). They highlighted, indeed, the predominance of the organizational/managerial approach (36 out of 50).

After confirming different CIOs' professional orientations, we attempt to answer our RQ1. To answer the RQ1, we correlate, in a preliminary way, the skills and personal features with the four approaches above mentioned (as shown in Table 2, 3, 4 and 5). To deepen features of different approaches, we carry out a comparative analysis among them. We decide to eliminate the marketing/relational approach, as

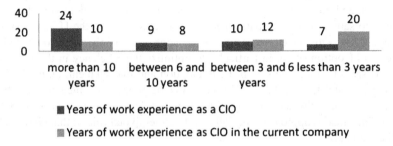

Fig. 2 Years of work experiences as a CIO and years of work experiences as CIO in the current company

Table 1 Professional orientations of the CIOs in our sample

	Organizational/managerial	Informatics	Engineering/process related	Marketing/relational
CIO	36	6	4	2

results demonstrates the low relevance of this profile (just two respondents choose this approach).

Table 2 underlines that CIOs' education could affect the way in which they adopt and manage ERP; the informatics profile is chosen especially by CIOs with a more technical background. Respondents who attended technical institutes seem to prevail among CIOs with the informatics approach. Comparing informatics profile to the others, we note that in the informatics one there is the highest percentage of CIOs without a degree. In the other two approaches, interesting considerations could arise from the analysis of the degree programme, as respondents with engineering or informatics degree seem to prevail among CIOs with an engineering profile, thus reflecting in the company, process setting of their studies.

Table 3 confirms, in general, a high turnover of CIOs, as they tend to have a long experience in this field, even if a short work experience in the current company.

In detail, analysing the three CIOs profiles, we find that respondents with informatics approach tend to have a lower turnover than respondents with the other two approaches and the engineering respondents tend to have a higher turnover than the other two profiles.

The identification of the three different CIOs' profiles is also confirmed by analyzing CIOs' activities (Table 4). We find, indeed, that each approach has its own main activities (with a percentage greater than 15 %), that are different from each other and seem to affect each specific profile.

In the informatics approach, main activities especially regard the IT area and IT structure. In particular, relevant activities for this profile seem the detection of the main informatics needs and the ability of building the most efficient and effective IT structure able to satisfy these needs, both in short and long term (through a proper management and maintenance of the IT structure). CIOs in organizational/managerial approach seem to prefer activities that allow CIOs to go beyond the technical IT area boundaries. These activities are useful to promote integration and interaction among the other organizational functions (first IT users) in order to satisfy their informatics needs and to contribute to the IT functionality. Finally, CIOs with an engineering/process approach mainly focus on activities related to IT optimization, in particular to optimize the efficiency in the IT area.

CIOs seem to affect the way of ERP adoption and management, on the basis of the their specific skills (Table 5). This confirms the presence of three profiles above mentioned. Main relevant skill for all CIOs is problem solving, even if just CIOs with an informatics approach especially declare the pivotal role of this kind of skill for their function.

In informatics approach, indeed, relevant skills regard IT area useful to solve technical problems. In the engineering/process related profile, main skill is the

Table 2 CIOs' education and CIOs' approaches

	Technical institute (%)	High school (%)	Engineering (%)	Informatics (%)	Economics (%)	Mathematics (%)	No degree (%)
Informatics	80[a]	20	20	20	20	0	40
Engineering	50	50	75	25	0	0	0
Organizational	44	56	42	17	11	3	28

[a]Percentage is equal to the sum of respondents that have an informatics approach and attended a technical institute divided by the total number of respondents with an informatics approach, expressed in percentage, and so on

Table 3 Work experience as a CIO in the life and in the current company and CIOs' approaches

		Years of work experience as a CIO			
		Less than 3 years (%)	Between 3 and 6 years (%)	Between 6 and 10 years (%)	More than 10 years (%)
Informatics	Life	20	0	20	60
	Company	60	0	0	40
Engineering	Life	0	25	25	50
	Company	25	75	0	0
Organizational	Life	12	22	19	47
	Company	42	22	19	17

Table 4 CIO's activities and CIOs' approaches

	Informatics (%)	Organizational (%)	Engineering (%)
Definition of investment plans	15	11	13
Design of the informatics structure	20	10	19
Control and monitoring of investment	0	8	13
Management and maintenance of the IT structure	15	8	6
Cost optimization of the IT area	10	10	19
Identification and enhancement of skills in the IT area	5	9	0
Promotion of organizational integration	5	13	13
Detection of the main informatics needs	15	8	0
Co-design and collaboration with other business functions	5	19	13
Supplier management	5	4	6
Other	5	1	0

ability to map business processes, consistently to previous analysis regarding CIOS' activities. Other pivotal skills within this approach are related to ability useful to achieve an organizational integration, such as the listening skill, the communicational skill and skills in raising awareness of the organizational structure. In particular, we find that listening skills is more relevant in this approach than in the organizational one, not consistently with our expectations. Skills useful for CIOs in the organizational profile are the ability to have a unique view of business processes (as in the informatics approach) and the communicational skills and skills in raising awareness of the organizational structure (as in the engineering approach). Some CIOs in this approach underline the relevance to have leadership in their own team and the need to know the business, the firm and the market. The organizational approach thus seem to be an intermediary approach among the others. Figure 3

Table 5 CIOs' skills and CIOs' approaches

	Informatics (%)	Organizational (%)	Engineering (%)
Technical-computing knowledge	25	7	6
Skills in having relationships with vendors	5	3	6
Skills in raising awareness of the organizational structure	5	13	13
Communicational skills	0	12	13
Motivational skills	0	9	6
Unique view of business processes	15	15	6
Ability to map business processes	10	10	19
Decision making	5	10	6
Problem solving	25	13	13
Listening skills	10	8	13
Other	0	1	0

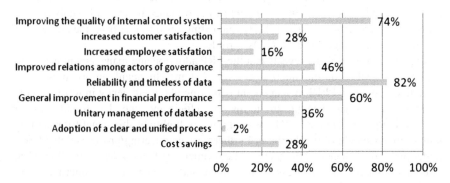

Fig. 3 Main advantages of a good ERP management: CIOs' perspectives

shows the main advantages of a good ERP management in the CIOs' perspectives, not affected by the CIOs' profile.

Most of the respondents identified as the main impact due to the ERP implementation, the traditional results concerning the reliability and timeliness of data. This impact is quite essential and unavoidable. However, around 60 % of CIOs aware that their role contributes to the overall financial performance improvement. A higher number of CIOs (74 %) declare that their role have a positive impact on the quality of the internal control system, confirming the pivotal role of CIOs in mapping and optimization of the processes. This aspect is consistent with the professional association's viewpoint [7]. A significant group of CIOs (46 %) underline an improvement of relationships among actors of governance due to their role.

Table 6 Main advantages of a good ERP management and CIOs' approaches

	Informatics (%)	Organizational (%)	Engineering (%)
Cost savings	15	7	0
Adoption of a clear and unified process	0	0	6
Unitary management of database	5	10	13
General improvement in financial performance	10	16	13
Reliability and timeless of data	20	22	25
Improved relations among actors of governance	20	13	6
Increased employee satisfaction	10	4	6
Increased customer satisfaction	5	7	13
Improving the quality of internal control system	15	21	19

To answer our RQ2, (Table 6), we find that regardless of the CIOs' approach, respondents emphasized an improvement of performance in terms of reliability and timeless of data, as we expected. More interesting results arise from the analysis of the highest percentage for each CIOs' profile.

In general, this analysis reveals that the ERP adoption and management is able to lead better quality of the internal control systems. In detail, informatics CIOs underline that a good ERP management can bring about efficiency in terms of cost savings. A similar benefit in terms of efficiency can be found among engineering/process related CIOs, who indirectly highlight this benefit through an unitary management of the database. Furthermore engineering/process related CIOs underline, among benefits, the increased customer satisfaction, as a reflection of an orientation based on a process management and oriented to the internal client satisfaction.

An interesting finding is linked to the fact that the advantage related to the adoption of a clear and unified process is just perceived by engineering/process related CIOs (even if with a low percentage), while respondents of the other two approaches do not observe it. Organizational/managerial respondents emphasize, among benefits, the general improvement in financial performance (as in the engineering/process approach) and the improved relations among actors of governance (as in the informatics approach). Finally, we analyze main words that CIOs used in the survey to describe their features (we asked them to use maximum three words). The main words used by respondents were: Innovation (12 CIOs); Vision (7 CIOs); Solution (5 CIOs); Collaboration (5 CIOs); Know-how (5 CIOs); Facilitator (4 CIOs); Patience (4 CIOs); Purposeful (3 CIOs); Planning (3 CIOs); Reliability (3 CIOs); Availability (3 CIOs); Listening-Skills (3 CIOs); Strategy (1 CIO), Practical (1 CIO), Timeliness (1 CIO), Flexibility (1 CIO).

6 Discussion

This research revealed some interesting findings (results are synthetized in the Fig. 4) about the skills and personal features of the CIO could affect the ERP implementation and management, thus answering our RQ1 (*In which way skills and personal features of the CIO could affect the ERP implementation and management?*).

In-depth pilot interviews allow us to elicit early qualitative feedback and to better refine our research design and the subsequent survey. All CIOs underline a deep need to have a wider approach than the classical technical IT one. In particular, these interviews allow us to define CIOs' role in the ERP adoption and management and we find 4 main CIOs' approaches in the ERP management:

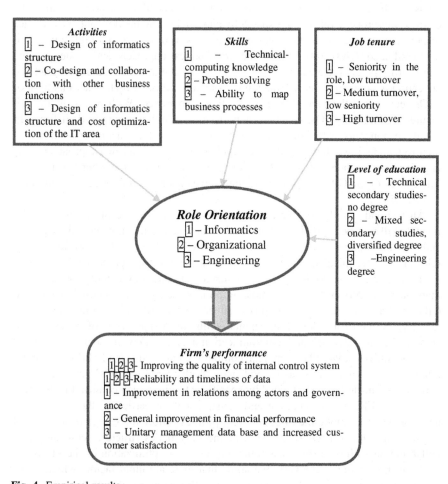

Fig. 4 Empirical results

(1) informatics; (2) engineering/process related; (3) organizational/managerial and (4) marketing/relational. From deep interviews, it emerges that CIOs are especially aimed to propose operational and technical solutions to the emerging problems from different firms' functions and they have strong relationships with other functional managers and other C-level managers.

In their perspectives, it emerges awareness of the CIOs' contribution to the firm growth and of the necessity to go outside the functional boundaries, improving relationships between CIOs and other managers. Preliminary findings about survey are also consistent with our expectations and with the previous step of the deep interviews. The survey confirms, in fact, the four main CIOs profiles above mentioned, even if we decide to delete the marketing/relational one, as results are not significant and just few respondents chose this approach. The survey highlights that skills and personal features of a CIO could affect the ERP implementation and management. In detail, we find that the informatics profile is chosen especially by CIOs with a more technical education in secondary school, while the engineering/process related is especially chosen by engineering and informatics respondents, as we expected. Relevant finding is also related to a high number of not graduated CIOs (40 % for the informatics approach and none for the engineering/process related one). This could mean that university and post-graduate education is not so relevant for the CIOs' role; as confirmed by the fact that a lot of CIOs recognized the pivotal role of the field experience. With regard to the job tenure, we find that CIOs, generally, tend to have a high turnover in their firms. In detail, respondents with informatics approach tend to have a higher seniority of their role and a lower turnover than respondents with the other two approaches. The engineering respondents tend to have a higher turnover than the other two profiles. The choice of the CIOs' approach by themselves is also conditioned by their skills and activities.

All respondents identify the problem solving ability as one of the most fundamental skill to a better ERP implementation and management, even if this specific skill has the highest value for the informatics CIOs. These CIOs also declare the relevance of technical computing knowledge. Engineering/process related CIOs confirm their concern to the processes management and they identify the ability to map business processes as the most important skill. Organizational/managerial CIOs prefer skills relative to improve an organizational integration. They, thus, identify, as one of the most fundamental skills, the unique view of business processes; the motivational and communicational skills. Few respondents identify more operative skills (like technical computing knowledge and skills in having relationships with vendors) as pivotal ones. With regard to CIOs' activities, each approach seems to be characterized by specific activities which confirm the different ways to the ERP implementation and management. In particular, the main CIOs' activities (19 %) among the three different profiles (informatics, organizational and engineering) are, respectively, design of the informatics structure; co-design and collaboration with other business functions and cost optimization of the IT area.

According to our framework, we argue that there are input factors which affect the different ways of ERP management and, furthermore, that the specific way chosen could affect firms' performance. The survey results allow us to answer the RQ2: *How the different ways of ERP implementation and management could contribute to the firm's performance?*

Respondents underline relevant impacts of the ERP on the firms' performance; thus confirming several prior studies about this issue. Interesting findings demonstrate that skills and personal features of CIOs affect the choice of different CIOs' profile and this facts affect several dimensions of firms' performance. Most of respondents (84 %) highlight an expected improvement in the reliability and timeliness of data, while 76 % of CIOs of all profiles unexpectedly identify the awareness of the ERP impact on the quality of internal controls. This could be due to the fact that classical internal control framework, like COSO and ERM (Enterprise Risk Management) give relevance to the Information Technology (IT). This pivotal role of the IT is then particularly underlined by a specific framework for IT, namely COBIT. Furthermore, we find other kinds of impacts that are different among the three profiles, above mentioned. These findings allow us to attempt to define impacts on firms' performance depending on different CIOs' approach. Informatics CIOs, indeed, underline the relevance of technical skills useful to solve problems of efficiency; informatics profile thus highlights an impact on firms' efficiency, as expected. This particularly impact is totally absent in the engineering profile. Engineering CIOs, instead, underline the relevance of an unitary management of database, pivotal condition to carry on an integrated process management and to reduce efficiency problems due to a not-unitary management of data. Another unexpected result for engineering CIOs is linked to the advantage of better relationships among top managers (6 % for engineering CIOs; 20 % for informatics CIOs and 13 % for organizational CIOs). This could be due to the fact that the ERP management allows the informatics CIOs to have more occasions for relationships with top managers. With regard to the organizational CIOs' approach, it does not seem to have any prevalent impacts and it underlines a general improvement of financial performance and an unitary management of database.

Finally, interesting findings are also linked to the advantage regarding a better customer satisfaction, underlined by engineering CIOs. We argue that these findings regard the traditional process management aimed at satisfying internal client and, finally, the final customer. The following figure confirms our proposed framework, reporting for each considered variable the higher value, obtained from survey. In order to appreciate the CIOs' perspectives about their role, we consider interesting that respondents used terms like innovation, vision, facilitator, patience, solution, purposeful, reliability, availability, know-how, listening-skills and collaboration. This result is particularly significant, as CIOs seem to give more emphasis to soft skills (organizational and strategic) rather than hard ones (technical). This confirms the recent evolution of the CIOs' role in the IT governance.

We are aware that results of this research could be distorted by the subjective nature of the deep-interview and the survey. This method could emphasize the positive CIOs' role and positive impacts on firms' performance, more than in the reality. Anyway, the survey is built with a questionnaire that asks CIOs to answer to several predefined options, restricting the discretionary of the respondent in order to highlight the actual relevance of chosen answers.

7 Suggestions for Future Researches

Future researches could be carried out extending the survey in Italy and in other countries. This allows researchers to compare different geographical and business contexts and to analyze the differences among CIOs that operate in "entrepreneurial" and "managerial" firms and in large and small firms. These researches should be carried out using a wider CIOs' sample useful to conduct advanced statistical analysis. Furthermore, our research highlights some interesting findings that deserve to be deepen into the future. For instance, we find that main previous work experience of CIOs are in the field of IT, in the internal audit, in the managerial control and in the organizational fields.

References

1. Sobol, M.G., Klein, G.: Relation of CIO background, IT infrastructure, and economic performance. Inf. Manag. 46, 271–278 (2009)
2. Lunardi, G.L., Becker, J.L., Maçada, A.C.G., Dolci, P.C.: The impact of adopting IT governance on financial performance: an empirical analysis among brazilian firms. Int. J. Account. Inf. Syst. 15, 66–81 (2014)
3. Li, M., Ye, R.L.: Information Technology and Firm Performance: Linking with Environmental. Strateg. Managerial Context Inf. Manag. 35, 43–51 (1999)
4. Earl, M.J., Feeny, D.F.: Is your CIO adding value?, Sloan Manag. Rev. 11–20 (1994)
5. Mithas, S., Tafti, A., Bardhan, I., Goh, J.: Information technology and firm profitability: mechanisms and empirical evidence. Manag. Inf. Syst. Q. 36, 205–224 (2012)
6. Banker, R.D., Hu, N., Pavlou, P.A., Luftman, J.: CIO reporting structure, strategic positioning and firm performance. MIS Q. 35, 487–504 (2011)
7. COBIT, Framework for IT Governance and Control, ISACA. http://www.isaca.org/Knowledge-Center/COBIT/Pages/Overview.aspx
8. Van Grembergen, W., De Haes, S., Guldentops, E.: Structures, processes and relational mechanisms for IT Governance. In: Van Grembergen, W. (ed.) Strategies for Information Technology Governance, pp. 1–36. Idea Group Publishing, Hershey (2004)
9. Brazel, J.F., Dang, L.: The effects of ERP system implementations on the usefulness of accounting information. Working Paper, Department of Accounting College of Management North Carolina State University, pp 1–37 (2005)
10. Gattiker, F.T., Goodhue, D.L.: What happens after ERP implementation: understanding the impact of interdependence and differentiation on plant level outcomes. MIS Q. 29, 559–585 (2005)
11. Glover, S.M., Prawitt, D.F., Rommey, M.B.: Implementing ERP. Internal Auditor, Feb, 40–47 (1999)
12. Hayes, D.C., Hunton, J.E., Reck, J.L.: Market reaction to ERP implementation announcements. J. Inf. Syst. 15, 3–18 (2001)

13. Shields, M.G.: E-Business and ERP: Rapid Implementation and Project Planning. Wiley, Hoboken (2001)
14. Al Sudairi, M.A.T.: Analysis and exploration of critical success factors of ERP implementation: a brief review. Int. J. Comput. Appl. **69**, 44–52, (2013)
15. Nicolaou, A.I.: Firm performance effects in relation to the implementation and use of enterprise resource planning systems. J. Inf. Syst. **18**, 79–105 (2004)
16. Markus, M.L., Axline, S., Petrie, D., Tanis, C.: Learning from adopters' experiences with ERP: problems encountered and success achieved. J. Inf. Technol. **15**, 245–265 (2000)
17. Jarrar, Y.F., Mudimigh, A.A., Zairi, M.: ERP implementation critical success factors—the role and impact of business process management. Proceedings of the 2000 IEEE International Conference on Management of Innovation and Technology, pp. 122–127 (2000)
18. Hunton, J.E., Lippincott, B., Reck, J.L.: Enterprise resource planning systems: comparing firm performance of adopters and non-adopters. Int. J. Account. Inf. Syst.s **4**, 165–184 (2003)
19. Nicolaou, A.I., Bhattacharya, S.: Organizational performance effects of ERP systems usage: the impact of post-implementation changes. Int. J. Account. Inf. Syst.s **7**, 18–35 (2006)
20. Brown, C.V.: Examining the emergence of hybrid IS governance solutions: evidence from a single case site. Inf. Syst. Res. **8**, 69–95 (1997)
21. Loh, L., Venkatraman, N.: Diffusion of information technology outsourcing: influence sources and the kodak effect. Inf. Syst. Res. **3**, 334–359 (1993)
22. Agić, Z., Tadić, M., Zdravko, D.: Tagger voting improves morphosyntactic tagging accuracy on Croatian texts. Information Technology Interfaces (ITI), 2010, 32nd International Conference on IEEE, 2010
23. Simonsson, M., Pontus, J., Ekstedt, M.: The effect of IT governance maturity on IT governance performance. Inf. Syst. Manag. **27**, 10–24 (2010)
24. Debraceny, R.S.: Re-engineering IT internal controls—applying capability maturity models to the evaluation of IT controls. In Proceedings of the 39th Hawaii International Conference on System Sciences, Hawaii, USA (2006)
25. IT Governance Institute (ITGI): Control objectives for information and related technology, 4.1st edn. IT Governance Institute, Rolling Meadows, IL (2007)
26. IT Governance Institute (ITGI): The Val IT Framework. IT Governance Institute, Rolling Meadows, IL (2007)
27. Krakar, Z., Žgela, M., Rotim, S.T.: CobIT–Framework for IT governance–analysis and experience. FOI, retrieved, 25–06 (2010)
28. Tiwana, A., Konsynski, B.: Complementarities between organizational IT architecture and governance structure. Inf. Syst. Res. **21**, 288–304 (2010)
29. Chan, Y., Reich, B.: IT alignment—what have we learned? J. Inf. Technol. **22**, 297–315 (2007)
30. Brown, A.E., Grant, G.G.: Framing the frameworks: a review of IT governance research. Commun. Assoc. Inf. Syst. **15**, 38 (2005)
31. Weill, P., Ross, J.: A matrixed approach to design IT governance. MIT Sloan Manag. Rev. **46**, 26 (2005)
32. Peppard, J.: Managing IT as portfolio of services. Eur. Manag. J. **21**, 67–83 (2003)
33. Ross, J.W., Beath, C.M., Goodhue D.L.: Develop long-term competitiveness through IT Assets. Sloan Manag. Rev. Fall **38**, 31–42 (1996)
34. Ward, J., Peppard, J.: "Mind the Gap": diagnosing the relationship between the IT organisation and the rest of the business. J. Strateg. Inf. Syst. **8**, 29–60 (1999)
35. Karahanna, E., Preston, D.S.: The effect of social capital of the relationship between the CIO and top management team of firm performance. J. Manag. Inf. Syst. **30**, 15–55 (2013)
36. Li, Y., Tan, C.H., Teo, H.H., Tan, B.C.: Innovative usage of information technology in Singapore organization: do cio characteristics make a difference. IEEE Trans. Eng. Manage. **53**, 177–190 (2006)
37. Guillemette, M.N., Paré, G.: Toward a new theory of the contribution of the IT function in organizations. MIS Q. **36**, 529–551 (2012)

38. Chen, Y.C., Wu, J.H.: IT management capability and its impact on the performance of a CIO. Inf. Manag. **48**, 145–156 (2011)
39. Khallaf, A., Skantz, T.: The effects of information technology expertise on the market value of a firm. J. Inf. Syst. **21**, 83–105 (2007)
40. Hambrick, D.C., Mason, P.A.: Upper echelons: the organization as a reflection of its top managers. Acad. Manag. Rev. **9**, 193–206 (1984)
41. Peppard, J.: The conundrum of IT management. European J. Inf. Syst. **16**, 336–345 (2007)
42. Chatterjee, D., Richardson, V.J., Zmud, R.W.: Examining the shareholder wealth effects of announcements of newly created CIO positions. MIS Q. **25**, 43–70 (2001)
43. Carpenter, M.A., Geletkanycz, M.A., Sanders, W.G.: Upper echelons research revisited: antecedents, top management team composition. J. Manag. **30**, 749–778 (2004)
44. Preston, D.S., Karahanna, E., Rowe, F.: development of a shared understanding between the chief information officer and top management team in U.S. and French organizations: a cross cultural comparison. IEEE Trans. Eng. Manage. **53**(2), 191–206 (2008)
45. Bharadwaj, A.S: A resource based perspective on information technology capability and firm performance: an empirical investigating. MIS Q. **24**, 169–196 (2000)
46. Khallaf, A., Majdalawieh, M.: Investigating the Impact of CIO competencies on IT security performance of the U.S. Federal Government Agencies. Inf. Syst. Manag. **29**, 55–78 (2012)
47. Ravarini, A., Tagliavini, M., Moro, J., Guimaraes, T.: Shaping CIO's competencies and activities to improve company performance: an empirical study. Proceedings of ECIS 2003 Conference, Naples, Italy (2003)
48. Peppard, J.: Unlocking the performance of the chief information officer (CIO). Calif. Manag. Rev. **52**, 73–99 (2010)
49. Spitze, J.M., Lee, J.J.: The renaissance CIO project: the invisible factors of extraordinary success. University of California, Berkeley **54**, 2 (2012)
50. Albrecht, W.D.: LinkedIn for accounting and business students. Am. J. Bus. Edu. (AJBE) **4**, 39–42 (2011)
51. Association of Accounting Marketing, Association for Accounting Marketing Social Media Survey, August 2010. from http://www.accountingmarketing.org/pdfs/2010/08162010_social_media_survey_results.pdf (2010). Retrieved 23 Feb 2011
52. Chen, J., Nairn, R., Nelson, L., Bernstein, M., Chi, E.: Short and tweet: experiments on recommending content from information streams. Proceedings of the SIGCHI Conference on Human Factors in Computing Systems. ACM (2010)
53. Yin, R.K.: Case Study Research. Design and Methods, London, Sage (1994)
54. Rubin, H.J., Rubin, I.S.: Qualitative Interviewing. The Art of Hearing Data, Thousand Oaks, Sage (1995)
55. Gable, G.G.: Integrating case study and survey research methods: an example in information systems. Eur. J. Inf. Syst. **3**, 112–125 (1994)

Determinants of Information Technology Audit Quality

Tatiana Mazza, Stefano Azzali and Lily Brooks

Abstract The research aims to measure the Information Technology Controls (ITC) quality and its determinants within the Internal Controls over Financial Reporting. Data are collected from questionnaires and financial reporting of Italian listed companies. The main objective of the research has been investigated using innovative method of evaluation of ITC quality: we used the characteristics of two of the main relevant phases of the audit cycle: ITC scoping and ITC risk assessment. Taking the determinants from previous audit literature and adding the specific variable "Information Technology Auditors", results show that industry, internationalization and diversification, outsourcing strategy, market capitalization, firm age and corporate governance play a relevant role in determining the efficiency and the efficacy of ITC.

Keywords Information technology controls · Internal control over financial reporting · Audit quality · Audit cycle

1 Introduction

The overall objective of the research is to analyze the Information Technology Controls (ITC) quality over Financial Reporting with an original method of measurement. The evaluation of the Internal Control System (ICS) to assess the

T. Mazza (✉) · S. Azzali
Università Degli Studi Di Parma, Via Kennedy 6, 43100 Parma, Italy
e-mail: tatiana.mazza87@hotmail.it

S. Azzali
e-mail: stefano.azzali@unipr.it

L. Brooks
Washington State University, Pullman, WA 99164-4750, USA
e-mail: lily.brooks@wsu.edu

T. Mazza
Free University of Bozen-Bolzano, Bozen, Italy

© Springer International Publishing Switzerland 2016
D. Mancini et al. (eds.), *Strengthening Information and Control Systems*,
Lecture Notes in Information Systems and Organisation 14,
DOI 10.1007/978-3-319-26488-2_17

reliability of the financial reporting includes the audit of the ITC. Sarbanes-Oxley (SOX) Act in USA and the law 262/2005 in Italy provide for the Chief Executive Officer (CEO) and the Chief Financial Officer (CFO) the responsibility to attest the reliability of the financial reporting, evaluating also the ITC. The significant role of Information Technology (IT) in the financial reporting process and the related high risks of errors or fraud show an important research area connected with Audit Quality: the purpose is to identify methods useful for the improvement of ITC quality through its determinants.

Following the previous literature, the control authority and the professional institution guides, this paper investigates the relation between ITC quality, measured with the phases of scoping and risk assessment within the internal audit cycle, and four classes of its determinants: ITC Staff, Complexity, Internal controls resources, Corporate governance.

Originality of the paper concerns both the dependent and the independent variables: ITC quality (dependent variables) is evaluated with two phases of the internal audit cycle (scoping and risk assessment) instead of material weaknesses or other indicators as mainly used in the previous literature [1, 8, 11]; the determinants of ITC quality (independent variables) are mainly taken from previous audit literature [1, 5–8, 11, 13, 21, 22, 27] and tailored to Italian context to discover peculiarities. We include the number of IT auditor's specialist as specific determinants for ITC quality.

Our focus is on Italy because, as in USA, after the great corporate scandals, like Parmalat and Cirio scandals, this country has adopted a regulation with the same objective of SOX: the improvement of internal control over financial reporting and the safeguard of stakeholders. Differently from SOX, Italian regulation do not provide compulsory auditing standard.

Results discover that ITC Staff (negative relation both for ITC scoping and ITC risk assessment), Complexity (positive relation for industry, internationalization and diversification, outsourcing) Internal Controls Resources (positive relation for market capitalization and firm age), Corporate Governance (positive relation) play a relevant role in determining the efficiency and the efficacy of ITC.

Next sections of the paper are related to literature review, research hypothesis, method, results, robustness and conclusion.

2 Literature Review

2.1 ITC Quality

The phases of Audit Cycle are scoping, risk assessment, testing design and operating effectiveness of controls, evaluation of control deficiencies and reporting (COBIT for SOX). Previous literature uses the output of the audit as indicator of audit quality: the phases of evaluation of control deficiencies and reporting. Literature proposes the material weaknesses (MW) as indicator of internal control over financial reporting quality and analyze its determinants [1, 8, 11]. This method is difficult in country, like Italy, that do not have public database on MW. Our research improves the literature proposing to use the input of the audit as indicator of audit quality: the phases of scoping and risk assessment for the evaluation of ITC. Instead to use the MW, we use two relevant phases of the Audit Cycle: scoping and risk assessment as shown to be important in planning ITC by COBIT for SOX. Their importance is key in designing the test of design and operating effectiveness to perform. Thus, we focus on the planning (scoping and risk assessment), rather than on testing.

The **scoping**, as the full audit cycle, follows a top-down approach, coherently with the request to reduce SOX compliance costs. O' Brien [28] writes that there are several ways to reduce it, including improving training, streamlining SOX processes, and automating controls: however, implementing a top-down, risk-based approach to establishing scope and testing strategies will have the largest impact on return on investment. Fogleman et al. [9] recommend a "stop-rethink-reuse" starting from the top level.

Some authors are critical to this proposal. Basilo [2] thinks that costs of SOX derives from the implementation of a new standard and from the update of the internal control documentation needed because the top-down approach used by external auditors had led to failure in keeping an internal control documentation for less riskily accounts covered by the top, concluding that the top-down approach is not a solution but it could be the cause of the corporate fraud because audits became predictable. Wilson [30] asks if for the audit planning it is better a top-down or a bottom up approach.

Although standards and frameworks underline its importance, the **risk assessment** is not developed as required and many researches show that the relation between the audit planning and the risk assessment is weak [10, 14, 24, 25]. Bedard [3] finds that audit plans are quite stable over a two-year period but the risk assessment is not included in the planning. O'Keefe et al. [29] find that labor inputs are significantly associated with client size, complexity, leverage and inherent risk, but not with control reliance, years on the engagement and non audit services suggesting that audit plans are responsive to inherent but not to control risks. Houston et al. [18] find that in the presence of errors, the audit risk model adequately describe audit planning decisions, in the presence of irregularities it did not.

Research after SOX shows the higher importance of risk assessment in planning. Hogan and Wilkins [16] find that auditors increase their fees when control deficiencies exist, particularly in cases where the problems are the most severe, that is they increase their effort in the presence of greater control risk. Bedard and Johnstone [4] report that audit planning responsiveness to risk increases considerably during the period immediately preceding and following the passage of SOX.

To implement the risk assessment, companies should identify the IT Inherent Risks. Despite IT is very helpful for accounting (for example they increase the accuracy and speed of calculus, they improve the update and the reconciliation, and they reduce the human influence), it could lead new risks linked by IT environment [23–25].

This research, based on previous literature, investigate the scoping and risk assessment phases of audit cycle and employ them to test the determinants of ITC quality.

2.2 Determinants of ITC Quality

The determinants of ITC quality, taken from previous audit literature, are classified in the following classes: (1) ITC staff; (2) Complexity; (3) Internal Controls Resources; (4) Corporate Governance.

1. ITC quality can have as determinant the number and the competences of the ITC Staff. The difficult communication, cooperation and integration between managers/evaluator and system designers is one of the major problem in IT audit cycle [27]. Therefore it is important that the companies assign the responsibility on compliance with SOX or Italian law 262/2005 to IT auditors together with the auditors on financial reporting. Hermanson et al. [15] find that the prevalence of computer audit specialists on the internal audit staff is associated with internal auditors' performance on IT evaluation. Other researches investigate the IT expertise on audit [6, 13, 22]. Cohen et al. [7] find that inherent risk assessments were not significantly affected by the resource dependence role, but control risk assessments and audit program planning judgments were significantly affected when the board played either a weak agency role or weak resource dependence role.

2. PCAOB, in the Auditing Standard 5, paragraph 13 suggests, as determinant, the scaling of the audit: complex company might achieve its control objectives differently than a less complex company. The Complexity for ITC increases when IT system are: (a) in outsourcing; (b) in the bank and insurance industry; (c) related to companies more diversified (segment) and internationalized (gain and losses from foreign currency translation); (d) older.

   When the company chose the strategy of outsourcing, the ITC can be transferred to the Outsourcer or to a Service Auditor, but the responsibility on the reliability of ICFR is always to the CFO or CEO that should evaluate the ITC outsourced, involving more actors in the audit process [5]. Hermanson et al. [15] find that the decentralization of IT system is positively associated with internal auditors' performance on IT evaluation (IT Asset Safeguarding). The strategy of outsourcing increase the risk assessment because the companies have to include in it many IT Inherent and Control Risks such as the level of detail of information flows in the description of controls, the timing, the standardization of audit methodology, the third part reputation. Laurent [21] shows that many organizations do not pay enough attention to the multitude of new risks. SOX obliged company to scrutinize any business or IT processes to consider these risks that may affect financial control and the accountability of those controls.

The complexity of IT general systems and applications is greater for banks and insurances because they include in scope applications for front office, interbank, method of payment process as credit card, ATM and POS management, which manufacturing and services companies do not have. Furthermore, banks and insurances have a more developed internal control system because they are subjected to a lot of requirements by Bank of Italy or IVASS.[1] Hermanson et al. [15] find that the finance industry is positively associated with internal auditors' performance on IT evaluation (System maintenance and program changes, IT Asset Safeguarding). Ge and McVay [11] find that disclosure of material weaknesses in internal control after SOX are different for industry: banking industry have the most common deficiencies in segregation of duties.

The intricacy of transaction toward more segments and international markets can lead to internal control problems. Ashbaugh-Skaife et al. [1], Doyle et al. [8] and Ge and McVay [11] find a positive relationship between the number of reported business segments, foreign sales and material weaknesses.

3. Because the evaluation of ICFR is costly, Internal control resources are important determinants. We use some variables that indicate the size and the profitability as proxy for the amount of resources that can be addressed to this process, as the market capitalization value, the presence of losses and the ratio CFO/A. Smaller firms, probably, have not sufficient resources to invest in ICFR. The firm profitability instead is an unsolved determinant, because great performances could leave free resources to invest in the ICS, but poor performance could incentive a big effort to control and discover the problems. Ge and McVay [11] and Doyle et al. [8] find a negative relationship between firm age and material weaknesses. We expect that older firms likely have more efficient ITC procedures.

4. Doyle et al. [8] find a negative relationship between Corporate Governance score and specific material weaknesses. We expect that the corporate governance quality helps in implementing a good ICS without material weaknesses.

3   Research Hypothesis and Model

Our model analyze the relation between the ITC quality (dependent variables) and their determinants (independent variables).

---

[1]IVASS: National Control Authority for the insurance industry.

3.1 ITC Quality

Following the US guidance, we investigate the ITC quality through the ITC scoping and ITC risk assessment quality.

ITC scoping quality can be improved building a MAP of elements, performing a LINK between elements and a CRITICAL EVALUATION ON FINANCIAL REPORTING. Better these actions are made, better is the ITC scoping quality. We investigate how to develop these specific actions. We investigate if the presence of a formal map help to identify elements to be evaluated, the linkage helps to have a systemic view of the company and the critical evaluation on financial reporting help to coordinate IT and FR competences. We also investigate the relative importance of these different actions assigning weights.

Firstly we built a measure of ITC scoping quality based on the definition of control authorities and frameworks. As defined by PCAOB and SEC the firm identifies which elements should be included in the audit cycle making a MAP of these elements. As defined by COBIT for SOX, a good process of scoping should LINK these IT elements with business processes and make a CRITICAL EVALUATION ON FINANCIAL REPORTING. Therefore we ask in the questionnaire if the companies include MAP, LINK and CRITICAL EVALUATION ON FINANCIAL REPORTING for the ITC scoping. We built a SIMPLE SCOPING SCORE that includes the three variables, weighed in the same way. If we assume a different impacts of the three components on the ITC scoping quality, we could also built a WEIGHETED SCOPING SCORE: the phase of mapping could have more influence (weighted 50 %) because let to identify and formalize the IT; next, the companies implement the critical evaluation on the risks related to the reliability of financial reporting only after having set up a map of IT possible risk (so with a lower weigh of 30 %) and finally companies link these IT elements to the business process as the final step (weigh of 20 %). We also change these weights to check if the results depends on the weights definition (see robustness).

We use these measures as dependent variables to investigate ITC scoping quality.

ITC risk assessment quality can be improved using a specific methodology to assign a RISK RATING and choosing a number of ITC PROCESSES, OBJECTIVES, CONTROLS following the trade off between the efficiency (low number) and effectiveness (high number). Better these actions are made, better is the ITC risk assessment quality. We investigate if the use of likelihood and impact of material misstatement is useful to improve the overall quality and if the compliance with the number suggested by US guidelines is useful also in Italy.

Secondly, we built a measure of risk assessment based on the definition of control authorities and frameworks. The first proxy is related to the method used to assign a risk rating: the firm should assign a risk rating considering the impact and the likelihood of financial statement error. Therefore we ask in the questionnaire if the companies use this method for the ITC risk assessment and we use the answers, variable called RISK RATING, as dependent variable, proxy for ITC risk assessment quality.

Next, we built a measure of risk assessment based on the number of ITGC processes, objectives and controls. The companies should identify the risky processes and the connected objective and controls that should cover at least the ITC problems of introduction, change management, access, security, and operation. We identify 5 level of risk assessment quality, coherently with Cobit for Sox requirements: 0, when company do not define the number of ITGC processes, objectives and controls; 1, when the company define a too low number of processes; 2, when company define too low number of objectives and controls, 3, when company define too high number of processes, objective and controls, without a risk based approach; 4, when company define a right number of processes, objectives and controls. This is the SIMPLE RISK ASSESSMENT SCORE.

Finally, we assign up and down thresholds to evaluate the number of processes and objectives too low, too high or adequate and we assign a different weight to the components of the ITC risk assessment quality. We assign the biggest weight (70 %) at the number of processes because it is the most objective and a lower weight at the number of objectives (20 %) and at the number of controls (10 %) because much more subjective and different among firms. This is the WEIGHETS RISK ASSESSMENT SCORE. We also change these weights to check if the results depends on the weights definition (see robustness), relaxing the hypothesis of a so high weight for the number of processes.

We employ these measures as dependent variables of the model to investigate the ITC risk assessment quality.

3.2 Determinants of ITC Quality

Following previous audit literature we grouped the determinants of ITC quality in the following classes:

1. **ITC Staff** is measured with the number of IT auditors;
2. **Complexity** is measured with IT Outsourcing, Industry, Segments, Gains and Losses from foreign currency translation;
3. **Internal Controls Resources** are measured with Market Capitalization, Loss, the index Cash Flow from Operations divided Assets, Firm Age;
4. **Corporate Governance** is measured with a composite measure of 7 factors encompassing 2 corporate governance categories: Board of Directors and the Audit Committee. This measure come from the output of a factor analysis using as input the number of directors, the number of independent directors, the number of annual meeting for both the categories and the number of expert directors for Audit Committee. The data have been hand collected from the corporate governance report 2011 public available on the web site of the firms. Expertise is defined by the certification, we used the number of certified public

accountants (CPA) or auditors: we check if the names of the directors in the audit committee are registered in the Italian CPA or auditors web sites. We base the measure of Corporate governance on the literature about the relation between Corporate governance and ICFR quality [12, 17, 19, 20, 26, 31]. The variables have showed a high correlation, as assumption of factor analysis and thus, we run this computation to have a factor score that aggregate all these variables in one indicator.

To analyze the relation between these determinants and the ITC quality, we use the following model:

ITC SCOPING QUALITY or ITC RISK ASSESSMENT QUALITY = $\beta 0$ + $\beta 1$ IT AUDITORS + $\beta 2$ OUTSOURCING + $\beta 3$ INDUSTRY + $\beta 4$ SEGMENTS + $\beta 5$ GAINS OR LOSSES FROM FOREIGN CURRENCY TRANSLATION + $\beta 6$ MARKET CAPITALIZATION + $\beta 7$ LOSS + $\beta 8$ CFO/A + $\beta 9$ FIRM AGE + $\beta 10$ GOVERNANCE SCORE

Table 1 shows the variables definitions. The model allows us to test the following Research Questions (RQ):

RQ1: Which are the determinants of ITC scoping quality?
RQ2: Which are the determinants of ITC risk assessment quality?

Following Hermanson et al. [15] we expect a positive relation between the quality of the ITC scoping and the number of auditors specialized in IT because the IT competences can increase the quality of ITC. Following Cohen et al. [7], we expect a positive relation between the ITC risk assessment quality and the number of IT auditors because the human resources have a strong impact on Control Risk assessment.

Following Cannon and Growe [5], Laurent [21], Ge and McVay [11], Doyle et al. [8] and Ashbaugh-Skaife et al. [1] finding, we expect a negative relation between the ITC quality and the complexity: industry more articulated (banks and insurances), the companies more diversified, internationalized and with the IT given in outsourcing because these characteristics show higher risk.

For the internal control resources there are not clear evidences of their relation with the ITC quality in the literature: the size and the performance could increase the ITC quality because they let free resources to assign at the ITC, but the presence of losses or low profitability could give more incentive to internal auditor to look for and discover problems implementing good quality procedures for the audit cycle. Following Ge and McVay [11], Doyle et al. [8] and Ashbaugh-Skaife et al. [1] we predict a positive relationship between the ITC quality and the firm age and governance score because the experience of the firms or of the components of the corporate governance organs can increase the ITC quality.

Table 1 Variable definition

Variables	Definition
Dependent	
ITC scoping	
Map	1 = if companies have a map for IT elements, such as processes, applications and layers 0 = otherwise
Link	1 = if companies link the IT risk and control matrix (map for IT elements) with the business risk and control matrix (map for accountability elements, such as companies controlled, financial reporting value and counts significant, procedures) 0 = otherwise
IT risks critical evaluation on FR	1 = if companies make a critical evaluation to decide the scoping with a financial reporting consideration 0 = otherwise
Scoping score	The sum of MAP, LINK and IT RISKS CRITICAL EVALUATION ON FR
Weighted scoping score	A score with the following weight 0.50 * MAP + 0.20 * LINK + 0.30 * IT RISKS CRITICAL EVALUATION ON FR
ITC risk assessment	
Risk rating	1 = companies assign a risk rating based on impact and likelihood of financial statement error 0 = otherwise
Simple risk assessment score	0 = number not defined 1 = too low number of processes 2 = too low number of objectives and controls 3 = too high number of objectives and controls 4 = adequate of processes, objectives and controls
Processes	0 = number not defined 1 = 1–6 (too low) 2 = 13–34 (too high) 3 = 7–12 (adequate)
Objectives	0 = number not defined 1 = 1–29 (too low) 2 = 66–130 (too high) 3 = 30–65 (adequate)
Controls	0 = number not defined 1 = 1–40 (too low) 2 = 326–800 (too high) 3 = 40–325 (adequate)
Weighted risk assessment score	A score with the following weight 0.70 * PROCESSES + 0.20 * OBJECTIVES + 0.10 * CONTROLS
Independent	
#Auditors on financial reporting	Number of internal auditors in the ICFR staff or designated for the ICFR attestation to comply with Italian law 262/2005 divided for total assets

(continued)

Table 1 (continued)

Variables	Definition
#IT auditors	Number of IT auditors in the ICFR staff or designated for the ICFR attestation to comply with Italian law 262/2005 that own competences on IT divided for total assets
Outsourcing	0 = IT and ITC is an in-house system 1 = IT and ITC system is in outsourcing
Industry	0 = {manufacturing and business service} 1 = {insurance, banking and finance}
Operating segments	Number of operating segments for which company express investments and income components following the requirement of IFRS 8
Gains or losses from foreign currency translation	1 = presence of other comprehensive income following the requirement of IAS 21 0 = otherwise
Market capitalization	1 = Index FTSE Italy Micro Cap 2 = Index FTSE Italy Small Cap 3 = Index FTSE Italy Mid Cap 4 = Index FTSE Italy Mib
Loss	1 = negative earning 0 = otherwise
CFO/A	Cash flow from operation scaled by total assets
Firm age	Number of years from the foundation year to 2010
Governance score	A composite measure of 7 factors encompassing 2 corporate governance categories
	Board of Directors
	– number of directors – number of independent directors – number of annual meeting
	Audit Committee
	– number of directors – number of independent directors – number of annual meeting – number of expert directors

4 Method

4.1 Study Design

Because we do not know the situation in Italy after the implementation of the model to comply with the Italian law 262/2005, we conducted exploratory interviews with a general open question: "How do you evaluate the ITC over financial reporting?" We asked this question at the internal auditor who has the responsibility to evaluate the ITC.

As in Italy there are not national general guidelines, companies implement a model that follows USA frameworks. For this reason we include in the questionnaire the phases of the ICFR evaluation process identified by these USA frameworks.

The questionnaire was prepared by academic researcher, internal auditors and external consultants. The help of internal auditors external consultants has been very important to assure a simple understanding language for the target companies. We include in the questionnaire questions about the procedures implemented for the evaluation process, without asking discretionary judgment on it. Then, we tested the questionnaire on three firms: a bank, insurance and a manufacturing firm who were within the target population. They answered the questionnaire and provided comments. This permitted us to make some adaptations to refine the study's design as well as the measurement of some of its constructs.

The questionnaires were mailed in 2011 addressing the evaluation process for the year 2010. The distribution procedure involved sending a survey package containing the questionnaire and a cover mail to underline the importance of the research and to motivate the participation. From the interview we have perceived the necessity of an Italian benchmark that let a comparison of the evaluation process. The companies complain the absence of this because in the market there are only USA benchmarks, too different from the Italian context, or expensive and biased benchmark prepared without a data control. Therefore, we use this problem to motivate the participation at the survey: in the cover mail we explain that the survey will be followed by an internal report for the participants that show the results of the evaluation process and give a benchmark sample in the Italian context with unbiased data. The results will be presented in a seminar at the university. After three weeks, we contacted by phone the companies that have not answered yet to increase the response rate.

We decided to assure at the answer of the questionnaire the confidentiality (we know the name of the company that answer at the questionnaire but we cannot disclosure this information, we can show the results only in the aggregation form). This decision lets us to link the data collected with other sources (financial reporting 2010, firm web site and web site of the Italian Stock Exchange). In addition, our association with the university was made clear to assure a greater response rate because the firms are protected from the disclosure of private information by a well-know and trust institute.

4.2 Sample

The population of this paper are the Italian listed company at Milan Stock Exchange implementing ITC that are explicitly targeted at monitoring and assuring compliance with law 262/2005.

The specific sample of the élite interview includes 3 companies, 1 company from each industry (the banking, the insurance and the manufacturing and service industries), because different industries have different IT systems and different internal control systems. Besides, the size (total assets) can influence the evaluation process because larger firms have more resources and more necessity to evaluate the controls. Therefore for each industry, we selected one firm from the top and one firm from the bottom quartile of the total assets.

The general sample for the sending of the questionnaire has been selected with the purpose to generalize the results at the Italian context. To exclude the companies that have not an ITC evaluation process we select the sample based on capitalization: it has been assigned a lager weight to company with lager capitalization. The variable used for the stratification of the sample is the capitalization because lower capitalized firms have not the ITC evaluation process implemented. We send the questionnaire at 122 companies. As we can see from the Table 2, the usable responses confirm the stratification hypothesis because larger firms respond more frequently at the questionnaire. The response rate was a 41.3 %. The population is limited, so a sample of 50 companies (21 % of the population) can be considered a sample with significance comparable with similar researches.

We assume that in the short period the procedure to evaluate the ITC does not change because they need high investments and a long process of training to be implemented. Then, we build a panel data including the questionnaire data for one year before (2009) and one year after (2011) the 2010: we match these data with the financial data for the relative fiscal year and we obtain the final sample of 150 observations (Table 2—Panel B Observations). We use (year) fixed effects models to control for the presence of repeated companies.

Table 2 Sample selection

Panel A—sample selection

Criteria	Total number of companies	Companies selection weighted for capitalization	Usable response 2010
Companies listed on the Milan Stock Exchange in 2011—Index FTSE MIB	38	30 (80 %)	17 (45 %)
Companies listed on the Milan Stock Exchange in 2011—Index FTSE Italy Mid Cap	59	35 (60 %)	11 (19 %)
Companies listed on the Milan Stock Exchange in 2011—Index FTSE Italy Small Cap	128	51 (40 %)	18 (14 %)
Companies listed on the Milan Stock Exchange in 2011—Index FTSE Italy Micro Cap	28	6 (20 %)	4 (14 %)
Total	253[a]	122	50 (20 %)

Panel B—observations

Year			Observations
2009			50
2010			50
2011			50
Final sample			150

[a]We have excluded 19 companies because we have missing data for the analysis. Because 17 listed companies are not included Index FTSE classification, we included them in this classification taking into account their capitalization

Table 3 Mean comparison

Variable	Sample mean	Control group mean	Two-groups mean comparison t test with unequal variances (two-tailed p-value)
Panel A—non-respondents			
Size (total assets)	30,173,207.46	27,845,841	−0.1134 (0.9099)
Profitability (operative income/total assets)	0.0143167	0.0307055	1.1608 (0.2480)
N	50	72	
Panel B—other firms of the population			
Size (total assets)	30,173,207.46	11,804,580.14	−1.6044 (0.1124)
Profitability (operative income/total assets)	0,0143167	0,0074759	−0.6131 (0.5406)
N	50	203	

We performed tests for non-response bias and for generalize the results to check whether our results were affected by unknown factors that systematically distinguished respondents from non-respondents (control group in panel A, Table 3) and respondents from the other firms of the population (control group in panel B, Table 3). We compare the mean for profitability and size. The data for the control groups have been collected from the financial reporting database DATASTREAM. The results in Table 3 show no sign of a non-response bias and of difference with other firms of the population according either to profitability or size.

5 Descriptive Statistics, Univariate Results and Correlation Matrix

Descriptive statistics are showed separately for financial and non financial industry, consistent with the methodology of the literature. We make this distinction also to better appreciate the difference by industry of the scoping methodology and the risk assessment based on the procedure to assign rating but overall, on the decision on the number of processes, objectives and controls.

Table 4 Descriptive statistics

	Financial industry				Non financial industry			
	Mean	Std. dev.	Min	Max	Mean	Std. dev.	Min	Max
Dependents variables								
ITC scoping								
Map	0.74		0.00	1.00	0.53		0.00	1.00
Link	0.81		0.00	1.00	0.53		0.00	1.00
IT Risks Critical evaluation on FR	0.58		0.00	1.00	0.37		0.00	1.00
Scoping score	2.13	1.01	0.00	3.00	1.42	1.05	0.00	3.00
Weighted scoping score	0.71	0.34	0.00	1.00	0.48	0.38	0.00	1.00
ITC risk assessment								
Risk rating	0.42		0.00	1.00	0.68		0.00	1.00
Simple risk assessment score	1.06	1.28	0.00	4.00	1.74	1.46	0.00	4.00
Processes	1.10	1.23	0.00	3.00	1.33	1.12	0.00	3.00
Objectives	0.68	0.90	0.00	3.00	1.37	1.14	0.00	3.00
Weighed risk assessment score	1.00	1.09	0.00	3.00	1.28	1.00	0.00	3.00
Independent variables								
#Auditors on financial reporting	6	8	0	40	7	5	0	23
#IT auditors	2	3	0	15	2	2	0	10
Outsourcing	0.61		0.00	1.00	0.68		0.00	1.00
Operating segments	3.11	2.05	0.00	10.00	4.14	1.43	1.00	7.00
Gains or losses from foreign currency translation	0.59		0.00	1.00	0.25		0.00	1.00
Market capitalization	2.65	0.94	1.00	4.00	3.37	0.82	1.00	4.00
Loss	0.29		0.00	1.00	0.28		0.00	1.00
CFO/A	0.05	0.08	−0.12	0.46	0.02	0.06	−0.28	0.31
Firm age	66.30	43.05	7.00	149.00	104.11	61.57	14.00	186.00
Governance score	−0.33	0.49	−1.73	1.05	0.53	1.33	−2.37	4.52

5.1 ITC Quality

ITC scoping. Map, link and critical evaluation on FR are implemented differently across industries: in financial industry 74 % of the companies implement the procedure of mapping the IT elements and 81 % execute the link with the business processes but only the 58 % of the companies apply a critical evaluation about the risks of misstatements on financial reporting that can come from the IT (Table 4).

The situation is worse in the non-financial industry where only the 53 % use an effective map and link and only the 37 % apply the critical evaluation. The critical evaluation is the worse component: companies do not evaluate specific risks related to the objective of the reliability of the financial reporting, they only focus on general risks on IT but they do not evaluate the misstatements or frauds that can impact on the financial reporting reliability.

The descriptive statistics are underneath the expectation because do not put in practice the three aspects of the scoping is an index of weak scoping quality. However, the scoping score in the sample is 2.13 out of 3 in financial industry and 1.42 over 3 in non financial industry consistent with the hypothesis of the literature that companies think to reduce compliance costs using the phase of scoping [9, 28]. In Italy the scoping is primarily realized following USA frameworks and its consideration is consistent with the scheme of PCAOB, SEC and COBIT for SOX. The same consideration could be done with the weighted scoping score.

ITC risk assessment. It shows critical results: only the 42 % of the companies in financial industry use a risk rating procedure. However 68 % of non-financial companies use it.

The evaluations considering ITC processes, objectives and controls are very low in the sample, both employing the simple risk assessment score (1.06 for financials and 1.74 for non financials) and the weighed risk assessment score (1.00 for financials and 1.28 for non financials). Consistent with literature the risk based approach is not developed as required [10, 24, 25]. The same consideration can be done for the individual score for processes, objectives and controls.

5.2   Determinants of ITC Quality

ICFR staff. For easy of interpretation, summary statistic for the number of auditors and IT auditors divided for the total asset is converted to an amount in Table 4.

The number of IT auditors is more stable (standard deviation of 3 against 8 in financial and 2 against 5 in non financial) and, as expected, it is lower than the number of auditor on financial reporting: it is in mean 2 because, independent from the size, different companies tend to have few IT experts (in median only 1 person is an expert in IT, untabulated). The number of auditors on financial reporting is nearly 6 for financial and 7 for non-financial industry in mean but with a greater volatility than the number of IT auditors: due to the company's size, different companies can have a different number of auditors.

Complexity. The majority of the companies use the strategy of outsourcing (61 % in financial industry and 68 % in non financial industry). Financial industry is more internationalized (59 %) than non-financial industry (25 %) resulting from the presence of foreign currency translation. The mean of operating segments number in which the companies operate is 3.11 in financial industry and 4.14 in non-financial industry. This information shows the degree of diversification of the groups considered in the research.

Internal control resources. The market capitalization shows the composition of the sample among the four segment of FTSE index: looking at the number of companies that have answer at the questionnaire the segment more represented in the sample is the index FTSE Italy small cap with 18 companies, followed by the index FTSE MIB with 17 companies (see Table 2—Sample Selection). This let us to conclude that our sample is enough uniform regarding the capitalization (2.65 or 3.37 out of 4). The CFO/A is positive (5 % in financial and 2 % in non financial industry) and not too much high, but it is acceptable high bearing in mind the period of crisis that influence the financial data in 2010. The other data about the presence of loss in the income statement is indirectly connected with the information on CFO/A: in the sample about the 30 % of the companies recognize losses and this probably is one of the causes that determine the reduction of the CFO/A index. The percentage of LOSS is similar among industries (0.29 and 0.28).

Our sample is composed of companies that are in mean nearly 66 years old in financial and 104 in non-financial industry (excluding the company that began its activity at the end of 1400).

Corporate governance. A high positive governance score means that firms have a high number of directors, independent directors, annual meeting for the Board of Directors and a high number of directors, independent directors, expert directors for the Audit committee over the mean. Non-financial industry has a better corporate governance quality than the financial industry.

5.3 Correlation Matrix (Data Untabuled)

The correlation matrix shows multicollinearity problems (threshold level of 45 %) for the variable number of auditors on financial reporting/assets. Because of this problem, we exclude this variable from the regression.

6 Regression Results

The columns 1 and 2 of Table 5 show the results for the simple scoping score and the weighed scoping score as dependent variables. The Adj. R^2 is, respectively, 40.8 and 39.5 %, showing that the determinants explain a significant percentage of the ITC scoping quality.

The columns 3 of Table 5 display the multivariate logistic regression with the dummy variable of risk rating as dependent variable. The columns 4 and 5 show the results for the simple and the weighed risk assessment score based on ITC compliance with COBIT for SOX. The Pseudo R^2 is from 9.4 to 13.4 % for the variables based on the number of processes, objectives and controls for ITC and 44.6 % for the dummy variable of risk rating.

Table 5 Regression Results

Independent variables		Simple scoping score	Weighted scoping score	Risk rating	Simple risk assessment score	Weighted risk assessment score
		OLS estimate	OLS estimate	Logit marginal effect	OLS estimate	OLS estimate
ITC staff						
#IT AUDITORS	+	−23,346.7	−8284.0	4043.0	−22,119.4	−18,423.8
		(−2.60)**	(−2.64)***	(0.53)	(−2.94)***	(−2.93)***
Complexity						
OUTSOURCING	−	−0.0959	−0.0440	0.340	0.451	0.177
		(−0.55)	(−0.73)	(1.92)*	(2.44)**	(1.17)
INDUSTRY	−	1.172	0.376	−0.0856	−0.0985	0.225
		(6.50)***	(6.01)***	(−0.59)	(−0.39)	(1.21)
OPERATING SEGMENTS	−	0.0449	0.0248	−0.0449	−0.0244	−0.0414
		(1.42)	(2.29)**	(−1.44)	(−0.51)	(−1.00)
FOREIGN CURRENCY TRANSLATION	−	0.277	0.123	0.0775	0.195	−0.0305
		(1.62)	(2.17)**	(0.61)	(1.04)	(−0.22)
Internal control resources						
MARKET CAP	+	0.273	0.103	0.423	0.699	0.616
		(3.50)***	(4.03)***	(4.47)***	(5.75)***	(6.50)***
LOSS	?	−0.314	−0.0594	0.105	0.112	0.159
		(−1.71)*	(−0.94)	(0.75)	(0.55)	(0.90)
CFO/A	?	−0.166	0.0803	0.387	0.141	0.502
		(−0.15)	(0.22)	(0.49)	(0.14)	(0.56)

(continued)

Table 5 (continued)

		Simple scoping score	Weighted scoping score	Risk rating	Simple risk assessment score	Weighted risk assessment score
FIRM AGE	+	0.00660	0.00159	0.00447	0.00357	0.00338
		(4.02)***	(2.67)***	(3.39)***	(1.93)*	(2.29)**
Corporate governance						
GOVERNANCE SCORE	+	0.0957	0.0485	0.173	0.0183	−0.0143
		(1.15)	(1.77)*	(1.88)*	(0.18)	(−0.17)
Intercept		−0.264	−0.122		−1.240	−1.089
		(−0.72)	(−0.99)		(−2.34)**	(−2.53)**
Year fixed effect		*included*	*included*	*included*	*included*	*included*
Sample size		150	150	150	150	150
Pseudo R²/Adj. R²		0.408	0.395	0.446	0.134	0.094

t-stat values in parantheses ***indicates significance at the 0.01 level or better, **indicates significance at the 0.05 level or better, *indicates significance at the 0.10 level or better

The results show that the number of IT auditors is negatively related to ITC quality (ITC scoping and risk assessment quality). Our results do not confirm in Italy previous findings [7, 15]: one possible motivation may be the difficulties of cooperation and integration between audit and IT competences. Without a strong integrated action, the audit teams could not understand the IT specialist suggestions and determine a negative effect on ITC quality.

Internationalization (gains and losses from foreign currency translation) and diversification (numbers of operating segments) increase ITC scoping quality: our results, opposite to the expectations, may mean that complexity increases the risks but also the internal control culture and the exigency of audit activities. In other words, companies may positively react to the increased complexity and risks coming from internationalization and diversification with an efficient ITC audit.

The outsourcing strategy is significantly related to ITC risk assessment quality with a positive coefficient: companies that outsource the ITC should include the outsourcing risks in the risk rating to increase ITC risk assessment quality.

When the dummy variable for industry goes from 0 (manufacturing and services) to 1 (banks and insurances) the ITC scoping quality increases: this means that ITC scoping quality is lower for manufacturing and services industry. We interpret that the activities of the control authorities (Bank of Italy, etc.) overpass the effect of the complexity and bring to a higher ITC scoping quality because of the strict requirements that they ask.

The market capitalization, the firm age and the corporate governance score have the expected sign. The results show that firms with higher market value guarantee more resources to control activities, included the ITC scoping and risk assessment and that older companies with higher corporate governance quality assure more expertise in the evaluation of IT risks and planning.

In summary, our results show that ITC staff, complexity, internal resources and corporate governance variables are relevant determinants of ITC quality, and affect the scoping or the risk assessment ITC quality.

7 Robustness (Data Untabuled)

First, we repeat the regressions also with only one year of data (2010), to see if the results are due to the choice to refer to a 3-years period. Significant coefficients confirm the results found in the main analysis.

Then, we repeat the analysis changing the weight in the weighted score for scoping and risk assessment.

Instead of 0.40 * MAP + 0:20 * LINK + 0:30 * IT RISKSCRITICAL EVALUATION ON FR, we change the score in 0.50 * MAP + 0.10 * LINK + 0.40 * IT RISKSCRITICAL EVALUATION ON FR.

Instead of 0.70 * PROCESSES + 0.20 * OBJECTIVES + 0.10 * CONTROLS, we change the score in 0.50 * PROCESSES + 0.30 * OBJECTIVES + 0.20 * CONTROLS.

Our findings confirm the same results obtained with the original data.

Prior literature exclude financial industry from the regression model because too different from the other industries. To control if the fit of the model depends only by this determinant, finally, we repeat the regressions separated by industry. This method decreases the number of observations but let us to support the results if the Adj. R^2 does not decrease too much.

The results show an Adj. R^2 from 39.5 to 38 % for simple scoping scores and from 44.6 to 36 % for risk assessment scores, supporting our results also for the other determinants.

8 Conclusion

The main objective of the research (to find relevant determinants of the ITC quality over Financial Reporting) has been investigated using innovative method of evaluation of the dependent variable (ITC scoping and risk assessment quality) and testing in Italy relevant determinants used by previous literature grouped in four classes of independents variables (ITC staff, Complexity, Internal resources, Corporate Governance Score).

For ITC scoping quality we propose a simple and a weighted scoping score constructed considering the map, the link with the business and the critical evaluation on financial reporting as defined in the COBIT for SOX. Looking at the descriptive statistics for the scoping, the companies of the sample demonstrate that they are working to improve the ITC quality in this phase of the audit cycle but they also have some deficiencies, overall in non-financial industry and in the critical evaluation on financial reporting.

For ITC risk assessment quality we propose a simple and a weighted ITC risk assessment score and a dummy variable for the ITC risk rating constructed considering the impact and the likelihood of financial reporting errors, the number of processes, objectives and controls defined in the COBIT for SOX. Also in this area the descriptive statistics demonstrate that the ITC risk assessment represents a critical area because too low companies follow the benchmark, overall in financial industry.

The results show that ITC quality is positive related to complexity, internal control resources and corporate governance and negative related to IT auditors specialists. Companies that aim to improve ITC quality must take into account of the probable benefits coming from internationalization, diversification and the outsourcing strategy. On the contrary, the IT auditors specialist seem to be not so determinant, overall when they do not work in an integrated way with the other auditors. The unexpected finding related to complexity variables may be justified with the positive reaction of companies to the increased complexity and risks coming from internationalization and diversification with an efficient ITC audit. Industry is another important determinants of ITC quality: our results show that financial industry present a higher ITC quality in comparison with manufacturing and services industry. This result may be due to the role of national and international control authority (Bank of Italy, European Central Bank) that introduced specific mandatory internal and external audit for these companies. Among the proposed Internal Control Resources variables, our results show that market capitalization and firm age represent significant determinants of ITC quality that confirm previous literature findings. Finally, the set of variables related to the Board of Directors and the Audit Committee included in the Corporate Governance Score reveals a positive association with ITC quality.

Limitations of the research may be connected to the variables used in the model, to the weight used in the score and the proxy used for some determinants, such as the variables used to measure the corporate governance score. Another limit may be the sample composition. Finally, the descriptive statistic for risk assessment could be understated because on 5 classes defined (0–4) only the class number 4 has a positive meaning and the statistics for outsourcing could be overstated because the research does not distinguish the true outsourcing from the intra-group one.

Taking into account of previous limitations, the results show that relevant determinants of ITC quality are industry, internationalization and diversification, outsourcing strategy, market capitalization, firm age and corporate governance.

Acknowledgments We thank Professor Dr. Henning Zülch for helpful comments and suggestions at the 74th Annual Conference of the German Academic Association for Business Research (VHB) held in Bozen, 2012, May 30–June 2, and the partecipants to the annual meeting of Italian Society of Accounting and Business Administration (SIDREA) in Modena—Italy, 2012, November 27–28. We are grateful to Professors Gerrit Sarens, Giuseppe D'Onza, Marika Arena, Arno Nuijten, Andrew D. Chambers for useful suggestions received at the XIIth Academic Conference on Internal Auditing and Corporate Governance held in Como, 2014, 9–11 April. Finally we thank professors John Hudson and Gareth Myles for helpful comments and suggestions at The International Conference Current Economic Trends in Emerging and Developing Countries, Timisoara (Romania), 2014, 12–14 June.

References

1. Ashbaugh-Skaife, H., Collins, D., Kinney, W.: The discovery and reporting of internal control deficiencies prior to SOX-mandated audits. J. Account. Econ. **44**(1–2), 166–192 (2007)
2. Basilo, T.A.: Reducing Sarbanes-Oxley compliance costs. CPA J. **77**(1), 6–9 (2007)
3. Bedard, J.: Archival investigation of audit program planning. Auditing J. Pract. Theor (Fail), 51–57 (1989)
4. Bedard, J.C., Johnstone, K.M.: Audit partner tenure and audit planning and pricing. Auditing **29**(2), 45–70 (2010)
5. Cannon, D.M., Growe, G.A.: How does Sarbanes-Oxley affect outsourcing? J. Corp. Account Finance **16**(3), 13–20 (2005)
6. Carnaghan, C.: Discussion of IT assurance competencies. Int. J. Account. Inf. Syst. **5**(2), 267–273 (2004)
7. Cohen, J.R., Krishnamoorthy, Ganesh, Wright, A.M.: The impact of roles of the board on auditors' risk assessments and program planning decisions. Auditing **26**(1), 91–112 (2007)
8. Doyle, J., Ge, W., McVay, S.: Determinants of weaknesses in internal control over financial reporting. J. Account. Econ. **44**(1–2), 193–223 (2007)

9. Fogleman, S.L., Peterson, B.H., Heninger, W.G., Romney, M.B.: Opportunity detected. J. Accountancy **204**(6), 62–65 (2007)
10. Fukukawa, H., Mock, T., Wright, A.: Audit program plans and audit risk: a study of Japanese practice. Int. J. Auditing **10**(1), 41–65 (2006)
11. Ge, W., McVay, S.: The disclosure of material weaknesses in internal control after the Sarbanes-Oxley Act. Account. Horiz. **19**(3), 137–158 (2005)
12. Goh B.W.: Audit Committees, Board of Directors, and Remediation of Material Weaknesses in Internal Control, Contemporary Accounting Research, vol. 26(2), pp. 549–579 (2009)
13. Greenstein, M., McKee, T.E.: Assurance practitioners' and educators' self-perceived IT knowledge level: an empirical assessment. Int. J. Account. Inf. Syst. **5**(2), 213–243 (2004). doi:10.1016/j.accinf.2004.04.002
14. Hackenbrack, K., Knechel, W.R.: Resource allocation decisions in audit engagements'. Contemp. Account. Res. (Fall). 481–99 (1997)
15. Hermannson, D.R., Hill, M.C., Ivancevich, D.M.: Information technology-related activities of internal auditors. J. Inf. Syst. **14**(Supplement), 39–53 (2000)
16. Hogan, C.E., Wilkins, M.S.: Evidence on the audit risk model: do auditors increase audit fees in the presence of internal control deficiencies? Contemp. Account. Res. **25**(1), 219–242 (2008)
17. Hoitash U., Hoitash R., Bedard J.C.: Corporate governance and internal control over financial reporting: a comparison of regulatory regimes. Account. Rev. **84**(3), 839–867 (2009)
18. Houston, R.W., Peters, M.F., Pratt, J.H.: The audit risk model, business risk and audit-planning decisions. Account. Rev. **74**(3), 281–298 (1999)
19. Krishnan, J.: Audit committee quality and internal control: an empirical analysis. Account. Rev. **80**(2), 649–675 (2005)
20. Krishnan G.V., Visvanathan G.: Reporting internal control deficiencies in the Post-Sarbanes-Oxley Era: the role of auditors and corporate governance. Int. J. Auditing **11**, 73–90 (2007)
21. Laurent, W.: Outsourcing governance. DM Rev. **16**(10), 14 (2006)
22. Leader, B.: Discussion of IT assurance competencies. Int. J. Account. Inf. Syst. **5**(2), 275–279 (2004)
23. Merhout J.W., Havelka D.: Information technology auditing: a value-added IT governance partnership between IT management and audit, communications of the association for information systems CAIS, 23 November, vol. 26, pp. 463–482 (2008)
24. Mock, T., Wright, A.: An exploratory study of auditor evidential planning. Auditing J. Pract. Theor (Fall), 39–61 (1993)
25. Mock, T.J., Wright, A.M.: Are audit program plans risk-adjusted? Auditing **18**(1), 55–74 (1999)
26. Naiker V., Sharma D.S.: Former audit partners on the audit committee and internal control deficiencies. Account. Rev. **84**(2), 559–587 (2009)
27. Norman, C.S., Payne, M.D., Vendrzyk, V.P.: Assessing information technology general control risks: an instructional case. Issue Account. Educ. **24**(1), 63–76 (2009)
28. O'Brien, P.: ReducingSOX section 404 compliance costs via a top-down, risk-based approach. CPA J. **76**(8), 36–39 (2006)
29. O'Keefe, T., Simunic, D., Stein, M.: The production of audit services: evidence from a major public accounting firm. J. Account. Res. (Autumn), 241–261 (1994)
30. Wilson, G.P.: Audit planning-top down or bottom up? Int. J. Gov. Auditing **26**(2), 8–9 (1999)
31. Zhang Y., Zhou J., Zhou N.: Audit committee quality, auditor independence, and internal control weaknesses. J. Account. Publ Policy **26**(3), 300–327 (2007)

E-Disclosure Key Drivers: An Empirical Analysis

Benedetta Gesuele

Abstract Transparency in Public Administration is an important topic for scholars. In the last time new communication tools have been changing the relationship between administration and citizens in order to enhance public accountability that is essential for Government transparency. The aim of this research is to analyze the e-disclosure key drivers in a sample of Spanish Local Governments, during 2012. The methodology used is Ordinary Last Square Regression Model. Eight key drivers are identified as size, financial autonomy, Internet visibility, media interest, citizens' wealth, political polar, gender of mayor and leverage. The results shows that size, Internet visibility, media interest, citizens 'wealth and leverage are able to influence the e-disclosure in the sample under investigation.

Keywords E-disclosure · Key drivers · Index · Local government authorities

1 Introduction

During the last time, new communication tools have been changing the relationship between Public Administration (PA) and citizens in order to enhance the transparency, participation process, and accountability. Nowadays the Local Government's websites has become the main channel, for communication with stakeholders and the most important disclosure tools. The aim of this research is to analyze the e-disclosure key drivers in a sample of Spanish Local Governments (LGs). The Spanish sample has been chosen because the Spanish Local Government is characterized by profound autonomy but, at the same time, the legislation about public communication is poor. In spite of this, the Spanish Local Governments seem to be moving forward e-disclosure. This paper is a further

B. Gesuele (✉)
Parthenope University, Naples, Italy
e-mail: benedetta.gesuele@uniparthenope.it

© Springer International Publishing Switzerland 2016   259
D. Mancini et al. (eds.), *Strengthening Information and Control Systems*,
Lecture Notes in Information Systems and Organisation 14,
DOI 10.1007/978-3-319-26488-2_18

development of a previous study about e-disclosure phenomenon in the Spanish Local Governments.

Transparency and accountability in PA are topics that have attracted the interest of several scholars, who have begun to investigate the key drivers of disclosure under the light of several theoretical frameworks. Agency theory and Neo Institutional theory represent the most commonly applied frameworks. Through these theoretical approaches the paper analyses e-disclosure key drivers, proposing the scoring system for the e-disclosure analysis. The structure of this paper is as follows. Section 2 introduces the theoretical background and presents several researches about e-disclosure. Section 3 presents the research model and hypotheses. Section 4 describes the research methodology and results of the analysis. Finally, Sect. 5 discusses the discussion, conclusions, limits and future research prospective.

2 Literature Review

In the last time, the disclosure via web (e-disclosure) in the public sector has been the object of interest of many studies through different theoretical background. The two major theoretical background used are the Agency theory and Neo Institutional theory. The scholars can validate that there are different key drivers are able to influence the e-disclosure practices.

Groff and Pitman [1], in their study, identified two e-disclosure key drivers of financial information: size and financial debt. Laswad et al. [2] examined as political competition, size, leverage, wealth municipal, visibility through the press and the type of government were the variables associated with voluntary disclosure. In similar way, Serrano-Cinca et al. [3] showed that size, political position and citizen's income level all affect e-disclosure. Styles and Tennyson' research [4] explored the relation that existed between accessibility of the information and size, debt level and financial condition of the municipality as well as the income level of residents. Jorge et al. [5], under the light of Institutional theory, analyzed socio-demographic, economic and political factors that affect municipalities' budgetary and financial transparency levels. Alvarez et al. [6] analyzed the important of political factors to influencing the e-disclosure. The Gandia et al. [7] research showed that disclosure levels depend on several social and political determinants as political competition, public media visibility and the access to technology and educational levels of the citizens. Similarly Bachmann [8] investigated the variables that affect the quality of Local Government Authorities websites. Guillamòn et al. [9] contributed to increase the literature on government transparency by analyzing the impact of political and socio economic factors on financial transparency under the light of Agency theory and Fiscal Illusion theory. Yu [10] highlighted how the size, wealth, local Authority' organization, procapita income and financial condition affect the e-disclosure. Lepore and Pisano [11] explored the determinants of Internet-based performance reporting (IPR) released by Italian Local Government

Authorities, they analyzed relationship between IPR and size, financial autonomy, voluntary disclosure, citizens 'wealth, press visibility, Internet visibility and media interest. Garcia-Garcia et al. [12] analyzed non-financial-reporting in the Spanish municipalities; the key drivers identified are used are: level of citizens 'economic development, life quality level municipalities size, municipality's budgetary, political stability, political strength, political rivalry.

3 Research Model and Hypotheses

With the aim to analyze the e-disclosure key drivers in a set of Spanish LG, under the light of Agency theory and Neo Institutional theory, this study identifies several key drivers as independent variables and builds one e-disclosure Index (eD Index)as dependent variable. The eD Index is based on websites contents in order to measure Local Governments' transparency level. The use of disclosure index to measure Local Governments' transparency level has been developed in many previous studies [5, 9, 13–18]. In this study the eD Index is composed by several items that explore three different areas of disclosure: institutional area (information about civil servants, organization chart and wages); management area (information about administration, investee companies, administration contact); financial and economic information (information about cash, financial-economic index, disclosure reports). Coherently with the disclosure areas identified, twelve items are chosen and the e-D Index is obtained by adding the items included in each of three sections (formula 1). For every item is assigned a score that assumes value 1 when this item was disclosed on the websites and a score of 0 otherwise. The final score assigned to each municipality varies from 0 to 12. Its average is 6.93 and its minimum value is 1 and its maximum is 12.

$$e - DIndex = \sum_{i=1}^{3} Ist_i + \sum_{i=1}^{3} Man_i + \sum_{i=1}^{6} FinEc_i \qquad (1)$$

Three groups of independent variables have been identified: citizenship and society development dimension, which can be explored in variables as size, Internet visibility and media interest, economic-financial dimension, which can be explored as financial autonomy index, citizens' wealth and leverage; political dimension that can be explored by political polar and gender of mayor (female).

Size is considered a e-disclosure key drivers in numerous theoretical and empirical studies [1, 4, 8, 10, 12, 16]. In other studies, the disclosure on Internet is considered an innovation and larger administration have greater possibilities of innovation than smaller cities [3, 9, 12]. So, in this study the size is considered as e-disclosure determinant and it can hypothesize that: **H1**: There is a positive relationship between size and e-disclosure Index.

The relationship between municipalities' financial condition and e-disclosurein literature, [2, 4, 9, 10, 12, 16] are considered. These studies obtained mixed results. The central idea is that financial condition reveals the ability of LGA management, which tends to show the results of their activities. In this study the Index of financial autonomy is a proxy of municipalities financial condition and the second hypothesis is that: **H2** There is a positive relationship between financial autonomy and e-disclosure Index.

According to the Agency theory the relationship between voters and politicians theInternet visibility iskey drivers factor of disclosure [2, 3, 11, 16, 17]. Concerning on the relationship between Internet visibility and e-disclosure, previous scholars obtained mixed results. In some researches the information disclosed via web are not focused on performances usually due to scandals and corruption; in a different way other studies consider that more visibility on the web encourages the municipalities to disclosure more information. Serrano et al. [2] considered Internet visibility as a measure of the popularity of a webpage or site, and for this reason it can be considered a key aspect in e-disclosure. In this research the Internet visibility is considered a key aspect in e-disclosure because the municipalities, which larger use of internet, are subjected to larger stress by Internet users. On basis of this, they are more disposed to disclosure information on webpage. The following hypothesis is proposed: **H3** There is a positive relationship between Internet visibility and e-disclosure Index.

The use of media, like that of newspapers or television, has an important role in influencing the agency relationship between voters and politicians [11, 16, 18]. In fact, politicians can use media to provide information to citizens concerning their activities [16] reducing the information asymmetry with voters. Ingram [15] argued that, "…a strong press might induce more disclosures to satisfy the information demands…". However, media have usually their own interests which could not coincide with those of citizens and politicians, and, as a consequence, they could decide to publish exclusively information about scandals and corruption in order to increase their circulation [12]. Other studies [16] showed that the media find a positive correlation between political visibility and disclosure, furthermore other studies [19, 20] argued that the most visible entities will disclose more information due to the pressures they face. In this scenario, Local Government Authorities could decide not to disclose information through Internet in order to avoid using such information in inappropriate and opportunistic way by media [2, 12]. In this research has been measured the media interest perceived by each municipality hypothesizing that: **H4** There is a positive relationship between media interest and e-disclosure Index.

The literature suggests that there is a relation between Local Government disclosure practices and citizens' economic status based. The central idea is that people have higher economic status have more access to new technology [3, 10]. Politicians have an incentive both to improve the economic conditions of the Country and they would like to show this improvement to stakeholders. Citizens with higher income per capita expect more services and performance information [2, 21, 11, 16], moreover they generally have more access to Internet and experience to use it [21]. In line with Ho [22], in the explicit case of e-disclosure, municipalities with a lower per capita income are less likely to adopt web to disclosure information. The fifth hypothesis is: **H5** There is a positive relationship between citizens' wealth and e-disclosure Index.

Municipalities are governed by politicians and they can influence the Local Authorities scenario and these may be reflected on many aspects of administration as e-disclosure [3]. According to Agency theory, Politicians are not encouraged adopting the most transparent practices [6, 9]. The dominant party affiliation of municipalities can affect e-disclosure because a different ideology may support a different e-disclosure style [6]. Alvarez et al. [6] argued that "…it is interesting to analyze whether the political trend of the ruling party can have any impact on e-disclosure…" Different studies [23, 24] showed that the political tendency of ruling party can be influenced the development of e-government. The following hypothesis is formulated: **H6** There is a positive relationship between political polar and e-disclosure Index.

Many studies consider the gender of mayor (female) as an important political determinant that influencing the e-disclosure level. The scholars investigate participatory inequality between men and women, they support that the gender is related to political activity [9, 18, 25]. The previous literature investigated about the differences in political participation between men and women [25] and showed that men were more active than woman [18]. Different scholars [26, 27] indicated that man have a higher level of political engagement than women but nowadays there are several initiatives for reducing the gender different and for considering the gender equal. In this study we considered that the gender of mayor aren't able to influence the e-disclosure level and we hypotheses that: **H7**: There is a relationship between female and e-disclosure Index.

According to literature, under the light of Agency theory, the politicians have encouragements to reduce the cost of debt [2, 17, 28], so that they would release resources and improve welfare. Many scholars showed that there is a positive association between public debt and disclosure of public information [9, 10, 12, 13, 18]. The following hypothesis is: **H8** There is a positive relationship between leverage and e-disclosure Index.

4 Methodology

This paper is a further development of a previous study about e-disclosure phenomenon in the Spanish Local Governments. In fact, in this wider analysis I develop other interesting variables to investigate the adoption of transparency standards through the innovative communication channels, more specifically the web sites. This section introduces the information about research context, data collection, analysis and results.

4.1 The Research Context: Spanish LG

The Spanish public sector is divided in three levels: the State, seventeen Regional governments and some Local Governments (fifty provinces and eight thousand one hundred and twelve municipalities). Between these entities there are some relationships based on competences and this system is characterized by a profound autonomy. In every municipality there are: a mayor, which is a head of executive elected by the citizens; a cabinet and professional administration. The electoral system is proportional and the elections are taken in place every four years. There are two main national political parties: socialist party (left) and the popular party (right).

There isn't a structured legal system about public communication or public services, but there is important law in the poor legislation for organizing and developing the public administration and public services there is the Law 71/1985. This Law, on the Regulation of the Bases of Local Government, regulates the minimum level services which town halls have to offer. This level has to depend on their population amount. However the municipalities' administrative management includes the preparation of budgets, presenting accounts and establishing relations with citizens and other stakeholders. In 2003, the Spanish Local Government reform started with the Law 57/2003. This Law, Measurement for Modernization of Local Government, emphasizes the need for using the ICT in order to contribute to accountability and transparency of government date.In Spain, as in great part of the world, the citizens' participation is promoted by government because it is an important principle for democratic progress of the country. From 2007, the Law 11 regulates electronic access by citizens to public services, fulfilling an important necessity of citizens (and all time of stakeholders).

4.2 Sample and Data Collection

The sample under investigation is a set of Spanish LG higher than 50.000 habitants, during 2012. The sample is composed by 145 Local Governments. The total of sample population is 24.216.938, and the minimum and maximum correspond about 50.098 and 3.2133e + 006. The average of income pro capita is 15.094 and the minimum and maximum are 10.173 and 27.004. Data were gathered from Badespe, a Spanish database of Spanish Ministry of Treasury.

4.3 Measurement

Size (size) is the number of inhabitants of the Local Governments [1, 4, 8, 10, 12, 16]. Financial Autonomy (FAut) is a financial autonomy index, which is calculated as proper revenues coming from taxes and fees divided total current revenues including grants [2, 4, 9, 10, 12, 16]. These data was collected by Badespe, the Spanish database of Spanish Ministry of Treasury. Citizens wealth (CiWealth) is measured by number that is citizens' wealth pro capita in every municipalities [2, 21, 11, 16]. It is taken from Badespe.

Media Interest (MediaInt) and Internet Visibility (IntVis) are data collected by google. MediaInt may be exploratory factors regarding on the interest of media about municipalities. In this study it is considered a dummy variable. It is measured as presence of news on google (the value assigned is 1) or absence of news on google in 2012 (the value assigned is 0). IntVis is considered the popularity of webpage, it is measured by number [2, 11, 16, 17].

Political Polar (Pol Polar) is considered as political ideology of municipal ruling parties. It is considered as dummy variable because in Spain there are two main national political parties: socialist party (left) and the popular party (right) [6, 9].

Gender of mayor (Fem) is considered as a mayor gender, this date is collected from municipalities' websites and assumes value 1 when mayor is woman and value 0 when mayor is man.

The variable leverage (Lev) is measured as municipal debt per capita taken from Spanish Ministry of Treasury in 2012. This variable is measured as natural logarithm [9, 18].

Table 1 provides descriptive statistics for our sample.

4.4 Results

In order to choose the appropriate statistic method we use two tests: Correlation test and White test. The Correlation test shows that there is not a strong correlation among the independent variables (Table 2), apart between leverage and size (0.9224).

The White test shows that the Heteroschedasticity is not present, but there is homoschedasticity (p-value = Chi-quadro (41) > 51.669578) = 0.122729). On the

Table 1 Descriptive statistics

Variables	Mean	Median	S. Dev	Min	Max
Size	1.67 + 0.0105	85.180	1.84	50.098	85.180
FAut	0.85	1	0.41	0	1
CiWealth	15.094	14.830	0.21	10.173	27.004
IntVis	43.22	42	0.23	3	209
MediaInt	0.77	1	0.54	0	1
PolPolar	0.77	1	0.54	0	1
Fem	0.77	1	0.54	0	1
Lev	1.61 + 0.005	58.794	3.89	0	7.42 + 0.006

Table 2 Correlation

Size	FAut	Media Int	IntVis	Lev	Ci Wealth	Pol Polar	Fem	
1	−0.0907012	0.1101	0.7548	0.9224	0.044	0.1124	−0.0668	Size
	1	0.0292	−0.1977	−0.02926	−0.0365	−0.0256	0.0912	FAut
		1	0.0719	0.0574	0.0604	−0.1299	−0.3703	Media Int
			1	0.5958	0.0847	0.1456	−0.0942	IntVis
				1	−0.0036	0.0738	−0.0421	Lev
					1	−0,1187	−0,1247	Ci Wealth
						1	0.0742	Pol Polar
							1	Fem

basis of these preemies, the Ordinary Last Square (OLS) regression model can be considered suitable for this type of analysis (Table 3).

We test the hypotheses on 145 Local Governments higher 50.000 inhabitants in 2012 through the following OLS regression model (formula 2):

$$eD = \alpha + \beta_1 Size + \beta_2 FAut + \beta_3 CitWealth + \beta_4 MediaInt + \beta_5 IntVis$$
$$+ \beta_6 PolPolar + \beta_{17} Fem + \beta_8 Lev \tag{2}$$

Table 3 White test

Const	−0.292073	1.58996	−0.1837	0.8546
Size_2012	−9.66824e−07	6.28645e−06	−0.1538	0.8781
F Aut ~	1.02050	1.51509	0.6736	0.5021
Media Int 2 ~	−0.136595	1.11859	−0.1221	0.9030
Int Vis~	0.0123961	0.0146252	0.8476	0.3986
Pol Polar ~	0.400274	0.793314	0.5046	0.6149
Fem	−0.659991	0.916265	−0.7203	0.4730
Lev	2.66543e−06	4.57134e−06	0.5831	0.5611
CiWealth	4.70421e−05	0.000108702	0.4328	0.6661
sq_Size_2012	5.48564e−013	4.32581e−012	0.1268	0.8993
X2_X3	2.83874e−06	3.69244e−06	0.7688	0.4438
X2_X4	−1.98716e−06	4.20347e−06	−0.4727	0.6374
X2_X5	1.85596e−09	1.15707e−08	0.1604	0.8729
X2_X6	5.83989e−07	1.65130e−06	0.3537	0.7243
X2_X7	7.16275e−07	1.74732e−06	0.4099	0.6827
X2_X8	−5.28343e−013	5.80666e−012	−0.09099	0.9277
X2_X9	1.65949e−011	1.84132e−010	0.09012	0.9284

(continued)

Table 3 (continued)

sq_F Aut ~	−1.50224	0.892912	−1.682	0.0955*
X3_X4	−0.0793755	1.12001	−0.07087	0.9436
X3_X5	−0.00862437	0.0122123	−0.7062	0.4817
X3_X6	−0.290894	0.698850	−0.4162	0.6781
X3_X7	0.214622	1.04056	0.2063	0.8370
X3_X8	1.52143e-06	2.61867e-06	0.5810	0.5625
X3_X9	6.81783e-06	4.75730e-05	0.1433	0.8863
X4_X5	−0.00950232	0.00675372	−1.407	0.1624
X4_X6	−0.0529190	0.332742	−0.1590	0.8739
X4_X7	0.261704	0.251693	1.040	0.3009
X4_X8	2.77548e-06	2.50290e-06	1.109	0.2701
X4_X9	2.32131e-05	3.75576e-05	0.6181	0.5379
sq_Int Vis ~	−1.36938e-05	2.50148e-05	−0.5474	0.5853
X5_X6	0.00315588	0.00509736	0.6191	0.5372
X5_X7	−0.00509384	0.00608161	−0.8376	0.4042
X5_X8	1.84703e-08	1.67819e-08	1.101	0.2736
X5_X9	−1.87970e-07	6.10743e-07	−0.3078	0.7589
X6_X7	0.210490	0.214970	0.9792	0.3298
X6_X8	−2.99600e-06	2.41407e-06	−1.241	0.2174
X6_X9	−5.16537e-06	2.95437e-05	−0.1748	0.8615
X7_X8	1.48950e-06	1.17005e-06	1.273	0.2059
X7_X9	−1.93585e-07	3.74594e-05	−0.005168	0.9959
sq_Lev ~	−6.03802e-013	1.89356e-012	−0.3189	0.7505
X8_X9	−2.87676e-010	1.76264e-010	−1.632	0.1057
sq_ CiWealth ~	−1.33361e-09	2.31139e-09	−0.5770 0.5652	
R2 = 0.356342				
Statistic test: TR^2 = 51.669578				
p-value = P(Chi-quadro(41) > 51.669578) = **0.122729**				

where: Size: **size** (number of inhabitants); **FAut**: Financial autonomy index; **CiWealth**: Citizens' wealth; **Media Int**: Media Interest; **IntVis**: Internet Visibility; **PolPolar**: Political Polar; **Fem**: Female; **Lev**: Leverage.

Table 4 shows the findings from the OLS regression. The relation between size (H1), CiWealth (H3), Intvis (H4), Media Int (H5), Lev (H8) and e-disclosure Index are supported. Otherwise, the relation between FAut (H2), Pol Polar (H6) and Fem (H7) and e-disclosure Index are not supported.

Table 4 OLS regression model

	Variables	Coefficient	Standard Error	*t*-student	*p*-value	
	Const	0.791696	0.295348	2.6806	0.00826	***
H1	Size	1.42934E-06	4.78074 e 07	2.9898	0.00331	***
H2	F Aut	0.179175	0.210506	0.8512	0.39617	
H3	CiWealth	2.40E-05	1.35E + 05	1.7817	0.7704	*
H4	IntVis	0.00269898	1.00145178	1.8591	0.06518	*
H5	MediaInt	0.227147	0.131081	1.7329	0.08538	*
H6	PolPolar	0.0871777	0.102913	0.8471	0.39843	
H7	Fem	0.000007	1.91E + 07	3.1463	0.00203	***
H8	Lev					
Observation: 145						
R^2	0.297246					
R^2 adjusted	0.255591					

***Error < 1 %; *error < 10 %

5   Discussion, Limits, Conclusions and Future Research Prospective

The aim of this research is to analyze the key drivers of e-disclosure in a sample of Spanish Local Government under the light of two theoretical frameworks: Agency theory and Neo Institutional theory. The results shown that the hypothesis H1, H3, H4, H5 and H8 are supported.

Size (H1) positively affects e-Disclosure (p-value = 0.00331). Literature frequently considers size as a determinant of e-disclosure [1, 4, 21, 9, 11, 25], according to Agency theory, the larger local entities are, the more information is issued. H3 is statistically significant (p-value = 0.07704). Literature suggests that there is the relation between disclosure in public entity and economic status based. The central idea is that people have higher economic status have more access to information communication technology [10]. According to the Agency theory framework, politicians have an incentive both to improve the economic conditions of the Country and they would show these improvements to stakeholders. H4 is supported (p-value = 0.06518). The municipalities, which have larger use of internet,are subjected to larger stress from Internet users [2, 10, 15, 16]. H5 is supported (p-value = 0.08538), the use of Media, like that of newspapers or television, has an important role in influencing the agency relationship between voters and politicians [11, 15, 17]. In fact, politicians can use media to provide information to citizens concerning their activities [15], reducing the information asymmetry with voters. There is a significant relation between e-disclosure index and leverage (p-value = 0.00203). According to literature, under the light of Agency theory and Neo Institutional theory, the politicians have encouragements to reduce the cost of debt, so that they would release resources and improve welfare.

This research has several limits, first one the object of observation as Internet usage is evolving over and over again. The sample under investigation is not more enough respect the key drivers investigated. Finally, the index don't consider the relevance, as quality, of the different items.

For the future we are collecting the data on other municipalities, in order to perform the analysis on a greater sample. Moreover, we are collecting data on environmental characteristics as the cultural level or the citizens' age, the tax revenue pro capita or the regional and central transfers pro capita. In addition, we would like to consider other type of political factors as turn of rate in last election, municipal political strength. Finally we would like explore the quality of e-disclosure index.

References

1. Groff, J.E., Pitman, M.K.: Municipal financial reporting on the world wide web: a survey of financial data displayed on the official websites of the 100 largest U.S. municipalities. J. Gov. Financ. Manage. **53**, 20–30 (2004)
2. Laswad, F., Fisher, R., Oyelere, P.: Determinants of voluntary Internet financial reporting by LGA. J. Account. Public Policy **24**, 101–121 (2005)
3. Serrano-Cinca, C., Rueda-Tomas, M., Portillo-Tarragona, P.: Factors influencing e-disclosure in local public administrations. In: Documento de Trabajo 2008-03, Facultad de Ciencias Economicas y Empresariales, Universidad de Zaragoza (2008)
4. Styles, A.K., Tennyson, M.: The accessibility of financial reporting of U.S. municipalities on the internet. J. Public Budgeting Account. Financ. Manag. **19**, 56–92 (2007)
5. Jorge, S., Moura, e Sá P., Pattaro, A.F., Lourenço, R.P.: Local Government financial transparency in Portugal and Italy: a comparative exploratory study on its determinants. In: 13th Biennial CIGAR Conference, Ghent, Belgium (2011)
6. -Álvarez, I.G., Rodríguez, D.L, andGarcía-Sánchez, I.M.: Are determining factors of municipal E-government common to a worldwide municipal view? An intra-country comparison. Gov. Inf. Q. **27**, 423–430 (2010)
7. Gandia, J.L., Archidona, C.: Determinants of web site information by Spanish city councils. Online Inf. Rev. Emerald **32**, 35–57 (2008)
8. García, A.C., Garcia, G.: Determinants of online reporting of accounting information by Spanish LGAs. Local Gov. Stud. **36**, 679–695 (2010)
9. Guillimon, M.D., Bastida, F. and Benito, B.: The determinants of local government's financial transparency. Local Gov. Stud. **37**, 391–406 (2011)
10. Yu, H.: On the determinants of Internet-based disclosure of government financial information. In: Conference Proceeding of Management and Service Science (MASS) (2010)
11. Lepore, L., Pisano, S.: Determinants of internet-based performance reporting released by Italian local government authorities. In Mancini D., Vaassen E., Dameri R.P. (eds.) Accounting Information Systems for Decision Making, pp. 63–72. Springer, (2013)
12. García-Sánchez, I.M., Frías-Aceituno, J.V., Rodríguez Domínguez, L.: Determinants of corporate social disclosure in Spanish local governments. J. Cleaner Prod. **39**, 60–72 (2013)
13. Caba, C., Rodriguez, M.P., Lopez, A.M.: E government process and incentives for on line public financial information. On line Inf. Rev. **32**, 379–400 (2008)
14. Pina, V., Torres, L., Royo, S.: Is e-government promoting convergence towards more accountable local governments? Int. Public Manage. J. **13**, 350–380 (2010)

15. Ingram, R.W.: Economic incentives and the choice of state government accounting practices. J. Account. Res. **22**, 126–144 (1984)
16. Lim, S., Mckinnon, J.: Voluntary disclosure be NSW statutory authorities: the influence of political visibility. J. Account. Public Policy **12**, 189–216 (2003)
17. Zimmerman, J.L.: The municipal accounting maze: an analysis of political incentives. J. Account. Res. **15**, 107–144 (1977)
18. Verba, S., Nie, N.H., Kim, J.O.: Participation and Political Equality: A Seven Nation Comparison. Chicago University Press, Chicago (1978)
19. Cormier, D., Magnan, M.: Corporate environmental disclosure: contrasting management's perceptions with reality? J. Bus. Ethics **49**, 145–165 (2004)
20. Magness, V.: Strategic posture, financial performance and environmental disclosure. An empirical test of legitimacy theory. Account. Auditing Accountability J. **19**, 540–563 (2006)
21. Giroux, G., McLelland, A.J.: Governance structures and accounting at large municipalities. J. Account. Public Policy **22**, 203–230 (2003)
22. Ho, A.T.: Economic incentives and the choice of state government accounting practices. J. Account. Rev. **56**, 410–420 (2002)
23. Càrcaba, A.C., Garcia, J.G.: Determinantes de la divulgation de information contable a traves de internet por parte de los gobiernos locale. Revista Espanola de financiacion y contabilidad **137**, 63–84 (2008)
24. Tolbert, C.J., Mossberger, K., McNeal, R.S.: Institutions, policy and e-government in the American States. Public Adm. Rev. **68**, 549–563 (2008)
25. Andersen, K.: Working woman and political participation. Am. J. Polit. Sci. **19**, 439–453 (1975)
26. Jennings, M.K.: Gender roles and inequalities in political participation: results from eight-nation study. West. Polit Q. **36**, 364–385 (1975)
27. Piotroswski, S.J., Van Ryzin, G.G.: Citizen attitude toward transparency in government. Am. Rev. Public Adm. **37**, 306–323 (2007)
28. Debreceny, R., Gray, G.L., Rahman, A.: The determinants of internet financial reporting. Int. J. Account. Public Policy **21**, 371–395 (2002)

Printed in the United States
By Bookmasters